The Black Sun

NUMBER TEN
*Carolyn and Ernest Fay Series
in Analytical Psychology*
David H. Rosen, General Editor

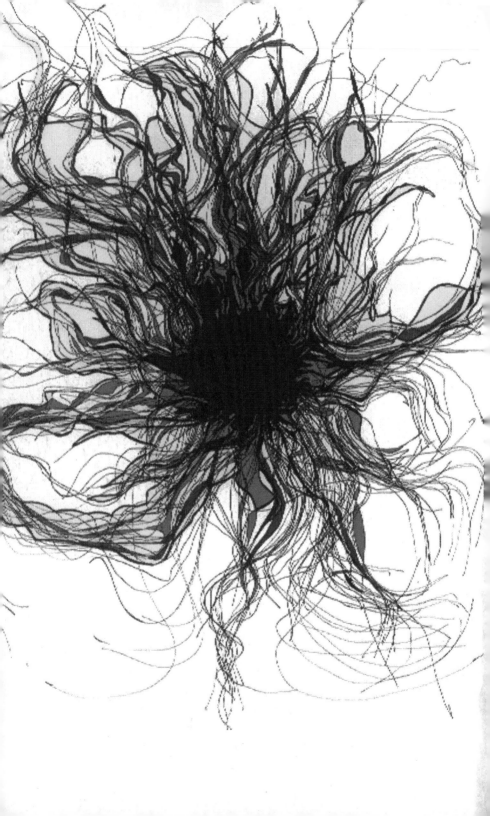

The Black Sun

THE ALCHEMY
AND ART OF DARKNESS

Stanton Marlan

Foreword by David H. Rosen

TEXAS A&M UNIVERSITY PRESS
COLLEGE STATION

The paper used in this book meets the minimum requirements
of the American National Standard for Permanence
of Paper for Printed Library Materials, Z39.48-1984.
Binding materials have been chosen for durability.

Library of Congress Cataloging-in-Publication Data

Marlan, Stanton.
The black sun : the alchemy and art of darkness / Stanton Marlan ; foreword by
David H. Rosen.—1st ed.
p. cm. — (Carolyn and Ernest Fay series in analytical psychology ; no 10)
Includes bibliographical references and index.
ISBN 1-58544-425-1 (cloth : alk. paper)
1. Jungian psychology. 2. Alchemy—Psychological aspects.
3. Shadow (Psychoanalysis). 4. Self. I. Title. II. Series.
BF175.M28345 2005
150.19'54—dc22
2004021663

ISBN 13: 978-1-60344-078-3 (pbk)
ISBN 13: 978-1-60344-585-6 (ebook)

I dedicate this book to my wife, Jan;
my children, Dawn, Tori, and Brandon;
my grandchildren, Malachi and Sasha;
and to my father Jack and my mother Sylvia.

I also dedicate this book to my patients and to
others who have suffered an encounter with the
black sun, and I hope that they may also come
to know something of Sol niger's shine and the
benevolence of darkness.

CONTENTS

FOREWORD

David H. Rosen

*As far as we can discern, the sole purpose of human
existence is to kindle a light in the darkness of mere
being.*

—C. G. Jung

Nearly six months before Stan Marlan's superb 2003 Fay Lecture series on the black sun, I had this dream: There was too much light and
brightness everywhere. I gave a talk on the need for darkness and its
healing value. I said I could always leave Star, a town at the periphery.
I realized that I could break off and leave and go to the Texas hill coun-
try and write haiku.

The dream is about *enantiodromia* and the restorative necessity of
darkness and its nurturing solitude. I became aware that I could leave
Star (a constant source of light) and end up alone in the Texas hill coun-
try writing haiku. This breaking off and leaving is what I call egocide
(symbolic death), which leads to transformation (rebirth) through
creativity.[1]

The black sun and the alchemy and art of darkness are subjects dear
to my heart and soul.[2] When I was in a psychic black hole contemplat-
ing suicide thirty-five years ago, my own darkness went through an alchemical process involving art.[3] I was able to transcend my despair and
later transform my depression, healing my soul through creativity. Art
is healing, and the shadow of despair is the fuel for creativity. Darkness
is critically needed in our too-well-lighted world. As Stan Marlan out-

lines in this important book, the secret is to engage in the alchemy and art of darkness, which yields creative endeavors through Jung's technique of active imagination. Usually I do this through painting and writing, most recently by completing a book on *The Healing Spirit of Haiku*.[4]

Given my experience with and affinity for darkness, I eagerly read Marlan's *Black Sun*, which explores darkness in vast and deep ways. Irvin Yalom states, "Everyone—and that includes therapists as well as patients—is destined to experience not only the exhilaration of life, but also its inevitable darkness: disillusionment, aging, illness, isolation, loss, meaninglessness, painful choices, and death."[5] Yalom also states that there is an "inbuilt despair in the life of every self-conscious individual."[6]

In the deep dark the person alone sees light.
—Chuang Tzu[7]

In the introduction, Marlan says that the black sun became a Zen koan for him. This got me thinking about the time I spent in Japan and the fact that in the Shinto religion the sun is considered a goddess. In other words, a black (yin) sun that glows and inspires creative works is *Sol niger* (black sun) functioning as a muse. Thus, in the land where darkness is praised, fear of the dark is overcome, and the black sun is a creative fire that heals.[8] Most striking—and a testament of the truth of an inner shine of darkness—is that blind people see light in their dark interior.

In chapter 1 Marlan begins with a focus on the sun as the source of light and its association with the King (a divine archetype). He gives several excellent alchemical examples of how the King must die in order to be born again. Closer to home, Elvis Presley, America's "King," illustrates the theme of this book in that he represents a dark King. He got stuck in the *nigredo* (darkness) and was poisoned. However, after Elvis died he continued to live on, reborn as a dark or blue King with an inner spiritual glow.[9]

In chapter 2 we descend with Marlan into the darkness and see the necessity of experiencing one's own "dark night of the soul." A case of a troubled woman is presented, which includes dramatic illustrations of the black sun. Her image of an "exploding black sun" is associated with "the madness of her suicidal feelings." It may also have foretold an aneurysm in the anterior region of her brain. She survived this near-death experience but lost sight in one eye. This case underscores the danger involved in getting close to the black sun. Marlan presents another case, also of a woman in long-term analysis who creatively transforms her suicidal feelings based on contact with the black sun. This patient's words and drawings are profound, and Marlan links the deep, dark work to powerful archetypal images from art, religion, and literature.

Chapter 3 outlines how analysis (breaking apart) is like the alchemical processes of *mortificatio* and putrefaction. Marlan describes brilliantly—and reveals through his alchemical psychological approach—how analyzing the ego to death opens the psyche to creative transformations involving the deep art of darkness. In essence, Marlan shows us how darkness heals by shining through.

In chapter 4 Marlan focuses on Jewish mysticism (primarily the kabbalah), Taoist alchemy, and illuminating pictures from artists and patients. Through these it becomes clear that darkness itself glows with a unique spiritual light. Marlan humbles us before a myriad of glimpses of Sol niger.

The last chapter concerns the mystery of Self and non-Self as One or Not-One. I think his position would be acceptable to both Lao Tzu and Jung, although Jung was more comfortable with the dark side of the Self rather than non-Self. For Jungian analysts who are Buddhists, such as Polly Young-Eisendrath, the paradox of Self and non-Self makes particular sense.[10] Jungian analysts who are Taoist in their spiritual orientation are also content with the irony of opposites: nothingness/fullness, dark/light, and evil/good.[11] Why? Because it is impossible to know one without the other. Transcendence of these opposites allows for the possibility of wholeness and emptiness. And, as we often see in this book, transformation of the opposites allows for creative art and healing.

In the epilogue, Marlan distills the essence of the journey he has taken us on from light to darkness and then to the light of darkness itself. I wholeheartedly support Marlan's maxim of preserving the mystery of Self and non-Self as a paradox. In the end it is both/and. Like Victor Hugo's last words, we see "black light":

> *Seeing into darkness is clarity.*
> *Knowing how to yield is strength.*
> *Use your own light and return to the source of light.*
> *This is called practicing eternity.*
> —*Lao Tzu*[12]

This volume helps us to understand the source of archetypal darkness and its relationship to a psychic crisis involving the black sun. As we know from Chinese philosophy, crisis involves both danger and opportunity. It is noteworthy that dreams of a black sun or an archetypal abyss can be both a warning of psychic and/or physical demise as well as the beginning of a significant renewal.

In alchemy the nigredo is first, and, according to Plato, the beginning is the most important part of the work. I agree with Marlan that darkness has neither been seen as primary nor valued for its inherent healing power and creative transformation.[13] The opportunity for healing through the art of darkness is ever present and extremely well illustrated in the text.

Another example of the alchemy and art of darkness as well as egocide and transformation is William Styron's eloquent memoir, *Darkness Visible*.[14] It is a book about his fall into a suicidal void and his struggle to climb out. Most likely he was guided by a healing glow coming from Sol niger.

On May 15, 2003, while I was editing this manuscript, there was a *luna niger*, a total eclipse of the moon by the sun's shadow. Marlan writes about the shadow of the sun and its darkness, and where is this more apparent than in a total eclipse of the moon? Perhaps in our time this represents the patriarchal Sun King and its shadow, which eclipses the feminine, whereas the black sun has no need to eclipse the moon because both have a soft glow, one from within and the other from outer reflection.

To conclude, this volume is extraordinary in its breadth and depth and in its objective and subjective scope. Stan Marlan's method of illustrating the alchemy and art of darkness with clinical cases, drawings, and paintings is rare and truly phenomenal. Clearly this book will enrich us all.

I close with the poet Wendell Berry's words, which seem connected to Sol niger:

> To go in the dark with a light is to know the light. To know the dark, go dark. Go without sight, and find that the dark, too, blooms and sings, and is traveled by dark feet and dark wings.[15]

Notes

1. D. H. Rosen, *Transforming Depression: Healing the Soul through Creativity* (York Beach, Me.: Nicolas-Hays, 2002), pp. xxi, xxiv, xxv–xxvi, and 61–84.
2. Ibid.
3. Ibid., pp. xvii–xxii.
4. *The Healing Spirit of Haiku* is coauthored with Joel Weishaus and illustrated by Arthur Okamura.
5. I. Yalom, *The Gift of Therapy* (New York: HarperCollins, 2002), p. 6.
6. Ibid., p. 7.
7. Chuang Tzu, "Readings from Chuang Tzu," in T. Merton's *The Way of Chuang Tzu* (Boston: Shambala, 1992), p. 147.
8. J. Tanizaki, *In Praise of Shadows* (New York: Leete's Island Books, 1998).
9. D. H. Rosen, *The Tao of Elvis* (San Diego: Harcourt, 2002).
10. P. Young-Eisendrath and S. Muramoto, eds. *Awakening and Insight: Zen Buddhism and Psychotherapy* (New York: Brunner-Routledge, 2003).
11. Rosen, *The Tao of Jung: The Way of Integrity* (New York: Penguin Arkana, 1997).
12. Laozi, *Tao Te Ching*, trans. S. Mitchell (New York: HarperCollins, 1988), p. 52.
13. Rosen, *Transforming Depression*.
14. W. Styron, *Darkness Visible* (New York: Random House, 1990).
15. M. Oman, ed., *Prayers for Healing: 365 Blessings, Poems, and Meditations from around the World* (Berkeley: Conari Press, 1997), p. 254.

ACKNOWLEDGMENTS

I am deeply indebted to David Rosen and Carolyn Fay for choosing me as a Fay lecturer and for giving me the opportunity to present my ideas at Texas A&M University. David was a superb guide through the entire process and an impeccable host during my stay at College Station. In addition, I am indebted to him for both his astute editorial suggestions and for his own scholarly work, which became important in my own reflection. In David I have found a fellow traveler into the depths of darkness.

In addition, I am indebted to many people who have played an important role in making and are a living part of the final product. Many mentors, both living and dead, colleagues, analysands, patients, students, friends, analytic and academic organizations, and family members have contributed to my writing and research in numerous ways. The final product is my own, but it would not have been possible without the ongoing engagement and generosity of others.

The work of C. G. Jung has been an essential foundation for these reflections. His contributions to a psychological approach to alchemy inform a sustaining passion and continuing impetus for my own work with the difficult and arcane materials of alchemy.

I am also indebted to Marie-Louise von Franz, Edward Edinger, and James Hillman, all of whom have made significant contributions to the continuation and development of Jung's work and therefore have played an essential role in the development of my ideas about the black sun.

I give special acknowledgment to Edinger and Hillman, who were both my analysts. Edinger's deep reflections on alchemical themes were essential in my development as an analyst. His early lectures, teachings, and writings, particularly in *Anatomy of the Psyche,* filled my heart and soul as I wrote. Likewise, Hillman's work has been formative and inspiring. His originality and critique of traditional ways of thinking put alchemical psychology on a new trajectory, reversing a tendency to reduce alchemical images to psychological constructs. Over the years as analyst, teacher, and later as colleague and friend, he has been a central influence in the formation of my ideas and the development of my imaginal life. I also want to thank my former analyst Anneliese Pontius, whose encouragement and faith in me first set me on the path to becoming an analyst, and to Harriet Machtiger, who made it possible to complete my training in Pittsburgh. I owe a debt of gratitude to my former analyst and now colleague and friend Thomas Kapacinskas for his years of deep insight, challenge, and support and whose depth of heart has been an essential ingredient in the development of the stamina necessary to engage the darkness of Sol niger.

I have also benefitted from the scholarly work and friendship of many gifted Jungian colleagues. I cannot mention them all, but I wish to thank my good friends James Hollis, Lyn Cowan, and Pat Berry, who have often offered their guidance when I found myself directionless and kept me in good humor as I descended into darkness. I also owe a debt of thanks to my good friend and colleague Maurice Krasnow, whose excellent critique of an early paper on the black sun opened new avenues for the furthering of my ideas. Thanks also go to my dear friends and colleagues Vocata George and Dianne Braden for their long-time support of my work and for the pleasure of our long talks about darkness and the life of the soul. I also thank Vocata for reminding me of the importance of the work of Anselm Kiefer, whose art resonates so strongly with my vision of the black sun.

I am also grateful to my good friends and colleagues Paul Kugler, David Miller, Wolfgang Giegerich, Robert Romanyshyn, Sonu Shamdasani, Ron Schenk, and David Perry, all of whom have inspired my writing over the years of our valuable friendship.

I would also like to thank Murray Stein, a friend and colleague who read an earlier paper on Sol niger and has made many supportive gestures over the years. He provided an opportunity for me to publish *Fire in the Stone: The Alchemy of Desire* and enabled me to present my work on Taoist alchemy in China.

I also acknowledge my appreciation of my old friend Donald Kalsched, with whom I began my training when we were students at the New York Institute. Don's current work on the defenses of the Self has been important in the formulation of my thinking about the black sun.

Thanks likewise go to my colleagues Brian Skea and Roger Brooke for their support and friendship over the years. Roger made it possible for me to present my work at Duquesne University. His *Jung and Phenomenology* has helped to clarify my own ideas.

I owe a debt of gratitude to kabbalistic scholar, philosopher, and psychologist Sanford Drob, whose wonderful support and critique of my work opened many new directions. I am also grateful to Bitzalel Malamid, who selflessly shared an untranslated Chasidic/kabbalistic text that richly amplified my understanding of black light. He has truly been a teacher to me though he insists we are simply learning together.

I likewise wish to thank alchemical scholar and my friend Adam McLean for his guidance and recommendations of research materials and for introducing me to the wonderful collection of alchemical texts and manuscripts at Glasgow University during my visit to Scotland. Thanks also go to alchemical teacher and scholar Dennis Hauck, from whom I have learned a great deal about the practical aspects of alchemy and its importance in the overall work of the alchemical opus.

I want to extend my heartfelt appreciation to those who have contributed materials for my research. Over the years, many people have generously shared their knowledge, ideas, references, and drawings, all of which have immeasurably enriched this book. To name all of the particular contributions would far exceed the format of these acknowledgments, but I wish to extend my sincere gratitude to Harry Wilmer, Marga Speicher, Michael Adams, Peter Thompson, Anu Kumar, Janice Markowitz, Suzanne Bailey, Tim Pilgrim, Dennis Charier-Adams, Thomas Hart, and Tyler Dudley.

Special thanks go to my good friends Lynne Connoy for her impressive artwork and to Keith Knecht, who has been so generous with his knowledge and talents.

I would like to express my appreciation to artist and friend Janet Towbin for inviting me to lecture on alchemy to her colleagues and for contributing her powerful black painting to this book. My deep appreciation goes out to artist Virginia Moore, who likewise has been generous in supporting my work and whose impressive art inspired many discoveries about the black sun.

In addition, I owe a debt of gratitude to my philosophical teachers, colleagues, and friends at Duquesne University. Thanks go first to philosopher Monique Roelofs for reading an early draft of my paper on the black sun. I appreciate her challenges, comments, and the rich dialogue that flowered into an important friendship. I also wish to express my thanks to my friend Bettina Bergo, Levinas scholar and translator, for her spontaneous generosity and astute, on-the-spot editorial suggestions. Thanks also go to Wilhelm Wurzer, chairperson of the philosophy department at Duquesne University, who read an early reflection on the black sun and who entered into many enjoyable discussions with me of Goethe's *Faust* and darkness.

Thanks go to my friend John Schulman—poet, bookseller extraordinaire, and owner of Caliban Books—who has continually gone out of his way to find and recommend obscure works and references on the black sun.

I am also grateful to Mark Kelly, librarian at the Pacifica Graduate Institute, for his help with references and to Maureen Porcelli and Patricia Sohl for locating many dramatic images from the ARAS collection.

I am indebted to both Claudette Kulkarni, friend, colleague, and feminist Jungian scholar who read my entire manuscript and made valuable suggestions. In addition, Claudette Kulkarni and Ravi Kulkarni both worked tirelessly to track down and obtain the many necessary permissions for the illustrations published here. I am deeply in their debt. Thanks also to Sharon Broll, whose professional editing helped to put my manuscript in its best possible form.

I give very special thanks to Bill Blais, without whose assistance, patience, skill, and scholarship I would have never completed the book. Bill, a graduate student in psychology at Duquesne University, was referred to me as an assistant and typist with computer skills. In all of these functions he proved invaluable, and it wasn't long before he became an intellectual partner and friend. He knows the book as well as I do and made many suggestions that I have incorporated into the text.

I give special thanks to my very closest friends, Susan and Terry Pulver, whose companionship over the years and during the writing of this book have been sustaining and nourishing. Terry, a Lacanian psychologist and faithful lover of psychoanalysis, has been a consistent intellectual partner and confidante. Our exchanges over the years on Lacan, Jung, and postmodernism have influenced me greatly. I am deeply indebted to him for his contributions to my thought.

I want to thank the Inter-Regional Society of Jungian Analysts, the C. G. Jung Institute Analyst Training Program of Pittsburgh, the Pacifica Graduate Institute, Duquesne University, and Texas A&M for their support of my work and for giving me the opportunity to lecture on the black sun.

I cannot end these acknowledgments without my heartfelt thanks and gratitude to my family: my wife, Jan; my daughters, Dawn and Tori; my son, Brandon; my son-in-law, Jeff Librett; my grandchildren, Malachi and Sasha; my father, Jack; my late mother, Sylvia; and my brother, David. I treasure their love, support, and interest far more than I can express.

My fatherly love and pride are immeasurable, and I am grateful to my children, who in their own ways have materially contributed to this book: Thanks go to Dawn for her sensitive support, her astute critique of what's left of my Jungian essentialism, and her and Jeff's scholarly responses to my questions about French and German translation. Thanks go to Tori for her kindness and for her examples of courageous research, fair mindedness, and editorial excellence. Thanks go to Brandon for his indomitable spirit, for keeping me in touch with the soul of music, and for his recommendation of the art of Alex Grey as it pertains to my work.

I end with my deep gratitude to my wife and Jungian colleague, Jan DeVeber Marlan, who has been my companion along the way. She has not only offered her support in innumerable ways but has also been my best critic, friend, and intellectual partner. Without her this work would never have seen the light of Sol niger.

The Black Sun

INTRODUCTION

I first became aware of the image of the black sun while reading Jung's alchemical works and later in a more personal way in my analysis of a woman whose encounter with the black sun was dramatic and life changing. What I initially thought was a rare and obscure phenomenon proved to be far more widespread than I had imagined. I have since found it to be linked to the deepest issues of our mortality and to both tragic and ecstatic possibilities.

The groundwork of my fascination with the black sun was laid down long ago—in childhood. I remember thinking about death, realizing that I would die along with everyone and everything I loved and valued. My thoughts about mortality took on an obsessive quality, and I wondered why not everyone spent all of their time trying to solve the problem of dying. Over the years I learned much about the historical and psychodynamic reasons for my obsessions, and even though the issue of personal mortality no longer aroused in me the same level of anxiety, I still struggled to find a stance in regard to this inescapable and existential truth of life.

I once had a dream of floating on a raft moving toward a waterfall. I was standing with my back to the direction of the flow but was bent over in order to see where the raft was going. I could see that it would at some point fall over a precipice, which would mean certain death. I heard a voice say, "Yes, you are going to die, but you don't have to bend over backward to see it." While the truth and humor of this dream gave me some relief from my obsession, I never quite stood up completely straight again.

My reflective turn toward death marks my melancholic character and, like the historical alchemist who has a skull on his bench as a memento mori, concern with mortality remains a part of my psychic reality. I now believe that these concerns prepared the way for my engagement with the black sun, a dark and burning ball of fire, an intensity of darkness and light that became like a Zen koan to me.

The Mumonkan, a classic collection of Zen koans gathered by the thirteenth-century, Chinese Zen master Mumon, speaks of the inescapability of the koan. It is like swallowing a red-hot iron ball that you cannot actively expel. However, you cannot passively leave it inside you either, or it will kill you. The Mumonkan describes the situation as one in which one's whole being has been plunged into great doubt. All of one's emotions are exhausted; one's intellect has come to extremity. Rinzai, a well-known, ninth-century Chinese Zen master, once described this state as the whole universe plunged into darkness.[1] This description fits my relationship with the black sun. Over the years spent in writing this book, I have taken in this black sun like a red-hot iron ball that I have been unable to expel. It has become not only my dark koan but also an enigmatic and infernal light referred to in alchemy as Sol niger.

Sol niger is an image that Jung wrote about in his late works on alchemy, and though it played a relatively marginal role in his reflections, I have found its implications to merit a far more extensive exploration. This image has shown itself in relation to the darkest and most destructive situations, in what the alchemists have called the blacker-than-black dimensions of the *nigredo*. The term *nigredo* is usually thought of as a beginning process in alchemy, roughly equivalent to a descent into the unconscious. In the face of this darkness and the suffering that sometimes accompanies it, there is a natural tendency to turn away from the psyche. While this defensive process is at times necessary, it may also inhibit or bypass a hidden potential in the darkness itself. The dark side of psychic life is both dangerous and at times tragic, but the acceptance of its tragic potential was for Jung a necessity. He noted that the cure for suffering might well be more suffering.

In the Visions Seminar of 1933, a participant, Dr. Baker, commented on Jung's ideas and offered the group a passage from Miguel de Unamuno's book *The Tragic Sense of Life:*

The cure for suffering—which is the collision of consciousness with unconsciousness—is not to be submerged in unconsciousness, but to be raised to consciousness and to suffer more. The evil of suffering is cured by more suffering, by higher suffering. Do not take opium, but put salt and vinegar in the soul's wound, for when you sleep and no longer feel the suffering, you are not. And to be, that is imperative. Do not then close your eyes to the agonizing Sphinx, but look her in the face, and let her seize you in her mouth, and crunch you with her hundred thousand poisonous teeth, and swallow you. And when she has swallowed you, you will know the sweetness of the taste of suffering.[2]

There will be little opium and plenty of salt and vinegar as we begin our descent into darkness. Nevertheless, you may also find some surprises as we follow Sol niger in clinical practice and through myth, literature, the creative arts, and various traditions at once philosophical, religious, and mystical. The black sun is a paradox. It is blacker than black, but it also shines with a dark luminescence that opens the way to some of the most numinous aspects of psychic life. It proffers a miracle of perception at the heart of what Jung called the *mysterium coniunctionis*. Considering the complexity of Sol niger will give us an opportunity to consider Jung's idea of the Self in a new way—one that both critiques and preserves its integrity as a central mystery of the psyche, which for Jung was always fundamental.

In chapter one we set the stage for our exploration by discussing the primacy of light as a metaphor for consciousness. We then consider the importance of the alchemical deconstruction of this light, which prepares us for our descent into the unconscious. There is a lot of dark material, and the descent is difficult and painful. In chapter two we follow a path, not from darkness into light, but from light into darkness and into the shine of darkness itself. Beginning with Goethe's *Faust,* we look at a series of vignettes—literary and clinical—in which the black sun appears and becomes important. These illustrations lead to the blacker-than-black aspects of Sol niger, and these serve as the foundation for our ongoing exploration.

The third chapter, titled "Analysis and the Art of Darkness," looks at the issue of trauma as one response to Sol niger. We examine some of Jungian analyst Don Kalsched's contributions to this theme from his work, *The Inner World of Trauma,* particularly the idea of the defenses of the Self as an archetypal process protecting the Self from disintegration. My reflection on the black sun explores a different perspective with regard to the archetypal functioning of psychological life. If we can for a moment project human intention onto the dark forces that attack the psyche, I believe their aim is not always to protect but rather to mortify the Self and to drive it into the unthinkable, which the idea of archetypal defense seeks to avoid. In this light we also look at the contribution of Jungian analyst David Rosen to this theme in his book *Transforming Depression* and his idea of egocide and the strange confluence of death and new life. From my perspective, this theme of renewal does not follow simply from symbolic death but is actually fundamental and at the core of Sol niger, which expresses itself in the simultaneity of blackness and luminescence, the central mystery of the black sun.

We then amplify this imagery by turning to the world of art and particularly to painters who have spent parts of their careers painting black suns and/or a kind of luminescent blackness. We look briefly at the works of Max Ernst, Mark Rothko, Ad Reinhardt, Pierre Soulage, and Anselm Kiefer and place their discoveries in the alchemical context of the *lumen naturae,* the dark light of nature. For the alchemists, the lumen naturae is a different kind of light that shines at the core of matter and within the ancient idea of the subtle or illuminated body. Chapter four explores a number of different, subtle body images from kabbalah, Tantra, Taoist alchemy, and contemporary art. These traditions serve as a background for looking at a patient's artwork, which Jung writes about in his *Alchemical Studies,* in which a black sun appears in her solar plexus, an important area in many subtle body traditions. It is a place to which, according to Jung, the gods have retreated in our modern era.

Finally we discuss the black sun as an image of the non-Self. This reflection focuses on a way of understanding the Self not so much as an ideal union of opposites but rather as paradox and monstrosity.

In writing this book, my childhood concerns about mortality are not resolved but show themselves in a new dark light that leaves me with a feeling of compassion and gratitude for each moment of life. This drives my spiritual and therapeutic sensibilities, and thus my work ends less with anxiety and more with wonder. I hope that the readers of this text will likewise discover darkness in a new way. It is not my goal to lead anyone beyond the darkness but instead to the illumination of darkness itself, and I hope that this will be a worthwhile experience in its own right.

CHAPTER 1

The Dark Side of Light

*When you see your matter going black, rejoice, for this
is the beginning of the work.*

—Rosarium Philosophorum

Jung considered alchemy in a way that few people, if any, before him
had imagined. Alchemy for the most part had been relegated to the status of a historical anachronism or hidden away within the confines of
esoteric occultism. To the contemporary mind, alchemists were viewed
as working in their laboratories, hopelessly trying to change lead into
gold. At best, their practice was seen as a precursor to the modern science of chemistry.

Jung began his reflections with a similar attitude, but as his inquiry
grew deeper, he concluded that the alchemists were speaking in symbols about the human soul and were working as much with the imagination as with the literal materials of their art. The gold that they were
trying to produce was not the common or vulgar gold but an *aurum
non vulgi* or *aurum philosophicum*—a philosophical gold (Jung 1961).
They were concerned with both the creation of the higher man and the
perfection of nature. In a 1952 interview at the Eranos conference, Jung
stated that "The alchemical operations were real, only this reality was
not physical but psychological. Alchemy represents the projection of a
drama both cosmic and spiritual in laboratory terms. The *opus magnum* had two aims: the rescue of the human soul and the salvation of

the cosmos."[1] This move brought alchemy into the realm of contemporary thought and was the beginning of a sustained psychology of alchemy.

To see alchemy in this way—as a psychological and symbolic art—was a major breakthrough for Jung and a key to unlocking its mysteries. The exploration and development of this insight led Jung eventually to see in alchemy a fundamental source, background, and confirmation of his psychology of the unconscious. His imagination was captured by the ideas and metaphors of alchemy, with its dragons, suffering matter, peacock's tail, alembics, athanors, red and green lions, kings and queens, fishes' eyes, inverted philosophical trees, salamanders and hermaphrodites, black suns and white earth, metals (lead, silver, and gold), colors (black, white, yellow, and red), distillations and coagulations, and a rich array of Latin terms. All of these images are, for Jung, the best possible expression of a psychic mystery that enunciated and amplified his maturing vision of the parallels between alchemy and his own psychology of the unconscious. Jung sees all of these as projected by the alchemists into matter. Their effort was to bring about unity from the disparate parts of the psyche, creating a "chemical wedding." Jung saw as the moral task of alchemy the unification of the disparate elements of the soul, symbolically represented as the creation of the lapis, or philosopher's stone. Likewise, Jung's psychology works with the conflicts and dissociation of psychic life and attempts to bring about the mysterious "unification" he calls Wholeness.

In *C. G. Jung Speaking,* Jung describes the alchemical process as "difficult and strewn with obstacles; the alchemical opus is dangerous. Right at the beginning you meet the 'dragon,' the chthonic spirit, the 'devil' or, as the alchemists called it, the 'blackness,' the nigredo, and this encounter produces suffering."[2] He goes on to say that in "psychological terms, the soul finds itself in the throes of melancholy locked in a struggle with the 'shadow.'" The black sun, Sol niger, is one of the most important images representing this phase of the process and this condition of the soul. Usually this image is seen as phase specific to the early part of the opus and is said to disappear "when the 'dawn' (aurora) emerges." Typically blackness is said to dissolve, and then "the 'devil' no longer has an autonomous existence but rejoins the profound unity of the psyche. Then the opus magnum is finished: the human soul is [said to be] completely integrated."[3]

In my experience, this is an idealized goal of alchemy, and there is a danger in bypassing the autonomous core of darkness that always remains as an earmark of the condition of any humanness. Thus, my approach to the image of the black sun pauses with the blackness itself and examines it in its own right, not simply as a stage in the development of the soul. As such we see that blackness itself proves to contain in its own realm the gold we seek in our attempts to transcend it. This focus contributes to a new appreciation of the darkness within.

Jung's exploration was influenced by the seventeenth-century alchemist Mylius, who refers to the ancient philosophers as the source of our knowledge about Sol niger. In several places in his collected works, Jung writes of Sol niger as a powerful and important image of the unconscious. To consider the image in the context of the unconscious is both to recognize its vastness and unknown quality as well as to place it in the historical context of depth psychology and of the psyche's attempt to represent the unrepresentable. Imagining Sol niger in this way is to see it in its most general sense, but Jung has also extracted from the alchemical literature a rich and complex, if scattered, phenomenology of the image. The black sun, blackness, *putrefactio, mortificatio,* the *nigredo,* poisoning, torture, killing, decomposition, rotting, and death all form a web of interrelationships that describe a terrifying, if most often provisional, eclipse of consciousness or of our conscious standpoint.

The nigredo, the initial black stage of the alchemical opus, has been considered the most negative and difficult operation in alchemy. It is also one of the most numinous, but few authors other than Jung have explored the theme in its many facets. In addition to the aspects just described, Jung also finds in this image of blackness a nonmanifest latency, a shadow of the sun, as well as an Other Sun, linked to both Saturn and Yahweh, the *primus anthropos.* For the most part, Sol niger is equated with and understood only in its nigredo aspect, while its more sublime dimension—its shine, its dark illumination, its Eros and wisdom—remains in the unconscious.

I imagine my work on the black sun as an experiment in alchemical psychology. It is concerned with this difficult and enigmatic image and with our understanding of darkness. My contention is that darkness historically has not been treated hospitably and that it has remained in the unconscious and become a metaphor for it. It has been seen primarily in its negative aspect and as a secondary phenomenon, itself constituting a shadow—something to integrate, to move through and beyond. In so doing, its intrinsic importance is often passed over. This attitude has also been perpetuated in alchemy, which places darkness at the beginning of the work and sees it primarily in terms of the nigredo. Yet in its usage of the black sun there is a hint of a darkness that shines. It is this shine of the paradoxical image that captures my attention. How is it possible to imagine a darkness filled with light or a shine that contains the qualities of both light and darkness?

Jung has noted that darkness "has its own peculiar intellect and its own logic which should be taken very seriously," and it is my intent to give darkness its due—not to rush beyond it but to enter its realm to learn more about its mysteries.[4] To turn toward darkness in this way is an odd reversal of our ordinary propensity. To more fully understand the turn toward darkness it is first important to pause and consider how much the historical primacy of light has infused our understanding of consciousness itself.

The image of light and its corresponding metaphor of the sun are fundamentally intertwined with the history of consciousness. Our language demonstrates the pervasiveness of these images, and it is difficult to envision a way of thinking that does not rely on them. In myth, science, philosophy, religion, and alchemy we find these metaphors widely disseminated. Our language is filled with metaphors of illumination: to bring to light, to make clear, to enlighten, and so on, all serve in these and in many other contexts.

In *Memories, Dreams, Reflections* Jung seems to have captured something of the primordial experience that must have been generative in the development of sun worship. While visiting the Elgonyi tribe of Africa, Jung writes, "the sunrise in these latitudes was a phenomenon that overwhelmed me anew every day."[5] He goes on to describe his observations a little before dawn, when he was in the habit of watching the sunrise:

At first, the contrasts between light and darkness would be extremely sharp. Then objects would assume contour and emerge into the light which seemed to fill the valley with a compact brightness. The horizon above became radiantly white. Gradually the swelling light seemed to penetrate into the very structure of objects, which became illuminated from within until at last they shone translucently, like bits of colored glass. Everything turned to flaming crystal. The cry of the bell bird rang around the horizon. At such moments I felt as if I were inside a temple. It was the most sacred hour of the day. I drank in this glory with insatiable delight, or rather in a timeless ecstasy.[6]

Jung goes on to say that "for untold ages men have worshiped the great god who redeems the world by rising out of darkness as a radiant light in the heavens. At the time, I understood that within the soul from its primordial beginnings there has been a desire for light and an irrepressible urge to rise out of the primal darkness."[7] Against this background it is evident to Jung why for the Elgonyi "the *moment* in which the light comes *is* God."[8]

Jung recognizes the importance of the sun and light in his alchemical writings, where he states that the soul is "an eye destined to behold the light."[9] Likewise, James Hillman, a Jungian analyst as well as the founder of archetypal psychology, wonders whether the "human eye prefers light to darkness" and whether human beings are "heliotropic, fundamentally adapted to light."[10] The power of this image is also recognized by the postmodern philosopher Jacques Derrida, who comments, "each time there is a metaphor, there is doubtless a sun somewhere, but each time there is a sun, metaphor has begun."[11]

The importance of the sun metaphor is further traced by Mircea Eliade, historian and scholar of religion, who finds a parallel between sun worship and the spread of civilization and kings. Eliade documents the predominance of sun religions: "Where history is on the march thanks to kings, heroes or empires, the sun is supreme."[12] The sun's majesty lent its power to the signification of the person and the office of the king. Both the Sun and the King archetypes are highly complex, archetypal images with multiple meanings. This theme has been extensively studied by Jungian analyst John Perry in his *Lord of the Four Quarters: Myth of the Royal Father;* Jungian analyst Robert Moore, and mythologist and therapist Douglas Gillette in *The King Within;* and more recently as the archetype of renewal in *Psychological Reflections on the Aging, Death, and Rebirth of the King* by Jungian analyst Stephenson Bond.

The sun has traditionally been associated with masculine attributes in patriarchal culture, but this attribution has been relativized and destabilized by studies such as Janet McCritchard's *Eclipse of the Sun,* which demonstrates a wide range of feminine attributes to the sun across time and culture.[13] Still, with regard to the "masculine" psyche, the sun, particularly in relation to the king, has been considered a representation of God on earth. Kings were considered sacred. Figure 1.1 shows an image of King Sol on his throne.

In general, the Sun King reflects a dominant force of historical, cultural, and psychic reality. As an inner figure, he is fundamental to life and a well-functioning psyche. There is a long tradition of the King and the Sun reflecting the qualities of rational order, stability, life force, vitality, blessing, joy, and light. The Sun and the King light up the world.

The work of Moore and Gillette argues that the inner King as an expression of mature masculinity should not be equated with the abuses of patriarchy and power and with the shadow of the King as Tyrant. As archetypal principles, the Sun and the King are not in themselves destructive or problematic to culture or the psychic life of people. On the contrary, as noted earlier, they enhance life and are essential to psyche. The problem begins when these archetypal forces overwhelm a developing or immature ego, inflating and corrupting it. When the ego identifies with the transpersonal power of the King and the ego becomes King, the Tyrant is near, and the King's energy can be devouring (cf. figure 1.2). In short, the King and the Tyrant are brothers in the archetypal psyche.

The devouring and oppressive shadow side of the King's energy has been linked in our time to patriarchy and to the one-sided Apollonian vision that has laid the groundwork for an angry critique of our psychological and cultural attitudes. If the Sun has led our way into the present, with all of the advances that have come with it, it has also led

Figure 1.1. King Sol on his throne. Fifteenth century. From Stanislas Klossowski de Rola, Alchemy: The Secret Art, *p. 67.*

to a massive repression and devaluation of the dark side of psychic life. "There are as many ways to be lost in the light as in the dark," says storyteller and poet Madronna Holden, who recognizes the peril that occurs when light loses touch with the principle of darkness.[14] On the cultural level we all too often have become lost in our spiritual, Apollonian, patriarchal, male perspective. Our roots in European languages and a Cartesian worldview have led to a personal and cultural elitism that have fueled charges of racism and colonialism. To the extent that these judgments have validity, they reflect a collective, cultural, and philosophical shadow. Has the light the eye was "destined to behold" displayed a blind spot with regard to vision itself?

Moore and Gillette have observed that, when the King sits on his

Figure 1.2. The king devouring his subject, 1625. From Johannes Fabricius,
Alchemy: The Medieval Alchemists and Their Royal Art, *p. 75.*

throne and is the center of the world, "world" becomes defined as that
part of reality that is organized and ordered by the King." What is outside the boundaries of his influence is noncreation, chaos, the demonic and non-world.[15] This situation sets the stage for a massive
repression and devaluation of the "dark side" of psychic life. It creates
a totality that rejects interruption and refuses the other from within its
narcissistic enclosure.

For a number of philosophers—Heidegger, Foucault, Derrida, and
others—there is a dangerous tendency in modernity toward closure
and tautological reductionism: "totalization, normalization and dom-
ination."[16] Levin has noted that behind our Western visionary tradition lies the shadow of phallocentrism, logocentrism, and a "heliopolitics" driven by the violence of Light. To put it more simply, the
concern about modernity is that it is governed by male desire and
power and by an egocentric rationality that serves political agendas

that conceal intrinsic violence. In his work *Writing and Difference*, Derrida speaks of the violence of Light and the imperialism of theory associated with it. He notes that this kind of violence also troubled the philosopher Emmanuel Levinas, whose work was aimed at developing an ethical theory freed as much as possible from the violence implicit in Western metaphysical thinking.[17] If one agrees with the philosophers and critics of our tradition, one might imagine our time as one locked into the tyrannical shadow of a Sun King who bears within himself the seeds of his own destruction.

Is it possible to imagine this situation as rooted in an unconscious identification with the King and the Light? If so, such unconscious identification colors the psyche and has important personal and cultural consequences.

On the most personal level, analysts have approached such concerns not so much philosophically but as they manifest themselves in clinical situations. In *The Anatomy of the Psyche,* Jungian analyst Edward Edinger, for instance, cites the expressions of unconscious kingly inflations in "outbursts of affect, resentment, pleasure or power demands."[18] The refinement of these affects is difficult. As an inner figure, the primitive King/ego must undergo a transformation not only in our culture but also in the lives of people. Alchemy recognizes this fact when it sees that the King is at the beginning—the raw matter of the philosopher's stone—and that he must be purified and refined by undergoing a series of alchemical processes, eventually dying and being reborn.

In alchemy, the process of dying, killing, and blackening is part of the operation of mortificatio. This operation is a necessary component of the transformative process of the King and other images of the prima materia such as the Sun, the Dragon, the Toad, and the condition of innocence. Edinger devotes a chapter of *The Anatomy of the Psyche* to this process. The mortificatio process was often thought of as tortuous and as the "most negative operation in alchemy."[19] "It has to do with darkness, defeat, torture, mutilation, death and rotting. The process of rotting is called *putrefactio,* the decomposition that breaks down organic bodies."[20]

Edinger has schematized and charted this operation reproduced in

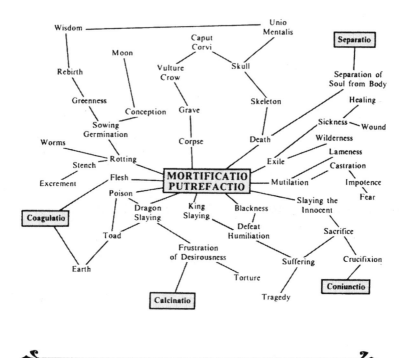

Figure 1.3. A map of alchemical processes. From Edward Edinger,
Anatomy of the Psyche: Alchemical Symbolism in Psychotherapy, p. 146.
Courtesy Open Court Books.

figure 1.3, an example of what he calls "cluster thinking"—thinking
that is concerned with elaborating a network of expanded meanings
derived from a central image. The process "goes back and forth, returning to the central image again and again, building up a rich asso-
ciative cluster of interconnected images, something like a spider web.
The result of such thinking is a rich tapestry of elaboration around a
central image."[21] Figure 1.3 shows the structural placement of related
images (e.g., the slaying of the King, the Dragon, the Toad, poison,
defeat, humiliation, torture, mutilation, the slaying of the innocent,

corpses, and rotting, as well as the placement of this operation in relation to other alchemical processes).

Alchemical engravings also help us to visualize the process. The ultimate goal of the king's mortification is purification, death, and transformation. This process is signified by a series of alchemical images that have been reproduced by Jung, Edinger, Von Franz, and others. These powerful and complex images lend themselves to multiple interpretations but generally seem to reflect the many aspects of the mortification process necessary for alchemical transformation. The subjects to be transformed are often represented by an old king, a dragon, a toad, or the sun in the process of being wounded or killed by club, sword, or poison; drowned; or devoured. The phenomenology of this process aims to displace or alter the old dominant function of the conscious ego or the underdeveloped, instinctual state of the unconscious psyche. It is a wounding or death that prepares the primitive self for fundamental change.

In the "Death of the King" from Stolcius, we see the king sitting on his throne.[22] Ten figures are uniformly lined up behind him preparing to club him to death. In another graphic titled "Sol and Luna Kill the Dragon," Sol and Luna likewise are about to club a dragon.[23] As noted, this creature is often a "personification of the instinctual psyche."[24]

The struggle with the unconscious is also portrayed in the *Book of Lambspring*, where a warrior with sword in hand encounters a dragon whose head he must cut off. A verse describing this image states:

> *Here you straightaway behold*
> *A black beast in the forest,*
> *Whose skin is of blackest dye, if any*
> *Man cuts off his head. His blackness*
> *Will disappear.*[25]

Dealing with the dragon requires both a slaying of and an incisive engagement with the instinctual ground of the psyche.

Figure 1.4 is from the *Dance of Death* by Hans Holbein. The image shows Death pouring a drink for the king.

The theme of poisoning is also linked to the alchemical image of the

Figure 1.4. The Dance of Death *(1538), woodcut by Hans Holbein.*
Death pours a drink for the king. From Edward Edinger, Anatomy of the Psyche:
Alchemical Symbolism in Psychotherapy, *p. 152*

Toad, which is a symbolic variation of the "poisonous dragon" and represents the outcome of unrestrained, unstructured life. "The toad as *prima materia* drowns in its own greed and hunger. It dies, turns black, putrefies, and is filled with poison."[26] The alchemist heats the remains of the toad, and its color changes "from black to many colors to white to red," indicating the transformative process.[27] The poison it contains is then transformed to a *pharmakon*, an elixir that can lead to death and/or regeneration.

Another well-known image of the king's mortification (figure 1.5) can be found in the alchemical work *Splendor Solis.* The king in the background is drowning and undergoing a *solutio* process. He represents the inflated ego dissolving in his own excessive waters. This process is said to make it possible for the king to rejuvenate. Other al-

Figure 1.5. The old father king drowning in the sea is reborn in his son and successor. From Solomon Trismosin, Splendor Solis, *1582. "Crowned figure with scepter and ball," Harley 3469 f16v. By permission of The British Library.*

chemical images such as the illustrations of seventeenth-century engraver Balthazar Schwan of the wounding of Sol by Luna depict the penetration of the unconscious into the body of the conscious ego. In a well-known graphic (color plate 1), Sol is wounded by the bite of the green lion, his blood flowing to the Earth as he is slowly devoured.

There have been many alchemical commentaries on color plate 1. The devouring aspect of the lion is represented in this emblem, which was first attached to a sixteenth-century manuscript of the *Rosarium Philosophorum*.[28] It shows the lion devouring the sun, with the blood of the lion issuing from its mouth. Abraham equates the sun with the alchemists' raw stuff, "'gold,' which is devoured and dissolved in order to obtain the 'sperm' of gold, the living seed from which pure gold can be grown."[29]

The idea is that the raw solar energy must darken and undergo a mortificatio process that reduces it to its prime matter. Only then can the creative energies produce a purified product. In this image the sperm of gold refers not to the ordinary seminal fluid of man but rather to "a semi-material principle," or *aura seminales,* the fertile potentiality that prepares the Sun for the sacred marriage with his counterpart, darkness, which is thought to produce a philosophical child or stone and is nourished by the mercurial blood that flows from the wounding encounter of the Lion and the Sun.[30] The blood—called red mercury—is considered a great solvent.

Psychologically, there is nourishment in wounding. When psychological blood flows, it can dissolve hardened defenses. This then can be the beginning of true productivity. In dreams the imagery of blood often connotes moments when real feeling and change are possible. The theme of the wound can also suggest a hidden innocence, which is also a subject of mortification. The green color of the lion, which is referred to as "green gold," suggests something that is immature, unripe, or innocent, as well as growth and fertility.

The alchemist imagined this innocence, sometimes called virgin's milk, as a primary condition, something without Earth and not yet blackened. Typical virgin-milk fantasies are often maintained emotionally in otherwise intellectually sophisticated and developed people. Unconsciously held ideas might include sentiments such as "Life should be fair," "God will protect and care for me like a good parent," "Bad things won't happen to me because I have lived according to this or that principle," "I have been good or faithful, eat healthy foods, and exercise," and so on. When life does not confirm such ideas, the innocent, weak, or immature ego is wounded and often overcome with feelings of hurt, self-pity, oppression, assault, and/or victimization.

The injured ego can carry this wounding in many ways. The darkening process can lead to a kind of blindness and dangerous stasis of the soul that then becomes locked in a wound, in hurt or rage, frozen in stone or ice, or fixed in fire. From the alchemical point of view, these innocent attitudes must undergo this mortificatio process—and innocent attitudes await the necessary work of alchemy. Hillman notes that the blackening begins in "scorching, hurting, cursing, rotting the innocence of soul and corrupting and depressing it into the nigredo, which we recognize by its stench [a mind lost in introspection about] its materialistic causes for what went wrong."[31]

Looking for what went wrong is often looking in the wrong place. What is not seen by the wounded soul is that what is happening under the surface and in the blackening process is a dying of immature innocence—a nigredo that holds a transformative possibility and an experience that opens the dark eye of the soul. As Edinger puts it, the soul "enters the gate of blackness."[32] Jung refers to the descent into darkness as *nekyia*. In *Psychology and Alchemy*, Jung uses this Greek word to designate a "'journey to Hades,' a descent into the land of the dead."[33] Mythically, as is the case throughout Jungian literature, there are many examples of such journeys. Jung mentions Dante's *Divine Comedy*, which Dante starts with a statement of the nigredo experience. He writes:

> *Midway upon the journey of our life*
> *I found that I was in a dusky wood;*
> *For the right path, whence I had strayed, was lost.*
> *Ah me! How hard a thing it is to tell*
> *The wildness of that rough and savage place,*
> *The very thought of which brings back my fear!*
> *So bitter was it, death is little more so.*[34]

The Dark Side of Light (23)

Figure 1.6. Leaden depression of a Benedictine suffering death in a valley of fading stars. From Johannes Fabricius, Alchemy: The Medieval Alchemists and Their Art, *p. 105.*

Jung also notes the classic Walpurgisnacht in Goethe's *Faust* and apocryphal accounts of Christ's descent into hell. Edinger gives further examples of the nekyia, citing descriptions from the book of Job, Bunyan's *Pilgrim's Progress,* and T. S. Eliot's "The Wasteland." His own contributions to this theme are in his study of Melville's *Moby Dick,* which he subtitles *An American Nekyia* and which he refers to as an American *Faust.*[35] Additional parallels are cited by Sylvia Perera, who notes the Japanese Izanami, the Greek Kore-Persephone, the Roman Psyche, and the fairy tale heroines who go to Mother Hulda or Baba Yaga. In *Descent to the Goddess,* her own work, she studies the theme from the perspective of the initiation of women and takes up the Sumerian story of Inanna and Ereshkigal, the Dark Goddess. One could go on citing numerous examples throughout history and across cultures. As Edinger notes, "the theme has no national or racial boundaries. It is found everywhere because it refers to an innate, necessary psychic movement

Figure 1.7. The nigredo. From Edward Edinger, Anatomy of the Psyche: Alchemical Symbolism in Psychotherapy, *p. 165.*

which must take place sooner or later when the conscious ego has exhausted the resources and energies of a given life attitude."[36]

The nekyia ultimately leads to the fading of the ego's light and a death that is captured in "The Hollow Men" by Eliot:

> *This is the dead land*
> *This is the cactus land*
> *Here the stone images*
> *Are raised, here they receive*
> *The supplication of a dead man's hand*
> *Under the twinkle of a fading star.*[37]

The image of Eliot's fading star or loss of light is given graphic representation in figure 1.6, which depicts a man in a "leaden depression" suffering death in a valley of fading stars.

The Dark Side of Light (25)

In alchemy, the loss of light renders the soul burnt out, dried up, and picked bare, leaving only skeletal remains. This is illustrated in figure 1.7, which Fabricius calls "The fears and horrors of the damned."[38]

In the alchemical text *Splendor Solis* (1582), death is portrayed by a black sun burning down on a desolate landscape (color plate 2). It is this burnt-out place of the soul that we must enter if we are to understand Sol niger and the nigredo process.

CHAPTER 2

The Descent into Darkness

Abandon hope, all ye who enter here!
—*Dante*, Inferno, *Canto 3*

What follows is difficult and uncomfortable. Hillman warns that the nigredo "speaks with the voice of the raven, foretelling dire happenings,"[1] and Dante tells us, "Abandon hope, all ye who enter here." Yet, in addition to these warnings, I would like to provide some encouragement. The artist Ad Reinhardt pointed out that we have a natural tendency to rush away from such experiences, yet he encouraged us instead to "wait a minute," to hold fast—because looking into blackness requires a period of adjustment. The reward for staying is available to those who have faith enough to withstand "infinite duration."[2]

Staying with the darkness allows something to happen that escapes us if we are hasty. If we resist our natural tendency to take flight before painful experiences, we can descend into the dark aspects of the unconscious, which is necessary if we are to make contact with what Goethe calls "infinite nature."[3] Turning toward such darkness requires a willingness to stay with suffering and to make a descent into the unconscious.

Goethe's great work, *Faust*, was essential to Jung, who once said that "one cannot meditate enough about Faust."[4] Edinger also remarked that this work is of "major importance for the psychological understanding of modern man."[5] For Jung, Goethe was in the grip of a descent, an archetypal process, a process also alive and active within him

Figure 2.1. The Forest, *by Gustave Doré (1832–1883).*
Dante preparing for the descent. From Gustav Doré, The Doré Illustrations
for Dante's Divine Comedy *(New York: Dover Publications, 1976).*

as a living substance, the great dream of the *mundus archetypus,* the archetypal world. It was Goethe's main business and essential to his goal of penetrating the dark secrets of the personality. In the opening of *Faust,* Goethe's magnum opus, Faust reflects on the nigredo of "night":

> I've studied now, to my regret,
> Philosophy, Law, Medicine,

and—what is worst—Theology.
from end to end with diligence.
Yet, here I am, a wretched fool
and still no wiser than before.
I've become master, and Doctor as well,
and for nearly ten years I have led
my young students a merry chase.
up, down, and every which way—
and find we can't have certitude.
This is too much for heart to bear!
I well may know more than all those dullards,
those doctors, teachers, officials and priests,
be unbothered by scruples or doubts,
and fear neither hell nor its devils—
but I get no joy from anything either,
know nothing that I think worthwhile,
and don't imagine that what I teach
could better mankind or make it godly . . .
No dog would want to linger on like this! . . .

Alas! I'm still confined to prison
Accursed, musty hole of stone
to which the sun's fair light itself
dimly penetrates through the painted glass.
Restricted by this great mass of books
that worms consume, that dust has covered
and that up to the ceiling-vault
are interspersed with grimy papers . . .

And still you wonder why your heart
is anxious and your breast constricted,
why a pain you cannot account for
inhibits your vitality completely!
You are surrounded, not by the living world
in which God placed mankind,
but, amid smoke and mustiness,
only by bones of beasts and of the dead . . .

The Descent into Darkness (29)

Sustained by hope, imagination once
soared boldly on her boundless flights;
now that our joys are wrecked in time's abyss,
she is content to have a narrow scope.
Deep in our heart Care quickly makes her nest,
there she engenders secret sorrows
and, in that cradle restless, destroys all quiet joy; . . .

You empty skull, why bare your teeth at me,
unless to say that once, like mine, your addled brain
sought buoyant light but, in its eagerness for truth,
went wretchedly astray beneath the weight of darkness.[6]

It is in this condition of the soul, in this cradle of darkness where the Sun's fair light barely penetrates, that we find Sol niger.

My first encounter with the image of the black sun began innocuously enough. It occurred while working with a woman who related the following dream:

I am standing on the Earth. I think: "Why should I do this when I can fly?" As I am flying I think I would like to find my spiritual guide. Then I notice, clinging to my waist, a person. I think this may be my guide. I reach behind me and pull the figure to the front so I can look it in the face. It is a young, borderline schizophrenic girl. I know this is not my guide. I put her aside and continue on my journey to the sun. Just before I get there, a wind comes and carries me back to Earth.

The journey skyward and Sun-ward is a common, if not universal, theme. James Hillman tells us that "Human life cannot keep from flying. . . . As we breathe air and speak air, so we are bathed in its elemental imagination, necessarily illuminated, resounding, ascending."[7] For him, "aspiration, inspiration, genius is structurally inherent, a pneumatic tension within each soul."[8] The function of the wing, Plato tells us, is to take what is heavy and raise it up into the regions above,

Figure 2.2. Faust *(ca. 1652), by Rembrandt van Rijn.*
Gift of R. Horace Gallatin, Image © 2004 Board of Trustees, National Gallery
of Art, Washington, D.C.

where the gods dwell. Of all things connected with the body, the wing has the greatest affinity with the divine.[9]

Similar themes are confirmed in art, folklore, classical mythology, sculpture, and poetry. The movement up and out seems to have a universal quality. In the *Feast of Icarus,* Sam Hazo writes:

> The poet imitates Icarus. He is inspired to dare impossibility even if this means that he might and possibly will fail in the attempt. His fate is to try to find silence's tongue, to say what is beyond saying, to mint from the air he breathes an alphabet that captivates like music. His victory, if it comes at all, must of necessity be a victory of the instant, a lyric split second of triumph, quick as a kiss.[10]

Hazo's study of Icarus values the necessity of flight—if a soul is to have a vibrant and creative life. It is important as an analyst to learn how to support such pneumatic and spiritual ascents, to know both the value of the *puer* spirit, while at the same time being aware of the dangers of inflation. Like a moth drawn to a flame, our Icarian souls are in peril when in our aspirations we forget our bodies on Earth and the call to an integrated life. For analysts, if not for poets, the "quick kiss" must be linked to a more stable relationship to our transcendent possibilities, so that our eyes are also fixed on waxen wings and on the danger of burnt souls and black holes.

We have had the benefit of the myths of Phaethon, Ixion, Bellerephon, and Icarus to remind us of the dangerous side of flying too high and too close to the sun, of becoming the prey of Poseidon. The problem for Icarus is not that he wishes to fly (for that is a natural and healthy emanation of our constitutional potential) but that there is an important difference between a grounded bodily imagination and a defensive or naive Gnostic flight that leaves the body and the darkness behind.

Analysts on the whole have learned to look at "flight" and "spirit" with Brueghel's eye rather than that of Ovid. In the *Metamorphoses,* Ovid describes "the amazement of a fisherman, a shepherd and a ploughman when they saw Daedalus and Icarus flying through the sky, an event that was interpreted as an epiphany of the gods."[11] This amazement is illustrated in the *Fall of Icarus* by Petrus Stevens and Joos de Momper.

Pieter Brueghel, on the other hand, in his "Landscape with the Fall of Icarus" (1558, Royal Museum of Brussels), "inverted Ovid's theme of placing the emphasis on the humble peasants who continue their labor without even a glance at the sky, or at Icarus, the latter reduced to an insignificant figure that had fallen into the sea."[12] For analysts to identify with either one of these perspectives has cyclopean consequences; it is important to look with two eyes, to see through the perspectives of both Ovid and Brueghel with an eye to epiphany and to earth-sea, or we ourselves are lost in one-sidedness.

My patient's desire to leave Earth may well have been spiritually motivated, but, if so, it was also a flight from the pain associated with the image of the borderline schizophrenic girl, a pathologized image of psychological distress. One might imagine the psyche saying to her, "Turn toward this figure of darkness that clings to you. That is your guide." This turning was not imaginable, and her pneumatic dream ego was driven with a single intent: to go skyward, sunward. Confronting this direction was the wind-spirit which blew her back to Earth and for the moment gently grounded her.

In alchemy, it is important that the pneumatic spirit remain in connection to Earth as imaged in Stolcius's *Viridarium Chymicum*. In figure 2.3, the high-flying bird is linked to the small, slow-moving creature of the Earth, which keeps the spirit from flying away.[13]

When the link to the Earth is not honored, grounding may emerge unconsciously and harshly. I cannot say whether what followed was in any way actually related to the neglect of the dark side of the psyche or was a part of her biological and spiritual destiny, but as our work continued we encountered a most destructive side of the Sol niger image. In an analytic session my patient reported that she felt something ominous in her chest. She described it as a dark ball that had long strands reaching throughout her body. Her inclination was to reach down and pull it up. Between sessions, in an active imagination she drew the image that she felt was lodged in her chest. It was a brilliant sun with a dense black center and long, fibrous tentacles (color plate 3).

The Descent into Darkness (33)

Figure 2.3. Alchemical image of the volatile and the fixed, ca. 1624. From Edward Edinger, Anatomy of the Psyche: Alchemical Symbolism in Psychotherapy, *p. 87.*

After drawing it, she felt the image was not menacing enough and felt a need to draw it again. She drew a second image, in which the black center had increased in size and the brightness of the yellow was replaced by a red field. The long, black fibers remained, and there were many circular black shapes that my patient described with horror as an explosion of dead, skeletal embryos (figure 2.4).

It was as if she had brought to the surface a compressed and exploding black sun that seemed to prefigure her ability to verbalize painful memories of her unassimilable distress and the madness of her suicidal feelings. In spite of this retrieval and the process that it initiated, the image, like a devouring demon, did not subside. Shortly afterward, she reported a dream in which she felt a nuclear war was inevitable. While grappling with these images, she suffered an aneurism of the anterior region of her brain and came close to death. She lost sight in one eye but

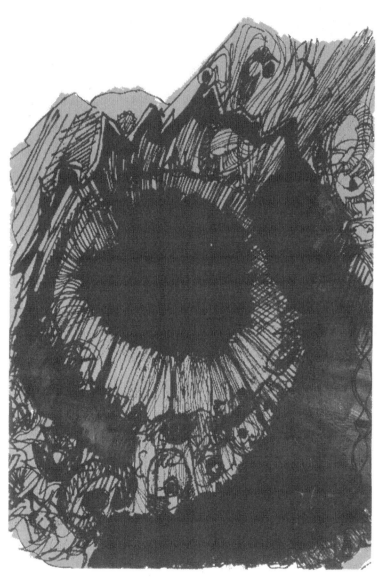

Figure 2.4. Menacing black sun. Artwork by analysand. Used by permission.

survived. I could not help but feel some connection between the image of the black sun and the medical incident, which almost cost her her life and led to partial blindness. This led me to wonder whether there were any documented incidents of a similar kind.

In researching the analytic literature, I came across the case of Robert, published by the Australian analyst Giles Clarke in *Harvest* (1983). His article is titled "A Black Hole in Psyche." In it he describes the case of Robert, a twenty-nine-year-old man who was struggling with something that seemed impossible to integrate or explain in terms of conventional, psychodynamic theories. Clarke describes a dream of Robert's in which there is an image of a black hole into which the whole world disappears. Astronomically, a black hole is a sun or star that has collapsed in on itself, creating a vacuum that sucks all matter into itself, a "scientific vision" of Sol niger. For Clarke, the psychology of the black hole is connected to the failure of psychic life and to something that is an inassimilable and intolerable object of anxiety and dread.[14] He connects it with a kind of chronic, psychic atrophy that can sometimes be literally fatal.

Robert's dream was followed by a series of disturbing images and debilitating physical symptoms. Clarke reports images of a "stillborn baby," a "mutant or monster birth," abortions, and a "miscarriage."[15] Robert "developed migraines, his eyesight suffered, his sense of taste and smell atrophied, and his legs tingled and ached."[16] Finally Robert became seriously ill and died of cancer.

Another encounter with the black sun is found in Ronald Laing's book *The Divided Self*, where he speaks of the emergence of the black sun in his treatment of Julie, who was diagnosed with schizophrenia. On the one hand, Julie imagined herself to be any one of a large number of famous personalities, but inwardly she had no freedom, autonomy, or power in the "real world." Since she could be anyone she cared to mention, she was no one. She was "terrified by life. . . . [L]ife would mash her to a pulp, burn her heart with a red hot iron, cut off her legs, hands, tongue, breasts." Life was conceived in the most violent and fiercely destructive terms imaginable. She stated that she was "born under a black sun," and the things that lived in her were wild beasts and rats that infested and ruined her inner city.[17] Julie's imagery is amplified in Von Franz's description of Sol niger as the destructive side of the Sun god, reminding us that Apollo is the god not only of the Sun but also of mice, rats, and wolves and that the dark side of the Sun is demonic and his rays burn life to death. He is a god without justice and brings death to the living.

Laing goes on to note that this ancient and very sinister image of the black sun arose, for Julie, quite independently of any reading; still, she described the way the rays of the black sun scorched and shriveled her, and under the black sun she existed as a dead thing. Her existence then was depicted in images of utterly barren, arid dissolution. This existential death, this death-in-life, was her prevailing mode of being in the world.[19] In this death there was no hope, no future, no possibility. Everything had already happened. There was no pleasure, no source of possible satisfaction, for the world was as empty and as dead as she was.

In *Alchemy,* von Franz writes about the shadow side of the Sun as destructive, unjust, and demonic. She refers to that aspect of Sol niger where the Sun is so hot that it destroys all plants. She recalls a story from Indochina that relates that a too-hot sun was shot at dawn by a hero figure linked to Saturn. For von Franz, the shadow of the Sun as "a Sun without justice, which is death for the living," reflects "a wrongly functioning consciousness" that rejects the dark side of God.[18] She states, "If consciousness works according to nature, the blackness is not so black or so destructive, but if the Sun stands still, it is stiffened, and burns life to death." When the psyche loses its natural rhythm and fixates into complexes, the unconscious becomes destructive.

This version of the black sun appeared in my long-term analysis of a Catholic priest. There had been significant progress in his analysis of a serious depression and ongoing suicidal desires, and he was for the most part functioning well with the exception of what seemed to be a chronic and deadly complex that still occurred regularly. In these moments he felt he was in a "black hole." He closed off the larger sense of his life and wanted to die. His heretofore rational sensibilities seemed to be growing delusional. He felt that his skin was too fair for him to really enjoy life and reported that he couldn't go out in the sun like ordinary people. For him, the Sun was vindictive, and there was a long series of dreams in which the Sun burnt him severely.

My patient recounted a dream:

> I was out resting in the sun for what I thought was not a long time. While I was there, the warmth penetrating my skin and my bones did feel good. Next I was showering and I could barely touch my skin at all. I looked with a sense of alarm, noticing that my skin was very red over every square inch. I did not know how that happened, except that the burn was thorough. My skin was fiery red and hot to touch, burned so badly that I could barely touch it. I would be in for a severe amount of pain and did not know what I was going to do.

In this dream, my patient thought of the sun as a hostile force, not unlike that portrayed by William Blake's painting in which it is "an angry, blood-red orb, unleashing its fury on an oppressed humanity"[20] (figure 2.5).

In this ongoing analysis, my patient and I were able to unpack a considerable amount of meaning related to this symptom/symbol/ image of the vengeful sun, including a significant father complex, his burning self-judgment, and the scorching demands of his perfectionistic expectations. We also discussed the idea of the Self as burning up his inflations and threatening his ego stance, making it painful even to move.

This work proved valuable. Over the years there were periods during which the Sun had become gentle, warming, and positive, and his skin had nicely tanned, integrating some of the darkness. In my judgment he was a priest who had come to terms with a good portion of shadow material, both personal and collective. But, in spite of this, his hostile Sun continued to return.

After one of our sessions, my patient wrote the following reflection in which he was trying to communicate his frustrations and the relentlessness of what he came to call his "skin barrier." He compared it to his work in scripture and to a "stubborn text," one that just will not go away:

Figure 2.5. The Body of Abel Found by Adam and Eve *(1826), painting by William Blake. Courtesy Tate Gallery, London/Art Resource, New York.*

It defies interpretation that satisfies me. My wish is to expunge the text but I cannot. I have no choice. The text confronts me and I have to deal with it. I often hate the text! I wish it had never been written. Yet I have to deal with it. My skin refrain is my stubborn text. I insist on bringing it up and coming back to it, because I am not satisfied with any interpretation. We have not yet come up with something I can live with. It is at this crucial moment that I say you can do nothing for me. I lose confidence in our work to solve this problem.

For my patient, whatever had been accomplished did not go far enough. He was ready to stop our work "unless we deal with my stubborn skin text so that I may live." Our capacity to relate to what truly became a threatening demon was tentative at best; it spoiled his life, and his world became ever darker and more depressed. He stated that "life stinks" and that "the Sun" continued to burn him. Since he felt there was no reason to live, death was the only thing that was real.

The Descent into Darkness (39)

Figure 2.6. Shame in the face of the monstrance. Artwork by analysand. Used by permission.

This aspect of Sol niger can show itself when consciousness becomes unconsciously critical. Alchemically, the heat is turned up too high, and the ego's skin is burnt, blackened, or tortured with stinging criticism, producing shame and threatening bodily integrity. Hillman describes a similar process of mortification—when the ego feels trapped or nailed down. It is a time of symptoms and the "grinding sadistic mortifications of shame."[21]

In figure 2.6, similar feelings are expressed at a point in analysis in which a woman was reexperiencing deep feelings of shame. She had lived "a sheltered childhood" and described "much censorship," "feeling constantly embarrassed," and inferior. The faces of masculine religious authority are "long, stern, gaunt, with unblinking eyes." In the painting she made, we see the unblinking eye of masculine authority, which seems like an evil eye or the dark side of "religious kings," clergy, and bishops with their miters and monstrance. On the far right, a figure holds up the monstrance, which appears traditionally as a sunburst. The monstrance is a utensil that is used to contain the presence of the consecrated Host, which is believed to be the living divinity, the Sun reflecting the transformed image of the God-man.

Matthew 17:2 says, "and he was transformed before them and his face shone like the sun, and his garments became white as light." For our dreamer, the brightness of the monstrance had turned monstrous, both words—monstrance and monstrous—sharing the same root, and was used to shame and attack her, functioning rather as a Sol niger, creating shame. The attack of her accusers was also a phallic probing about to goose her (note the cross behind her).

Another image of the destructive aspect of Sol niger can be seen in the life of the poet Harry Crosby. The poet's life is in his diaries, titled *Shadows of the Sun,* and in Wolff's biography of him, entitled *The Black Sun: The Brief Transit and Violent Eclipse of Harry Crosby.* Crosby is described as a handsome, wealthy aristocrat who with his wife, Caresse, scandalized Boston society. Caresse divorced her first husband, Richard Peabody, nephew of the legendary headmaster of Groton, to marry Harry. Together, they founded the *Black Sun Press* in Paris, which published exquisite editions of the works of Lawrence, Crane, Pound, Proust and others.[22] One of Harry's romances is portrayed by Edward Germain in his introduction to *Shadows of the Sun.* There, Germain suggests

it is almost impossible not to read these diaries as a poet's eight-year romance with death, consummated late in the afternoon of Tuesday, December 10, 1929, in a borrowed New York apartment in the Hotel des Aristes. Harry Crosby and one of his mistresses took off their shoes and lay on a bed together fully clothed. Then Harry pressed a .25 caliber Belgian automatic pistol to Josephine Rotch Bigelow's left temple and blew her head apart. For two hours Harry may have lain alive beside her with his arm beneath her head. Then he pointed the pistol at his own forehead and pulled the trigger.[23]

For our purposes, one of the remarkable connections to our theme is Harry's obsession with the sun, which is evident in his work titled *Chariot of the Sun*. Some of the titles of his poems are "Quatrains of the Sun," "Sun Rhapsody," "Angels of the Sun," "Sundrench and Sons," "Sun-Ghost," and "Suns in Distress." Many of these verses are obsessed with death, and one might imagine with Crosby's biographer Geoffrey Wolff that "the sun had truly struck Harry down, inspired him and blinded him too."[24]

One of the most poignant images of Harry's obsession with the Sun is portrayed in his poem "Photoheliograph." Here one finds the Sun in the midst of blackness:

> *black black black black black*
> *black black black black black*
> *black black black black black*
> *black black black black black*
> *black black* sun *black black*
> *black black black black black*
> *black black black black black*
> *black black black black black*
> *black black black black black*
> *black black black black black*[25]

Wolff is aware that "the black sun was no invention of Harry's," and he equates it with the *Sol niger* of the alchemists, "prime matter, the unconscious in its unworked, base state."[26] What Germain suggests that Harry sought but was unable to find, was the need, like the Sun, to resurrect beyond his own sunset, a project filled with paradox and ambiguity. He notes:

[T]he sun that gave sea, soil, and life also stared down without pity on its creations and withered them, dried them out, burnt them, failed to shine, winking while life failed. Where the sun is, there also find the death principle, the chaos that reigned before light dispelled it, the chaos that Harry's life and work replicated in miniature.[27]

Harry Crosby was not the only poet to struggle with Sol niger. In her work titled *The Black Sun: Depression and Melancholy*, Julia Kristeva, a French linguist and Lacanian psychoanalyst, writes about the poet Gerard de Nerval and his poem "El Desdichado," or "The Disinherited" (1859). Kristeva believes the poem was written in a fit of madness in an attempt to overcome a sense of deprivation and darkness. It seems that Kristeva may even have derived the title of her book from a chilling stanza in Nerval's poem that contains the image of Sol niger. The stanza reads as follows:

> *I am saturnine—bereft—disconsolate,*
> *The Prince of Aquitaine whose tower has crumbled:*
> *My lone star is dead—and my bespangled lute*
> *Bears the Black sun of Melancholia*[28]

Nerval's poem most likely is his response to the loss of a loved one: "My lone star is dead." For Nerval, the loss of this figure is the loss of the light of his life, without whom he is bereft and his world collapsed; his "Tower has crumbled," as it were, into the "Black Sun of Melancholia." For Kristeva, the "Black sun" is a "dazzling metaphor," an imagined sun, "bright and black at the same time," a "Thing" that is cherished in the absence of the loved one and marks an impenetrable loss.[29] Traditionally, it is thought that what is lost in ordinary mourning is eventually let go in the grieving process, the result of which is to hold what is lost in memory or, according to Kristeva, in symbolic language.

However, some people who cannot let go and who deny the loss create a situation of impossible mourning and a fundamental sadness to which they become attached. For Kristeva, such a situation can express itself as an attachment to a dark sun buried in a crypt of inexpressible saturnine affect. This kind of inner presence is really an absence, a light without representation, a sadness that is "the most archaic expression of an unsymbolizable, unnameable narcissistic wound" that becomes the depressed person's "sole object" of attachment.[30]

Throughout this process of mislaid grief, the relationship to a loved one is transformed into an attachment to an inexpressible affect, cryptically incorporated. This affect takes the place of the other; its numinous quality is held on to with mystical adherence. Thus, ultimately, for Kristeva, the black sun is such a "Thing," a mark of pathological mourning, whose brightness seems to sum up the "blinding force of a despondent mood."[31]

Kristeva is aware of the alchemical associations with Sol niger and situates Nerval's melancholia and the black sun in the context of the alchemical nigredo, which "asserts the inevitability of death" and which, in this case, "is the death of the loved one and of the self that identifies with the former."[32]

For Kristeva, Nerval was a "tireless wanderer" who, after a "fit of madness . . . withdrew for a while into the crypt of a past that haunted him."[33] His world was filled with "graves" and "skeletons" and "flooded with irruptions of death."[34] It was in such a context, says Kristeva, that Nerval wrote *The Disinherited*. Kristeva calls Nerval's poem his "Noah's ark," albeit a temporary one—temporary because Nerval appears to have committed suicide.[35] At dawn on January 26, 1855, Nerval was found hanging in the Rue de la Vieille-Lanterre.

In Kristeva's analysis, though Sol niger may have served to inspire Nerval's creative process, it ultimately signifies massive repression and death. For Nerval, the harshness of Saturn foreclosed human life and linked the god to the literal death aspect of the black sun and to his role as Ogre and the terrible father.

This aspect of Sol niger—destruction as the inevitable outcome of creation—may have been at the origin of the myth of Saturn devouring his children as soon as Rhea gave birth to them. In the painting *Saturn and His Children* by Marten van Heemskerck, Saturn is portrayed as beginning to devour his children, a process that has been linked to melancholia, which is written on the image next to Saturn. His color is said to be black and is also associated with winter, night, death, and distance.[36]

18

Plate 1. The green lion devouring the sun. Sixteenth-century woodcut.
From Stanislas Klossowski de Rola, Alchemy: The Secret Art, *plate 20.*

Plate 2. A portrayal of putrefaction. From Salomon Trismosin, Splendor Solis, *1582. Harley 3469 f30v. By permission of The British Library.*

Plate 3. An image of the black sun created by an analysand. Used by permission.

Plate 4. Picture of Kali as painted by Maitreya Bowen.
From Ajit Mookerjee, Kali: The Feminine Force, *p. 93.*
© *Maitreya Bowen, reproduced with her permission.*
maitreyabown@yahoo.com

Plate 5. Woman falling from sun. Illustration by Ul de Rico. From R. Wagner,
The Ring of the Nibelung, *plate 45.*

Plate 6. The goddess Kali. Kalighat painting, 1845.
© *V&A Images/V&A Picture Library/Victoria and Albert Museum, London.*

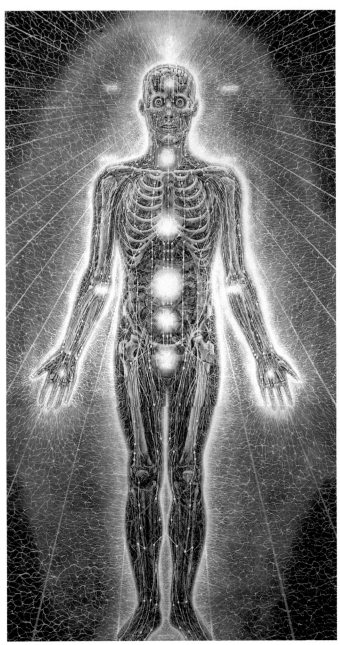

Plate 7. Alex Grey, Psychic Energy System *(1980), painting by Alex Grey.*
84" × 46" acrylic on linen. © www.alexgrey.com. Used by permission.

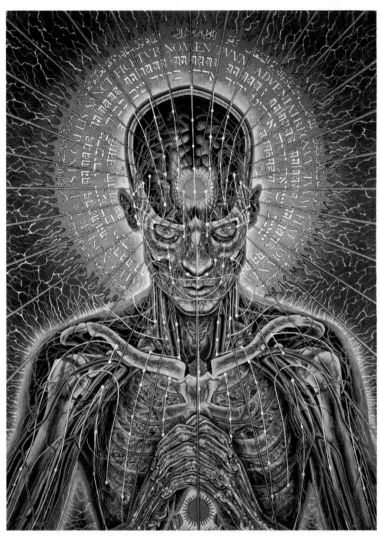

Plate 8. Praying *(1984), painting by Alex Grey. 48" × 36" oil on linen*
© www.alexgrey.com. Used by permission.

Plate 9. Seventeenth-century Nepalese scroll painting. From Ajit Mookerjee,
Tantra Art: Its Philosophy and Physics, *p. 128. Courtesy of*
Ravi Kumar, Publisher, Paris.

Plate 10. The Awakened Female: The Beginning of the Coniunctio.
Artwork by analysand. Used by permission.

Plate 11. Black birds turn to white around the philosophical tree. From Salomon Trismosin, Splendor Solis, *1582. "Golden tree with crown." Harley 3469 f15. By permission of The British Library.*

Plate 12. Flaming red sun. Artwork by analysand. Used by permission.

Plate 13. The alchemist who has achieved illumination. From Andrea de Pascalis,
Alchemy: The Golden Art. The Secrets of the Oldest Enigma, *p. 32. Used by*
permission of Gremese International.

PYTHON

Plate 14. *The spirit of Mercurius, ca. 1600. From C. G. Jung,*
Alchemical Studies, *frontispiece.*

Plate 15. Spiritual World: The Light That Shines beyond All Things on Earth *(1985–1986), by Alex Grey. Sandblasted mirror with illumination. © www. alexgrey.com. Used by permission of artist.*

Plate 16. Color transformations of alchemy. From Andrea De Pascalis, Alchemy, The Golden Art: The Secrets of the Oldest Enigma, *p. 142. Used by permission of Gremese International.*

Plate 17. (a) Black Hole. *Yarn painting. Courtesy of Harry Wilmer. Used by permission; (b) image of black hole and companion star rendered from Hubble telescope image. Courtesy NASA and STSci.*

Jung and Von Franz have both linked Saturn with Sol niger,[37] and Hillman has pieced together a rich phenomenology of the god's characteristics "from astrology, from the medicine of the humors, from lore and iconography [and] from the collections of the mythographers. . . ."[38] Hillman confirms the deadly aspect of Saturn: "The senex emblem of the skull signifies that every complex can be envisioned from its death aspect, its ultimate psychic core where all flesh of dynamics and appearances is stripped away and there is nothing left of those hopeful thoughts of what it might yet become, the 'final' interpretation of the complex at its end."[39]

In addition, and in connection with its death aspect, Saturn is also linked to ideas about Earth and time. At times Saturn is a great teacher, as was the case with a man who, approaching midlife, was concerned about "time passing," "growing older," and ultimately with "death" (figure 2.7).

A former patient in my practice illustrates some of these themes. The patient had just turned forty and was struggling with what we have come to call midlife issues, including a confrontation with illness, aging parents, and the loss of a loved one. These conflicts preceded the following dream:

I'm in an open space. The ground is a tawny color, and there is a large, very dark circle many feet, perhaps forty or so, in diameter. It is uniformly dark (like the skin of an African) with barely visible concentric bands that radiate from the center. Many tall African men appear with staffs. They are so coal black that they almost have a bluish sheen. I get a staff, too, and find that we are going to do some type of dance around this circle. There is one other white man, and neither of us is familiar with this dance so we try to stick together so as not to stick out individually. However, other African men quickly fill the space between us, and we are separated.

The Africans are friendly, but they are fierce looking. Everyone gets down on their hands like we're ready to do push-ups, heads pointed toward the center of the black disc. Our legs radiate outward like the spokes from a wheel. Now we must scurry

Figure 2.7. Death and the Landsknecht, *by Albrecht Dürer (1471–1528).*
From W. L. Strauss, ed., The Complete Woodcuts of Albrecht Dürer
(New York: Dover Publications, 1973).

along clockwise in the push-up position somewhat like a crab.
It's very hard to do; it takes considerable strength. I'm glad I've
been doing my push-ups. I realize that we are doing some kind
of a sun dance and that we represent the rays of the sun as we
scuttle along its perimeter.

The patient drew the dream image, which has the appearance of a
black sun (figure 2.8).

The patient had many associations and memories linked with this
image. Here I want to focus on his angst about becoming forty. He

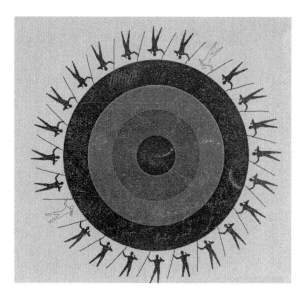

Figure 2.8. Image by an analysand after a dream. Used by permission.

noted that he had not been feeling well and reported a terrible, nagging sinus condition, headaches, and many trips to the doctor. He states that he was beginning to feel the effects of time and loss and that recently he had also had a lot of exposure to mortality. He wanted to "make peace" with his fears or felt they might rob him in ways "other than the obvious." He commented that "when your life is full . . . then you feel the shadow as a thief" and remembered someone saying that "it is a fearsome thing to love what the hand of death can touch."

As he participated in the temporal ritual of moving clockwise around Sol niger, the patient found himself in a relationship with the very things he fears. Being thus was hard, like doing an exercise in which he let himself down close to the dark core and then pushed up and away from it, all the time moving sideways like a crab along with the flow of time. It is noteworthy that his sun sign is Cancer, the crab, and that the dreamer came to feel that his movement reflected his own identity and destiny. At the bottom of the original image were two photos not shown here for the purposes of anonymity: one of the dreamer wearing sunglasses, with his dog, and the other of an African man, so dark black that he has a bluish shine. As the dreamer reflected on the dream, he felt he was being initiated into time and into his human mortality. He had to connect with this darkness and join in the primordial human dance with the cycle of time.

The importance of dance as a primal form of ritual enactment is described by the poet Gary Snyder, who states that dance once had a connection with "ritual drama, the miming of animals, or tracing the maze of the spiritual journey."[40] Snyder believes that we have lost touch with this connection and that it is the task of the dancer and the poet to regain it—"to put us in touch with our archaic roots, with the world in its nakedness, which is fundamental to us all: birth—love—death; the sheer fact of being alive." The importance of ritual and initiation as themes connected to dance is also richly elaborated by Steven Lansdale, who notes that initiatory ceremonies and dances are intended to teach the initiates what they need to survive in harsh environments.[41] For our dreamer, facing the issues of midlife were indeed harsh realities, and, in this instance and on a personal scale, one might imagine the artistry of the dream serving a singular function to the creative artist in drawing the ascensionist spirit down into the body, feeling, and time. Such a downward movement also requires a kind of dying, in which we come close to the mysterious forces of both creation and destruction.

Spontaneous expression of the black sun can also be found in the art of traumatized children. In their work, researchers Gregorian, Azarian, DeMaria, and McDonald studied Armenian children who were traumatized by earthquakes and who had witnessed "overwhelming death and destruction."[42] In these images, the black sun often appears over the location in which the trauma was experienced. A particularly striking example is shown in figure 2.9, an image made by a seven-year-old girl, Varduhy, who was traumatized by an earthquake. Here the black sun is in the sky above destroyed buildings surrounded by red clouds of smoke. It was reported that she began to fear everything in her world: the sun, rain, lightning, hail, animals, buildings, and so on.

The authors noted their astonishment at finding this "somewhat unusual" image in their study of children's art but also commented that references to it "can be found in many different sources."[43] "For

Figure 2.9. Varduhy's black sun. Reprinted from Gregorian et al., "Colors of Disaster: The Psychology of the 'Black Sun'" Arts in Psychotherapy 23 (1996): 1–14, fig. 6. Used with permission from Elsevier.

instance, there are various kinds of black suns used with different meanings in the mythological traditions and metaphors of poetry around the world. . . . First of all, the black sun has been referred to as an apocalyptic image indicating darkness and gloom, fear and terror, death and non-being, retribution and oblivion."[44]

It is noteworthy that, in Biblical passages, the dark sun is linked with earthquakes:

> The earth quakes before them,
> the heavens tremble.
> The sun and the moon shall be dark.[45]

And, again, in the Book of Revelations:

> When he opened the sixth seal, I looked, and behold, there was a great earthquake; and the sun became black as sackcloth.[46]

The authors of the children's study mentioned earlier conclude that "when earthquakes and other natural disasters" occur, "one's core sense of belonging and security is challenged and thrown into question."[47] "The sun itself has always been synonymous with light, understanding, the rational, the logical, life-giving. However, for these children the sun is painted black. The life-giver has turned dark. The rational has turned irrational, the clear lucidity of the sun has been eclipsed by the darkness and night of disaster and trauma."[48]

This description is pertinent to the next series of paintings, which were made by a woman in a long-term analysis. Her first image has an odd twist. The black sun above is surprising since the scene, reproduced here in gray scale (figure 2.10), in the original painting appears pleasant and colorful. The green mountains, blue waters, and aquatic life at first glance can give the impression that all is well, leaving one to wonder about the appearance of Sol niger in such a context.

On closer inspection, it is important to notice that the mermaid's face is highly stylized, made up with eyeliner, rouge, lipstick, and so on. This persona was an important factor that covered up her inner darkness. Another detail that one might link with Sol niger is the black anchor on the mermaid's tail, which is, perhaps, pulling her down toward deeper feelings and which interestingly calls our attention to a shark that appears to be attacking or ready to attack. The face of the mermaid, like the face of my patient, does not register the pain within.

In another painting (not included in this book) a similar theme is continued in a portrayal of a childlike woman with a noose around her neck and a dark sky behind her. Like the mermaid, the figure has an incongruent smiling face and seems totally unaware of the horrifying implications of her situation.

Later, the patient wrote the following poem:

Shattered
Shattered like a window pane
broken by a storm
each tiny piece of me lies only
and scattered far beyond repair
all my shining dreams just lying there

Figure 2.10. *Picture by an analysand of a mermaid. Used by permission.*

I'm broken but I'm laughing
it's the sound of falling glass
I hope that you won't mind if I
should cry and come in while I
wait for this to pass

Oh God, I'm shattered into fragments common gray
Sweep the pieces all away
And then no one will know how much it matters
Something deep inside of me is shattered!!!!

Something deep inside of me is shattered
Something deep inside of me is shattered

The angst in this poem is further amplified in a drawing she did of
a figure who appears to be screaming, an image very reminiscent of
Edward Munch's well-known painting, *The Scream*. This theme is continued by an image she titled "Whispered Screams"—of a child with a
downcast look on her face, carrying luggage from which items are

falling out. What fell out in the course of the analysis was the story of a horrific childhood involving emotional, physical, and most likely sexual abuse. My patient reported that her mother chained her to her crib, abandoned her, and told her that she wished she had never been born. Her birthdays were always marked by this statement of her mother's, and instead of feeling that her birth was something to be celebrated, she felt nothing but shame.

Events such as these left the patient feeling very small and alienated, locked out, and disregarded, dumped in the garbage as it were, waiting for the other shoe to drop. With considerable talent, she painted these feelings: The first is an image of a diminutive child in a gigantic chair with huge closed doors in the background; another painting depicts a child in a garbage can with a mother figure seemingly throwing a shoe out a window. It appears that, for her, the shoe has dropped.

Following these dramatic self-expressions were two self-portraits. In the first, she is a stripped-down tree; all of her leaves are blue. She writes in one of the branches, "No self respect," and the blood of her heart pours out over her head as the redness of shame and growing anger. Over time, platitudes and clichés of the false self no longer worked for her, and her sarcastic humor came to the fore. In response to those who would say things to her such as "It's better to have loved and lost than never to have loved at all," she wrote alongside her second self-portrait these lines: "Yeah, right. And it's better to have skied and broken every bone in your body than to have never gone skiing! And it's better to have raised pit bulls and gotten torn to shreds than to have never raised pit bulls! And I suppose it's better to have drunk drain cleaner and dissolved your insides than to have never drunk drain cleaner?"

The weight of these feelings contributed to her feeling alienated from herself and from God, not knowing where to turn. At times these feelings led to suicidal ideation and the desire to say good-bye to this world. At one point in our work she produced the following drawing (figure 2.11), which summed up her feelings of being overwhelmed by her emotions.

This work resembles a personal mortificatio in which she emphasizes her feelings of inadequacy, entrapment, grief, immobilization,

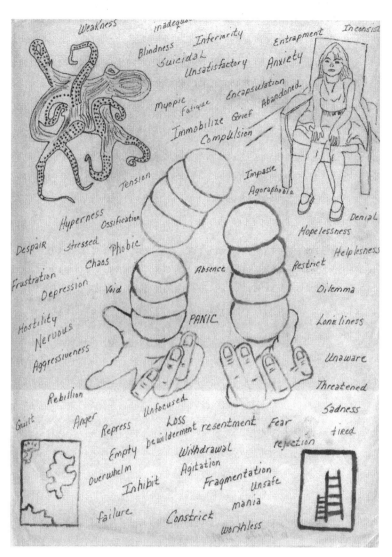

Figure 2.11. Picture made by an analysand expressing overwhelming emotions.
Used by permission.

hopelessness, worthlessness, fragmentation, bewilderment, resentment, loss, chaos, and voidness. The octopus in the upper left-hand corner of the image reflects all of these emotions, which, like tentacles, grab at her and are linked to one dark center. I think it is not far fetched to see the octopus, with its dark center and penetrating, raylike tentacles, as another version of Sol niger.

As my patient struggled with these emotions, she dreamed of being in a primitive old house. In the dream she stood in what appeared to be the kitchen or cooking area, with an ancient-looking, cast-iron pot on a wood-burning stove. She recalled the flames burning high and bright. She was dressed in rags and looked down at the floor and saw mice, cockroaches, and a crab scurrying across the floor. At first she felt frustrated and angry that she could not corner or catch them with her bare hands. Then she found herself holding what appeared to be two large shells, and, stooping forward, she began to scoop up a black mouse between the shells and then the cockroaches and the crab in the same manner. She began to skin and prepare the critters; when everything was cooked it all looked white and puffy like scallops.

I believe that what is happening in this dream follows Jung's observation in the *Mysterium*—that when consciousness descends into the unconscious, it at first has frightening results.[49] To begin with, it produces poisonous animals such as dragons, serpents, and scorpions. At first my patient could not come to terms with either the overwhelming octopus or the irritating creatures of her soul, but when she was able to get hold of them and cook them, they became whitened and potentially assimilable. This process might be seen in terms of traditional alchemy as a move from the blackness of the nigredo to the whiteness of albedo, but it is also the case that, for this patient, the continuing engagement with darkness was pronounced. Cooking became a part of the way she struggled with her darkness and took it in, but the darkness itself was never left behind. Sol niger remained as the dark light of the creatures of the night. The instinctual, poisonous remains of Sol niger remain fundamental and are not bypassed.

In figure 2.12a we see a copperplate engraving in which an alchemist is "processing a scorpion."

"In the past centuries, the most hazardous experiments with animal

Figure 2.12. (a): For Luck, by Ferdynand Landerer (1730–1795), after a painting by Johan Martin Schmidt (1718–1801), photo engraving, 7″ × 5″. Courtesy Fisher Collection, Chemical Heritage Foundation, Philadelphia, Pennsylvania. Photo by Will Brown. (b): The Five Poisons. From C. A. S. Williams, Outlines of Chinese Symbolism and Art Motives (Rutland, Vt.: Charles Tuttle, 1974), p. 188.

poisons were sometimes attempted for medical purposes."[50] These poisons are intrinsically related to healing, as darkness is to light. In Chinese symbolism, "five poisonous reptiles, viz. the viper, scorpion, centipede, toad and spider, [are] a powerful combination which has the power to counteract pernicious influences."[51] Sometimes images of these creatures are used for worship and meditation. Pictures of them are made with black silk, and children often swear that these pictures protect them. They are found on brass castings used as charms against evil spirits.

Figure 2.12b shows a "paper charm known as the five poisons, and endowed with protective and exorcising efficacy. It is suspended from the cross-beams of the roof on the fifth day of the fifth moon (vide also T'ai Chi and eight diagrams)."[52]

The Descent into Darkness (55)

In our analysis and descent into darkness, we have found Sol niger to be present in its most literal and destructive forms, in incidents of physiological and psychological destruction, brain aneurisms, blindness, cancer, schizophrenia, delusion, despair, depression, narcissistic mortification, humiliation, pain, murder-suicide, trauma, and death— it is a general spoiler of life. We can begin to imagine what the alchemists referred to as the "blacker than black" domain of the nigredo experience. "Nicholas Flamel stated that at the time of the nigredo, which is 'the black of the blackest black,' the 'Matter is dissolved, is corrupted.'"[53] Such experiences have been with us from time immemorial; life can be cruel, and the barbarism of human beings toward each other reflects this savagery. The universe—for all its creative light and beauty—gives little solace to ravaged souls as they journey through life. In the cold light of the black sun, we understand what Conrad calls the "heart of darkness" and the horror of the "cry" so vividly portrayed by Eduard Munch and the alchemists.

The cold face of Sol niger is, as Jungian analyst Sylvia Perera notes, "totally uncaring" and acts like a sniper or terrorist with dark abandon in the name of some infernal sun to destroy light and life itself. For Perera, this is the realm of the Sumerian goddess Ereshkigal, queen of the Netherworld and the dead, "unbounded, irrational, primordial."[54] She says, echoing what has been documented thus far, that this realm contains

> an energy we begin to know through the study of black holes and the disintegration of elements, as well as through the process of fermentation, cancer, decay and lower brain activities that regulate peristalsis, menstruation, pregnancy, and other forms of bodily life. . . . Ereshkigal is like Kali, who through time and suffering . . . 'pitilessly grinds down . . . all distinctions . . . in her undiscriminating fires'. . . . She symbolizes the abyss that is the source and, the end, the ground of all being.[55]

In this black aspect, Kali, the Hindu goddess associated with death and described as "one of the most intoxicating personifications of primal energy in the cosmic drama," is worshipped by the Tantrics.[56] The

Figure 2.13. The goddess Kali in her hideous aspect copulating with Siva (eighteenth century). From Indra Sinha, Tantra: The Cult of Ecstasy, *p. 52.*

Tantrics believe that "sitting next to corpses and other (ghastly) images of death" in the cremation grounds speeds their efforts to free themselves from attachment to ego and body.[57]

Color plate 4, an image painted by artist Maitreya Bowen, portrays the horrific aspect of Kali in a form reminiscent of the black sun.

In one of her left hands, Kali holds a severed head, indicating the annihilation of the ego, and in an another she carries the sword of physical extinction. Around her neck are many human skulls, which reflect the process of dying, which she represents. Imagine each one of these skulls as representing a case where Sol niger ended in a reduction of the human soul to its bare bones.

In figure 2.13 we see Kali in her hideous aspect copulating with Siva. Their lovemaking takes place on the body of a corpse that is burning in a funeral pyre. Cemeteries were the favorite places for Tantric rites because the spiritual human being arises shining out of the symbolic death of the body.

In the poem "Kali the Mother," Swami Vivekananda, a famous disciple of Sri Ramakrisna, who brought the ancient teachings of Vedanta to the West, writes of the terror and the need to embrace their goddess:

KALI THE MOTHER

The stars are blotted out,
The clouds are covering clouds
It is darkness vibrant, sonant.
In the roaring, whirling wind
Are the souls of a million lunatics
Just loosed from the prison-house,
Wrenching trees by the roots,
Sweeping all from the path.

The sea has joined the fray,
And swirls up mountain-waves,
To reach a pitchy sky.
The flash of lurid light
Reveals on every side
A thousand, thousand shades
Of Death begrimed and black—
Scattering plagues and sorrows,
Dancing mad with joy,
Come, Mother, come!

For Terror is Thy name,
Death is in Thy breath,
And every shaking step
Destroys the world for e'er.
Thou 'Time,' the All-destroyer!
Come, O Mother, come!

Who cares misery love,
And hug the form of Death,
Dance in Destruction's dance,
To him the Mother comes.[58]

For poet May Sarton, what we need to embrace or must stay open to is further expressed in a poem called "The Invocation to Kali":

> *The kingdom of Kali is within us deep.*
> *The built-in destroyer, the savage goddess,*
> *Wakes in the dark and takes away our sleep.*
> *She moves through the blood to poison gentleness.*
>
> *She keeps us from being what we long to be;*
> *Tenderness withers under her iron laws.*
> *We may hold her like a lunatic, but it is she*
> *Held down, who bloodies with her claws.*
>
> *How then to set her free or come to terms*
> *With the volcano itself, the fierce power*
> *Erupting injuries, shrieking alarms?*
> *Kali among her skulls must have her hour.*
>
> *It is time for the invocation, to atone*
> *For what we fear most and have not dared to face:*
> *Kali, the destroyer, cannot be overthrown;*
> *We must stay, open-eyed, in the terrible place.*[59]

Color plate 6 shows a nineteenth-century image of Kali. In this terrible realm, healing and transformation remain in doubt. Hillman distinguishes between the hero's night sea journey and the descent to the underworld. The main distinction Hillman makes is that the hero "returns from the night sea-journey in better shape for the tasks of life, whereas the nekyia takes the soul into the depth for its own sake so that there is no 'return.'"[60] There is no obvious benefit to justify the descent into darkness. Hillman, with Jung, sees with a dark eye that refuses to look at the ravages of the human soul through any simple teleological or innocent salvationist perspective. His vision is icy cold and compares the deepest hell with the marsh realm of Cocytus, the frozen lake of Dante's ninth circle, where there is an absence of all human warmth

Figure 2.14. Cocytus – Traitor, *by Gustave Doré (1832–1883). Dante's lake of the eternally frozen. From Gustave Doré,* The Doré Illustrations for Dante's Divine Comedy *(New York: Dover Publications, 1976), p. 67.*

and where the feeling of darkness is conveyed through the absence of contrast in the dim light (figure 2.14).

Scholar Dorothy Sayer says it well: "Beneath the clamour, beneath the monotonous circlings, beneath the fires of Hell, here at the centre of the lost soul and the lost city, lie the silence and the rigidity and the eternal frozen cold."[61]

One of the most profound descriptions of this state of affairs has been written by the Romanian philosopher Emil Cioran (1911–1995) in *On the Heights of Despair.* Cioran has been called the "connoisseur of apocalypse, a theoretician of despair."[62] Here is an extended passage from his reflection "on death":

Why don't we want to accept that one can entertain lively meditations on death, the most dangerous issue existing? Death is not something from outside, ontologically different from life, because there is no *death* independent of life. To step into death does not mean, as commonly believed, especially by Christians, to draw one's last breath and to pass into a region qualitatively different from life. It means, rather, to discover in the course of life the way toward death and to find in life's vital signs the immanent abyss of death. For Christianity and other metaphysical beliefs in immortality, the passing into death is a *triumph,* an opening toward other regions metaphysically different from life. Contrary to such visions, the true sense of agony seems to me to lie in the revelation of death's immanence in life . . .

To see how death spreads over this world, how it kills a tree and how it penetrates dreams, how it withers a flower or a civilization, how it gnaws on the individual and on culture like a destructive blight, means to be beyond tears and regrets, beyond system and form. Whoever has not experienced the awful agony of death, rising and spreading like a surge of blood, like the choking grasp of a snake which provokes terrifying hallucinations, does not know the demonic character of life and the state of inner effervescence from which great transfigurations arise. Such a state of black drunkenness is a necessary prerequisite to understanding why one wishes the immediate end of this world. It's not the luminous drunkenness of ecstasy, in which paradisal visions conquer you with their splendor and you rise to a purity that sublimates into immateriality, but a mad, dangerous, ruinous and tormented black drunkenness, in which death appears with the awful seduction of nightmarish snake eyes. To experience such sensations and images means to be so close to the essence of reality that both life and death shed their illusions and attain within you their most dramatic form. An exalted agony combines life and death in a horrible maelstrom: a beastly Satanism borrows tears from voluptuousness. Life as a long agony on the road to death is nothing but another manifestation of life's demoniacal dialectics, in which forms are given birth only to be destroyed . . .

The feeling of the irrevocable, which appears as an ineluctable necessity going against the grain of our innermost tendencies, is conceivable only because of time's demonism. The conviction that you cannot escape an implacable fate and that time will do nothing but unfold the dramatic process of destruction is an expression of irrevocable agony. Isn't nothingness, then, salvation? But how can there be salvation in nothingness? If salvation is nearly impossible through existence, how can it be possible through the complete absence of existence?

Since there is no salvation either in existence or in nothingness, let this world with its eternal laws be smashed to pieces![63]

Cioran, like Hillman, attempts to see beyond salvationist fantasies. His description wounds our narcissism and affronts our egos and is a violence to our complacent identities. For Jungian analyst Wolfgang Giegerich, such a hurtful cut is necessary; the soul must be torn away, turned around and inside out in a violent reversal of orientation.[64] For him, the mortificatio and putrefactio are logical operations in material and chemical imagery, but if they are so, it is important not to lose sight of the fact that these operations are excruciatingly personal and painful and resist our uplifting dialectic. Cioran's last sentiment is echoed in Job in Stephen Mitchell's excellent translation. Job cries out:

God damn the day I was born
   and the night that forced me from the womb.
On that day—let there be darkness;
     let it never have been created;
     let it sink back into the void.
Let chaos overpower it;
     let black clouds overwhelm it;
     let the sun be plucked from its sky.
Let oblivion overshadow it;
     let the other days disown it;
     let the aeons swallow it up.
On that night—let no child be born,
     no mother cry out with joy.
Let sorcerers wake the Serpent
     to blast it with eternal blight.
Let its last stars be extinguished;

Figure 2.15. *The stone of solar and lunar conjunction turned into the black sun of death.* From Johannes Fabricius, Alchemy: The Medieval Alchemists and Their Royal Art, *p. 103.*

let it wait in terror for daylight;
    let its dawn never arrive.
For it did not shut the womb's doors
    to shelter me from this sorrow.
Why couldn't I have died
    as they pulled me out of the dark?
Why were there knees to hold me,
    breasts to keep me alive?
If only I had strangled or drowned
    on my way to the bitter light . . .

. . . Why is there light for the wretched,
    life for the bitter-hearted,
who long for death, who seek it
    as if it were buried treasure,

The Descent into Darkness (63)

who smile when they reach the graveyard
and laugh as their pit is dug.
For God has hidden my way
and put hedges across my path.
I sit and gnaw on my grief;
my groans pour out like water.
My worst fears have happened;
my nightmares have come to life.
Silence and peace have abandoned me,
and anguish camps in my heart.[65]

In this world, Sol niger is both bitter cold and scorching heat, darkness and infernal light, encompassing both the truth of life and death. As figure 2.15 illustrates, Job's words leave us stripped bare where the only ground left to stand upon is the rotundum of Sol niger.

CHAPTER 3

Analysis and the Art of Darkness

*Push painting beyond its thinkable, seeable,
graspable, feelable limits. . . .*

—*Ad Reinhardt*

In the last two chapters we examined the primacy of light and the dark alchemy of descent, emphasizing the "blacker than black" aspects of the nigredo process in its most literal and destructive forms. This descent was an excruciating initiation into the most negative dimensions of Sol niger and an entrance into the domain of Hades and Ereshkigal, Dante's world of ice, and Kali's cremation grounds. Our king's ego has been spoiled, our virgin's milk has soured, and we have drunk the poison of Holbein's dance of death and seen the black sun of Splendor Solis. The sun has blackened, and we have met Jung's Dragon. Our dark eye is opened, and we have entered Edinger's "gate of blackness." Hollowed out with Eliot, ranting with the philosopher Cioran, and lamenting with Job, one may wonder why we were ever born. In the face of such a devastating vision, analysis stands still—shocked. Salvationist fires are fanned but are held back; the heart is wrenched. Job's comforters are quieted, and no platitudes or new analytic techniques will do. Biological remedies, primal screams, and spiritual fantasies are hollow. There is no rush to cure; perhaps there is no cure at all. Silence is in the soul of patient and analyst alike: a quiet pair sitting in the grip of Sol niger, dark and light, burning and ice cold, standing on ground that is no ground, a self that is no self and that has been devoured by a green lion or a black hole. We ended our last reflection with an image of Sol niger taken from Mylius's *Philosophia Reformata*. The image, which pictures a skeleton standing on a black sun, eerily echoes the culmination of our dark alchemy of descent. Standing in such a place signifies that the mortificatio has been achieved. In alchemy, putrefaction follows the mortificatio process. It is an aspect of the death experience and is thought to be the agent whereby change occurs. Only through the experience of dying and decomposition is new life possible. In this chapter we follow the potentially devastating consequences of an encounter with Sol niger. In so doing, we look first at depth psychology's idea of defense as a protective gesture and then beyond to a psychology of dying that is richly amplified in both alchemical art as well as the work of contemporary artists. Through depth psychology and art, we hope to gain an understanding of the meaning of a symbolic death in which dying and renewal together form the central mystery and paradox of the black sun.

Edinger speculates that "witnessing the putrefaction of a dead body . . . was not an unusual experience in the Middle Ages [and] would have had a powerful psychological impact. The effects of this experience might then be projected into the alchemical processes."[1] Whether the phenomenology of such experiences are observed in outer life and then projected onto alchemical processes or whether, on the other hand, such experiences emerge from an attention to psyche's intrinsic movement toward decay and decomposition, they nevertheless reflect a process and a place in the psyche.[2]

Bosnak describes the place of nigredo and putrefaction as

a dark, often repugnant underworld . . . [as] an incipient process of rot, rot that is necessary to permit a stagnated process to reach a state of dissolution. A period of stench, disintegration, repulsion and depression . . . [of dissolution and decay.] . . . Things must rot thoroughly like garbage, before they can be reduced to . . . rubble. . . . The future is dark and confused. It seems as though the feelings of emptiness and isolation will last forever. . . . All energy drains out of consciousness. In this bottomless pit, one finds death, death as the only reality. . . . It is a bottomless pit. . . . In this realm there is no light, no possibility for reflection. . . . The heart is heavy and in the lowest state of the *nigredo*, there are no images.[3]

Although I believe Bosnak is correct that at the "bottom" of this darkness there are "no images," in another sense, as we have seen, the images of dying and dissolution are endlessly imagined in literature, poetry, painting, and psychology. Sol niger is one such image that is not an image in the conventional sense at all. The very nature of such extreme darkness seems to call forth an endless proliferation of attempts to describe this void, no matter how unsuccessfully. In Virgil's *Aeneid*, a Sibyl, or priestess of the sun god Apollo, who accompanies him on his journey to the underworld, says, "If I had a hundred tongues and a hundred mouths and a voice of iron, I still could not describe all the . . . varieties of punishment awaiting the dead," yet Virgil describes Aeneas's encounter with a monstrous hydra—a beast with fifty heads—and a swarm of wilted, marooned spirits "wandering aimlessly along the marshes of the Styx," spirits who have to wander for a hundred years—awaiting putrefaction.[4] Many such visions of the underworld are widely disseminated across time and culture, from Egypt to Greece, in Homer's *Odyssey* and Plato's *Gorgias*, from the paintings of Bosch to fire-and-brimstone preachers who depict an image of the soul in the throws of the nigredo. Contemporary sources such as *Star Wars* and the *Lord of the Rings* continue to resonate with this image.

Given the repulsive and devastating impact of Sol niger, it is not surprising that there is a desire to escape its consequences and to move away from and out of its grip. Peter Tatham, a Jungian analyst, comments that it is best to avoid such experiences when possible (1984). He believes that in so doing we may enable ourselves and our patients to deal with their darkness in "acceptable doses, or to put it another way, we are helping them towards an incarnation of the death and rebirth process rather than being devoured by it."[5] However, he also acknowledges that there "will be times when the pull of the black hole is too great and our attempts to avoid it will be of no avail. Then we may have to be mere witnesses to a violent ending of physical" and/or psycho-logical life. Then there is "no alternative but to submit to its embrace, knowing what it means and without hope. There are some experiences into which we can enter willingly, while into others we can only fall screaming."[6]

The horror is exemplified in the Egyptian underworld by Ammut, the Egyptian "eater of the dead," "the monster [that] is part crocodile, part lion, and part hippopotamus." Ammut sits "at the feet of King Osiris in the Hall of Justice where the recently departed must face final judgment. As the soul gives an account of its life, Ammut tries to trick and confuse it, hoping to bring about an unfavorable ruling. If the soul is judged unworthy . . . Ammut devours it, sometimes with slow cru-elty."[7] Ammut has many brothers and sisters in the dark underworld of psyche. The bite of Ammut is much like the crocodile in figure 3.1, which appeared in the images drawn by a woman artist whose journey into the underworld we discuss in the next chapter.

The horror of such experiences breaks down our rational ideas and naïve visions of light and eternity. Saturnian time and scythe are the order of the night, and here we might imagine with Blake that

> *In stony sleep [Urizen has separated from Eternity and will be*
> *hatched as the body of the world:]*
> *Ages on ages rolled over him! . . .*
> *In a horrible dreamful slumber*
> *Like the linked infernal chain,*
> *A vast spine writhed in torment*
> *upon the winds, shooting pain*
> *Ribs like a bending cavern,*
> *And bones of solidness froze*
> *Over all his nerves of joy*[8]

In such instances, if death does not follow wounding, trauma often does. If Jungian analyst Donald Kalsched is right, the psyche has natu-ral defenses against such trauma. In *The Inner World of Trauma*, he describes the psyche's response to "unbearable psychic pain and anxi-ety."[9] By "unbearable," he means what comes into play when our or-

Figure 3.1. This picture, painted by an analysand, recalls Ereshkigal. Artwork by analysand. Used by permission.

dinary defenses fail. He goes on to describe how the psyche compensates for catastrophic and life-threatening experiences, what the psychoanalyst Winnicott calls "primitive agonies" and self psychologist Kohut refers to as "disintegration anxiety," an unnamed dread that threatens a dissolution of a coherent self. For Kalsched, beyond our ordinary defenses postulated by Freud and others, "*a second line of defenses* comes into play to prevent the 'unthinkable' from being *experienced*." These defenses and their elaboration in unconscious fantasy are the focus of Kalsched's investigation. He shows how a spontaneous symbolic process holds the fragmenting pieces of psyche together in what he calls a traumatic organization. Because this protects the inner core of the Self, this process has been referred to as a defense of the Self and constitutes an interesting story of psychic organization beyond the ego.[10]

Kalsched describes a split between the vulnerable and shamefully hidden remainder of the "whole Self," often portrayed as a child or animal, and "a powerful, *benevolent or malevolent great being*"[11] who protects the innocent being. What seems counterintuitive in his description is that this "protector" should show itself also as a malevolent force in the psyche, one that often persecutes the personal spirit and shows itself to the dream ego as a daemonic and terrifying force. He notes that most "contemporary writers tend to see this attacking figure as an internalized version of the actual perception of the trauma."[12] However, for Kalsched, this is only half correct since "the internal figure is often even more sadistic and brutal than the actual 'outer world perpetrator.'" For Kalsched, this indicates that we are dealing with something that is contributed from the psyche, a psychological factor and "an archetypal traumatogenic agency within the psyche itself."[13]

It is strange to think of such a brutal force as a "protector." Kalsched explains that the intention of this daemonic force is to prevent at all costs the reexperiencing of the horror at the genesis of the traumatogenic organization. The daemons of the inner world, like the temple lions at the entrance of sacred spaces, serve to keep away the unprepared. They will "disperse [the self] into fragments (dissociation) or encapsulate it and sooth it with fantasy (schizoid withdrawal) or numb it with intoxicating substances (addictions) or persecute it to keep it from hoping for life in this world (depression)."[14] Hope would open the soul, leaving it vulnerable to what is imagined as an even more painful experience than that which the "protective daemon" enforces on the wounded "personal spirit."

It is often the case, however, that the cure is worse than the "illness," even if this cannot be seen from within the experience of the overwhelming threat that continues in the wake of trauma. The fact that the ego does not notice the problematic character of the cure sets the stage for the fact that "the primitive defense does not learn anything about realistic danger. . . . Each new life opportunity is mistakenly seen as a dangerous threat of re-traumatization and is therefore attacked. In this way, the archaic defenses become anti-life forces which Freud understandably thought of as part of the death instinct."[15]

This is not surprising since the "self-care system" will "go to any length to protect the Self" in spite of the continual masochistic suffering involved, "even to the point of killing the host personality in which this personal spirit is housed (suicide)."[16] As a result, what was intended to be a defense against further trauma now becomes itself destructive in a variety of ways: "The person survives but cannot live creatively."[17]

Such consequences also manifest themselves in the ravages of depression and melancholic affect "engineered by our self-care system."[18] Kalsched cites Julia Kristeva, a Lacanian psychoanalyst who speaks of the black sun. Kalsched's interest is not in the archetypal image of the black sun per se but in contributing to a Jungian understanding of defense processes and to the operation of the psyche as a whole. For him, the image of the black sun via Kristeva remains a "pathological" product of the self-care system and a "primitive" expression and image of defense in the face of unbearable, unreachable, and even invisible narcissistic wounds.

For Kalsched and Kristeva, a person attaches to a thing that is intended to protect the personal spirit from the unthinkable. In so doing, the person is cut off from the "spontaneous expressions of self in the world."[19] Living in this devastation, the soul is in a suspension from life, a dark enclosure seemingly safe but isolated and stuck in terms of further individuation. In describing this process, Kalsched seems to equate the "personal spirit" with the inner core of the Self, and from this perspective he speaks of the Self as "coherent" and as the "total human personality." He sees the child or animal images as reflecting the hidden remains of the "whole self." In symbolic imagery Kalsched sees a larger operating dynamic of the psyche, not just of ego dynamics as such. In this way of imagining it, he gives a Jungian, archetypal basis to the psychoanalytic ideas of others such as Fairbairn, Guntrip, and Klein.

As we already noted, Kalsched's contemporary vision of Sol niger places it in the realm of pathology and of the defensive and traumatic organization of the psyche. Although his contribution reflects the working of the archetypal dimension, his focus is on the way archetypal dynamics protect and preserve the remaining fragments of what he calls the self or "personal spirit." But can the archetypal image of Sol niger be adequately understood as the product of defense?[20] If understood strictly in this way, Sol niger can be imagined only as a kind of black hole whose gravity draws the vulnerable "ego" or Self into a fascination, a spider web that traps it into a doomed stasis.

My contention is that such a description is only part of the story and that it does not yet take into account a more fundamental, archetypal role played by Sol niger in the transformative dynamics of psychic life. One question here is the status of the ego or the self. Does Sol niger have an important role to play in breaking defensive bewitchment and in the deconstructing of the ego or the Self itself? Does the ego require a dying process, as the themes of myth and alchemy suggest? Kalsched's analysis is focused on the preservation and release of the fractured ego. This does not address those moments when the dissolution of the ego is required and constitutes a genuine possibility for a nondefensive initiation that aims at far more than self-preservation, fascination, and the return of the more integrated ego into the flow of life. As important as this process is—and Kalsched's contribution to our understanding of it—the emergence of Sol niger requires a reflection on that which is beyond the humanism of ego psychology and which attempts to take on questions of the death of the ego or perhaps even the Self as part of psychic possibility.

In the classical and developmental psychologies, the unity of the healthy ego is the essential structure of the psyche. The question of the dissolution of the ego or Self is almost always seen as regressive and detrimental, a fusion, or a return to the mother. Some analysts, however, have raised a different perspective, one that has challenged ego psychology and the humanistic position it requires. Such approaches lend themselves to a different understanding of Sol niger and to our interpretation of the "death instinct" as being beyond biological assumptions, or defensive operations of the psyche, or the death of the ego as a regression.

One such position is that of French psychoanalyst Jacques Lacan, who imagines the aggressive energy directed toward the ego not at all as a defense of an ideal unity of the Self, but rather as a rebellion against it.

For Lacan, this ideal unity is itself the problem, and the idea of the ego is a distortion of reality. The aggressive energy—the "brutal force"—directed against the ego is not, as Kalsched suggests, to preserve the Self but actually to break down its defensive function. Psyche's telos may not be to protect the ego from reexperiencing trauma but rather to push it toward the feared unthinkable—to the core of its voidness. The intention of the "death instinct" may be to move psychic organization *beyond* the interests of maternal or paternal preservation of the ego's survival and its humanistic concerns of health and wholeness.[21]

Jungian analyst David Rosen's work *Transforming Depression* contributes to our understanding of such a death process. In that book Rosen coins the term "egocide" to describe the symbolic death necessary to the transformative process, a process in which the psyche is pushed beyond its defenses. He states that symbolic death "leads to a . . . greater fall, which actually feels like death."[22] It is like entering an eternal void and requires a suffering through a death-rebirth experience. Rosen images the dying process alchemically, comparing it to a fertile ground—"the underground psychic soil"—in which the seeds of the true self are embedded ans from which they ultimately can germinate."[23] If the soul in depression is nurtured properly, the results will be new life for the psyche. This process is similar to what the alchemists understand as mortification. Figure 3.2 shows the relationship between life, death, and the soil as illustrated in the image of the sun in the shape of a black skull with a golden headdress. The figure—called the Lord of the Soil—is a sixteenth-century image from the Kye Monastery in Ladakh, India.

In another image (figure 3.3) from *The Hermetic Museum*, grain is seen to be growing out of the grave and "corresponds to the alchemical idea that death is the conception of the Philosopher's Stone," the mystical goal of alchemy. For Rosen, this deep "organic" process sets in motion a kind of mourning for the now lost, dominant ego, and he gives examples of this kind of journey through the dark night of the soul, in which part of the individual psyche must die or be symbolically killed. Egocide makes possible a psychic transformation and constitutes a death-rebirth process. In that process, ego identity dies or is symbolically killed along with one's former perspectives of oneself and

Analysis and the Art of Darkness (73)

Figure 3.2. "The Lord of the Soil," photo by Madanjeet Singh.
From Madanjeet Singh, The Sun: Symbol of Power and Life, *p. 132.*

of life. Still, for Rosen, what Jung calls the Self is not destroyed. What is killed or analyzed to death is the negative (destructive) ego or false (inauthentic) Self. The primary Self as an archetypal image of the Supreme Being remains connected to the secondary, reconstituted ego and the true (authentic) self, which can be renewed and live its personal myth with joy.[24]

In Rosen's study, egocide is thus closely tied to rebirth and creativity, and one can begin to reimagine what has been called the "death in-

*Figure 3.3. Grain growing from the grave, symbolizing resurrection.
From Edward Edinger,* Anatomy of the Psyche: Alchemical
Symbolism in Psychotherapy, *p. 163.*

stinct" as something more than a biological drive toward physical death. For Kalsched, too, there is a death that breaks through sterility, bewitchment, and defensive mystical devotion. In his approach an analysis of defense helps the person to suffer through blockages, and in the best instances this can lead to a deep sense of compassion that mediates the experience of the "whole Self and its embodied incarnation."[25] What Kalsched does not consider is that the death instinct and the archetypal image of Sol niger might themselves lead toward a breakdown of the defensive stasis.

The work of psychologist Mark Welman lends itself to this conclusion. The death instinct has been "conspicuously absent in Jung's psychology."[26] Welman notes that it is seldom recognized that Jung "saw death as the ontological pivot" point in the process of psychic unfolding. Welman, therefore, sets out to explicate a Jungian phenomenology of death. He sees Jung's thought as going beyond Freud's idea of the death instinct as a search for literal death. He suggests via Lacan and in resonance with Rosen that its intent is rather a "deconstruction" of the literalist ego in favor of a symbolic order. He points out that for Jung as well, "death" is already a psychological rather than a corporeal event.[27] He notes that from the point of view of the ego, death is a brutal and frightening reality, but "from the perspective of the Self death appears," as it does for Rosen, as "a joyful event . . . a *mysterium coniunctionis* [through which] the soul . . . achieves wholeness."[28] For Welman, understanding the meaning of death in terms of the archetype of the Self offers a way of seeing it in a broader and more adequate way than Freud's conception of Thanatos. From the existential point of view, death is not some "actuality" outstretched in time to be experienced later, but rather, as Heidegger, Hillman, Lacan, the Buddhists, and others suggest, as something always already happening in the "now" as an "existential immediacy."

For Jung, this "now" of death is an "imaginal reality: a dark and pervasive presence and a primordial abyss" that obliterates the light of consciousness even as *it opens up and frees one for the symbolic life.*[29] In short, the power of the death demon at an archetypal level aims at *both* the deconstruction of the ego and the creation of new life. In Welman's elaboration of Jung via philosopher Martin Heidegger and other existential thinkers, death fertilizes the imaginal and works to open a poetic space that brings depth and meaning to everyday life. Welman's ideas closely follow Heidegger's account of death as a "shrine of nothing," by which Heidegger means a kind of ontological emptiness, an emptiness within which Being is grounded and through which Being may be recollected. For many analysts, this way of speaking is unfamiliar and difficult to understand within the traditional frameworks.

I believe, however, that what Welman, through Heidegger, is suggesting is not far from Jung's idea that the Self can be discovered and recollected through the nothingness of the mortificatio process. The mortificatio process eventually leads to "nothingness," a nothingness that is not literal but existential, imaginal, symbolic, and poetic. For an analyst to speak in this way by no means bypasses the defensive processes or the horror of an analysand's terror of the unthinkable nothingness that Kalsched and others so well describe. The point is not to idealize the destructive potential of nothingness and death but to shift our focus toward the possibility that the psyche itself may call us to the "unthinkable" dissolution of the ego and that this is *not always* what we imagine. Therefore at times the job of an analyst may be not to collude with the restorative function of defense but rather to help the psyche dissolve them.

As we move from egocide toward the reevaluation of the ego and the death instinct, we move from a simply biological or traditional psychological understanding toward a symbolic and metaphoric one and from literal death to a deconstruction of the literalist ego, which is part of the teleological aspect of the psyche itself.

In *Dreams and the Underworld,* James Hillman moves us further in this direction and speaks of death as a metaphor, separating it from literal death and linking it more to what goes on in the subtle body and in the psychic life.[30] For him, "the death we speak of in our culture is a fantasy of the ego," and from that perspective we lose touch with subtlety. "For us, pollution and decomposition and cancer have become physical only."[31] He notes that in the great art of other cultures there is a different kind of sensibility with respect to dying, one that has faded from our attention and become part of the modern unconsciousness and of the psychic underworld. For him, it is in the world of depth psychology "where today we find the initiatory mystery, the long journey of psychic learning, ancestor worship, the encounter with demons and shadows, the suffering of Hell."[32] He describes the experience of this underworld as a journey that "must be made."[33] Describing one such journey, he says "it comes as violation, dragging one out of life and into the Kingdom that the Orphic Hymn to Pluto describes as 'void of day.' So it often says on Greek epitaphs that entering Hades is 'leaving the sweet sunlight.' "[34]

In this instance, Hillman is describing the underworld of Hades against the mythic background of the Greek Demeter/Persephone mythologem and the psychological mysteries of Eleusis, which, he notes, we still experience today. He refers to our "sudden depressions, when we feel ourselves caught in hatefulness, cold, numbed, and drawn downward out of life by a force we cannot see . . . We feel invaded from below, assaulted, and we think of death."[35]

The world of Hades is an important focus for Hillman, but this, too, is only one way to imagine this metaphoric space of dying. Other mythologems help to constitute other experiences. Hillman's "underworld" is a "mythological style of describing a psychological cosmos."[36] For him, "underworld is psyche"; it is a world that can be seen when "one's entire mode of being has been desubstantialized, killed of natural life . . . and [is] devoid of life." To know the psyche for Hillman, then, is to "die," to make the "descent to Hades."[37]

For him, underworld images are ontological statements about the soul and how it "exists in and for itself beyond life." In light of this, Hillman reads "all movement towards this realm of death, whether they be fantasies of decay, images of sickness in dreams, repetitive compulsions, or suicidal impulses, as movements towards a more psychological perspective."[38] In this way he, too, takes up what Freud called the "death instinct" and reenvisions this dark side of the soul as a movement toward psychological depth and as an "invisible background that breaks us 'out of life' as we know it." In this way one might imagine the death of the "ego" as a death of the materialist perspective and of the humanism of a naturalistic psychology. For him, the idea is not to return a stronger ego to life or to the constellation of the "true self," which is just as suspect. Rather, what is called for is a "shift in consciousness" and a descent to the underworld that "must be made." This descent is necessary even for the most integrated egos. In dreams and psychic life there is for Hillman an *inherent* opposition within the psyche, and no amount of good-enough parental care should protect the soul from dying into psychological life. Ultimately, for Hillman, "death" is the most radical way of expressing a shift in consciousness.

For most depth psychologists, the journey to the underworld is for the purpose of a return to life as, one hopes, a more integrated self, but for Hillman this does not go far enough. The return of the repressed still does not address the deeper meaning of "death itself" and the underworld psyche.[39] Hades as a figure of his concern reflects a radical shift in our view of psychological life, which is qualitatively different from that of our modernist tradition; Hades does not represent a movement into life and wholeness but rather a movement out of life in which the literal ego loses its fixed substance. This is a difficult perspective for modern consciousness to understand. How it differs from the perspectives of Jung, Kalsched, Rosen, Welman, Lacan, and others remains to be further elaborated, but on the surface Hillman's vision seems to be one of a very different sense of psyche.

Whatever the differences and similarities between the positions we have outlined, all of us would agree that the "death experience" must be understood metaphorically and psychologically. We have already seen that alchemy has placed the death experience at the heart of the alchemical process. Without entering into the nigredo and undergoing the mortificatio experience, no transformation is possible. Alchemical literature is replete with descriptions, arcane as they may be, of the phenomenology and symbolism of dying, often illustrated with highly complex images and symbolic drawings.

The Art of Mortificatio

Symbolic images of the mortificatio have appeared throughout the ages, from the alchemists to the postmodern artists of today. The metaphor of death is richly elaborated in arcane graphics in which corpses, coffins, and graves are containers for the mysterious workings of the psyche. The *Rosarium Philosophorum*, for instance, contains a series of such images in which the coffin functions as a container for the process of transformation. Jung writes that in these images, the "*vas hermeticum* . . . [has] here become sarcophagus and tomb."[40] This theme also appears in a series of drawings (figure 3.4) that began to appear in alchemical manuscripts during the Renaissance.

For Jung as well as for the alchemists, "death" is part of a process of transformation in which strange and symbolic events take place. It was important to the alchemists and for Jung to illustrate the process through images. Because the work of alchemy is concerned with the dying process and a linking of the ego and the unconscious, Jung felt that this experience could best "be expressed by means of symbols" or images "born of nature's own workings."[41] For Jung, a natural symbol is "far removed from all conscious intention."

Jungian analyst Jeff Raff rightly points out that "alchemical pictures were not simply illustrations for a text, but attempts to communicate" complex realities and "were a profound expression of the alchemical imagination."[42] Alchemical emblems "represent the mysteries of

Figure 3.4. Image of the coniunctio from the Rosarium Philosophorum.
From Vladilav Zadrobilek, ed., Magnum Opus *(Prague: Trigon), p. 72.*

alchemy so powerfully and concisely that their study can lead to a profound understanding of its nature."[43] Alchemical scholar Stanislas Klossowksi De Rola echoes this recognition in his study of alchemical engravings of the seventeenth century. Noting that these engravings "transcend both illustration and decoration," he argues that they constitute an independent pictorial language that, in silence but not without eloquence, conveys the secrets of alchemy.[44] De Rola sees these images as a kind of alchemical language that "plays [on] . . . double meanings, natural analogies and hermetick interpretations of classical mythology."[45] He calls this way of communicating "the Golden Game." The *Rosarium* pictures illustrating the dying process are one grouping among several others. The death experience was pivotal, and Sol niger was often intimately linked to the nigredo and mortificatio aspects of the process.

The metaphoric expression of the dying process is also found in other alchemical manuscripts. For example, chapter two ends with an illustration from Mylius's *Philosophia Reformata* (1622), in which the image of a skeleton is standing on a glowing black orb marking the nigredo/putrefactio stage in the death-rebirth process. Other alchemical manuscripts likewise place images of the black sun in similar positions in the process. For instance, alchemist Edward Kelly, in his paper "The Theatre of Terrestrial Astronomy," comments that "the beginning of our work is the black raven which, like all things that are to grow and receive life, must first putrefy. For putrefaction is a necessary condition of solution, as salvation is of birth and regeneration."[46]

In figure 3.5 we see an image of conjunction in which a black sun is contained in an alchemical vessel. Behind the furnace is a field of green barely springing up out of the earth, again linking death with regeneration. This process is beautifully described in the alchemical manuscript *Cabala Mineralis*, in which Sol is described as undergoing "sophic calcinations, and putrefaction." The common Sun is watered with new mercury and made "one body black and not porous." Then germination takes place. The Sun is changed from its black color and becomes green and is spread out into the vegetation.

Another image (figure 3.6) of Sol niger is found in *The Hermetic*

Figure 3.5. The black sun contained in an alchemical vessel, from "The Theater of Terrestrial Astronomy," series of emblems by Edward Kelly, 1676. From Adam McLean, http://www.levity.com/alchemy/terrastr.htm.

Garden of Daniel Stolcius.[47] This is an essential, seventeenth-century sourcebook in the symbolic and meditative tradition in alchemy and one of its most important emblem books.[48]

A translation of the Latin inscription accompanying the emblem reads as follows:

> *Let the highest point of your magistery*
> *Be to remove the earth born shade from*
> *the rays of the Sun.*
> *Let the bird die, and rise up again into the air*
> *So that it may know how to increase its life.*[49]

In these alchemical images, the symbology of dying is pivotal, complex, and closely linked to transformation. Images of Sol niger and death seem to bring what we think of as opposites into proximity. Black orbs glow with intense light, graves are filled with green barley, and death is linked to an increase in life. These alchemical images might be imagined to reflect what Welman calls an ontological "pivot point," a perspective in which death is also *jouissance* and egocide is linked to

Figure 3.6. Image of Sol Niger, 1627. From Adam McLean, ed.,
The Hermetic Garden of Daniel Stolcius, *emblem 99, p. 108.*

creativity. Likewise for Hillman, death is also the death of a materialist viewpoint, freeing us for imaginal and poetic life, a life beyond life, and a movement into psychological depth.

We have seen that images have played an important role in the expression of complex psychological processes, processes that seem to exceed our traditional ways of speaking and imagining. The attempt to explore ontological "pivot points" and to penetrate paradoxes like Sol niger are aided not only by allegorical images but also by the study of artistic expression in general. How can we understand a death that means new life or a darkness that shines? Images such as these have long interested artists and writers, even "after alchemy itself had fallen into disrepute as a natural science."[50] The death of the ego, blackness, and the transformation of the soul, which were so important in alchemy, were also concerns for a number of artists. Mona Sandqvist writes that "alchemy has been kept alive in art, music, and literature by a chain of masters: painters like Bosch, Brueghel the Elder, Max Ernst and Rene Magritte; musicians like Mozart, Scriabin, and Schönberg; and writers like E. T. A. Hoffman, Balzac, Gerard de Nerval, Mallormé, Autard, Yeats and Joyce."[51]

The paradox of the black sun is that it is an image that simultaneously expresses what traditionally has been held to be a pair of incompatible and opposing phenomena: darkness and light, blackness and luminosity. Yet, in the image of Sol niger, they are intimately linked. This luminous paradox at the heart of the black sun has been a theme both explicit and implicit in the work of painters who have painted in black.

Explicitly, there have been a number of artists who have painted black suns, including Motherwell, Matisse, Ernst, Calder, and others. More implicitly, the theme of painting luminous blackness has been an important part of the history of painting and would require a book-length study in its own right. Malevich, Rothko, Reinhardt, Soulages, Stella, and Rauschenberg are well known for their focus on blackness and the dialectic of light and dark and have dedicated a part of their careers to exploring this theme.

Figure 3.7 shows a primitive and powerful rendition of the black sun by Motherwell. Matisse expresses a very different aspect of the black sun. He thought of black as a luminous color and went on to experiment with the idea of black light, with black as luminosity. "The concept of black as a colour (not simply as a darkener) had been debated in painterly circles since the Renaissance, and had been more or less generally accepted by the close of the nineteenth century."[52] Still, as art historian John Gage points out, the notion of black as a light is "so paradoxical and so radical" that it invites a more careful examination.[53] Gage's reflection on Matisse considers a number of possible influences on him, including that of the philosopher Henri Bergson and the mathematician Henri Poincaré, who held that movement exists only by means of "the destruction and reconstitution of matter," a provocative idea relevant to our exploration of Sol niger. Gustave LeBon, a nineteenth-century scientist, was also interested in the idea of the instability of matter and likewise began to develop a theory of black light as well.[54] Although the term "black light" was not generally accepted, it became clear that visible light accounted for less than one tenth of

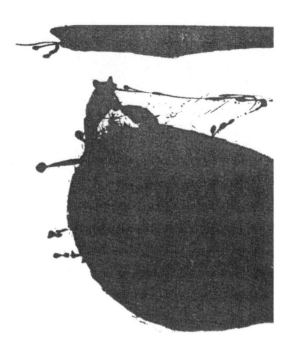

Figure 3.7. Black Sun *(1959), painting by Robert Motherwell.* © *Dedalus Foundation, Inc./Licensed by VAGA, New York, N.Y. Used by permission.*

the spectrum and that the invisible portion constituted a far more "important portion of the light," even though the human eye was not sensitive enough to perceive it directly.[55] "Black Light was not a concept which had any lasting [scientific] impact," but "Matisse's 'black light,' on the other hand, propelled partly by the inner turmoil brought about by illness and war, had a long life ahead of it. . . . What proved to be contingent and provisional in science has revealed itself as enduring in art."[56]

The oddly titled "Black Sun" by Max Ernst (figure 3.8) was literally painted in blues and yellows. Ernst was a member of the surrealist movement for which the black sun was an important image. In the introduction to his book, *Max Ernst and Alchemy,* M. E. Warlick writes about the prime matter of the alchemist and notes that "it is composed of two essential properties, Philosophic Sulphur and Philosophic

Figure 3.8. Black Sun *(1927–1928), painting by Max Ernst.* © *2004 Artists Rights Society (ARS), New York/ADAGP, Paris. Used by permission.*

Mercury, polarized masculine and feminine aspects of matter often pictured as King and Queen, or as the sun and the moon."[57] In the laboratory, these two properties are separated, refined, and purified. Warlick describes how as the alchemical process unfolds, these opposites combine, and, through their sexual union, the birth of the philosophical child or philosopher's stone emerges.

I am uncertain what Ernst had in mind in his painting of Sol niger, but it is not hard to imagine in this image the conjunction of opposites in the lower plane and the rounded image of a transcendental possibility above. In this case, a black sun, which is a "union" of Sun and Moon, gives off a strange luminescence or dark light, perhaps emerging from a crossing of opposites that is difficult to describe.

The theme of "bridging opposites" and of dark light is also found in the art of Mark Rothko. Rothko is well known for his powerful black-on-black paintings (figure 3.9). In 1961, John de Menil and Dominique

Figure 3.9. Untitled *(1964–1967), painting by Mark Rothko.* © *1998 Kate Rothko Prizel and Christopher Rothko / Artists Rights Society (ARS), New York. Used by permission.*

de Menil asked him to produce murals for a chapel in Houston, now named after him: the Rothko Chapel. While the black sun never became an explicit theme for him, the binary opposition between light and dark, subject and object, presence and absence, and life and death were fundamental to his art. Rothko's own reflections on this theme are of interest because for him the opposites are "neither synthesized, nor neutralized . . . but held in a confronted unity, which is a momentary stasis."[58] This confrontation creates a "structure" not unlike Ernst's *Black Sun* in that it calls the very status of "opposition" into question by overlapping their "terms." In essence, he finds a way to paint a "brink or border between" opposites and this was the focus of his subject.[59] In his so doing, Rothko's art expresses the "affective power of a state of irresolution or undecidability."[60]

The idea of undecidability helps to amplify what was earlier called an "ontological pivotal point," a point that Rothko continued to approach as he broke away from surrealism and turned toward what has been called "abstract painting." What he did in these paintings was to further what he had been struggling with all along. Art theorist Anna Chave describes this process as "at once inscribing and erasing . . .

working with the structure of traces, constructing a play between presence and absence."[61] In his black-on-black paintings, however, "known pictorial conventions were more 'under erasure' . . . than ever before."[62] In both Rothko's paintings and Chave's Derridean critique are new ways of continuing to understand what the alchemists tried to express in their mortificatio process and in their paradoxical image of Sol niger. One might likewise see the black sun as an image under erasure, undecidable in terms of presence or absence. For Chave, Rothko's black-on-black paintings are "directed against the closure of metaphysics," that is, the kind of thinking that binds one into binary hierarchies and ontological commitments to presence over absence. In Rothko's paintings, Chave concludes, "absence had come to the fore."

Chave notes that postmodern philosopher Jacques Derrida's terms for this gesture of effacing the presence of a thing is writing *(écriture)* and that a "text, whether 'literary,' 'psychic,' 'anthropological' or pictorial, is precisely 'a play of presence and absence,'" a kind of artistic *fort-da*, "'a play of the effaced trace.'"[63] Rothko's attempt to paint this pivotal point between presence and absence was also an attempt to paint the void. This led some of his critics to consider him a religious man or mystic, a description that he himself denied. One might also imagine Rothko struggling with the "death instinct," as we have described it, as an urge toward the unthinkable. In 1958, while lecturing on his art, he declared that "tragic art . . . deals with the fact that a man is born to die." For Chave, his art "engaged the emotions most subject to repression, those insufferable intimations of mortality and that invasive sense of nothingness that permeates modern experience."[64] Chave cites Adorno: "The greatness of works of art lies solely in their power to let those things be heard which ideology conceals." Rothko's black paintings, rather than creating a hysterical defense or fascination, served as revelations of a kind—"less reassuring than troubling."[65] As we have seen, engaging this realm of darkness can have tragic consequences, and so it was ultimately the case with Rothko. In February, 1970, he was found in a pool of blood on the floor of his studio, where he had committed suicide, and so he might be seen as yet another victim of the darkest side of Sol niger.

Another important painter who painted black-on-black paintings is Ad Reinhardt. For twelve years beginning in the early fifties, he painted only black paintings. He also wrote a good deal about his work, and a selection of his writing has been edited with commentary by prominent art critic Barbara Rose in a work called *Art-as-Art: The Selected Writings of Ad Reinhardt.*[66] Shortly before Reinhardt's death, he reflected on his painting and stated that his purpose was to "push painting beyond its thinkable, seeable, graspable, feelable limits."[67] Reinhardt's idea was that his painting represented "both the end of the Western tradition and the beginning of a new mode of perception."[68] According to Reinhardt, his black paintings created perceptual demands radically different from those of Western painting because his images require both the time to see and an act of focusing so demanding that it changes the state of the viewer's consciousness. For him, "the black paintings are icons without iconography. They function like the hypnotic patterns of the abstract diagrams of tantric Buddhism: they induce a state of contemplation which may be defined as meditative. . . . The black paintings, although not specifically 'religious,' are an effort to retrieve the dimension of the spiritual in a secular culture."[69]

In the last ten years of Reinhardt's life, his paintings became "black, black, black, black, black."[70] "Nothing in the painting: 'No realism, no impressionism, no expressionism . . . no texture, no brushwork, no sketching or drawing, no forms, no designs, no calm, no light, no space, no time, no size or scale, no movement, no object, no subject.'"

For writer Richard Smith, Reinhardt's dozens of published statements like this one "burn on the page like a demonic chant." Like the "neti neti" of the Hindus or the inability to name God in Christian mysticism, there seems to be no way to adequately capture any object of Reinhardt's paintings.

Ultimately, though, for Smith, "this endless chain of negations [does] not lead to nihilism" but actually reverse the negative association that the color black usually connotes. Although Reinhardt himself and many of his critics reject the religious intention of his paintings, writer Naomi Vine notes that, in his own jottings on the mandala, he wrote this of his paintings:[71] "Holy ground, sacred space, fixed point, threshold, limit, entrance, 'gate,' sign, ritual, pure region; holy of holies, breakthrough from plane to plane . . . no change, no exhaustion, re-

Analysis and the Art of Darkness (89)

coverable, repeatable, starting over at the beginning, eternal return, repetition."[72]

For Vine, such statements indicate that Reinhardt saw his paintings as an entry point to an attainable, repeatable spiritual experience, an experience that went beyond nihilism.

Pierre Soulages, a twentieth-century French abstract artist, also painted black images, which art historian and critic Donald Kuspit has called "unsettling, undigestible, out of sight, unseeable, ironically invisible."[73] Like Rothko and Reinhardt, Soulages's paintings "do not submit to the usual process of perception" and have the effect of displacing and minimizing the ego subject. For philosopher Theodor Adorno, Soulages's images lead to an "emaciation" of the subject and constitute a "blackness that is too extreme to become the site of human fantasy."[74] Such statements bring to the fore the tension between a humanistic ego psychology and a psychology that could do justice to "postmodern sensibilities" of abstract art. The complexities of such a psychology must go beyond binary opposition and approach the kind of undecidability that opens the psyche to a process of creativity and the sacred.

Even though Kuspit finds it oversimplifying, he still characterizes Soulages's purpose as being to "find the light in the dark, more particularly the light that dwells in the darkness and that, at the moment of revelation, is secreted by it, as it were."[75] Such a moment is reminiscent of the Elgonyi as noted in chapter 2, for whom such a moment is sacred. Kuspit goes on to suggest that what Soulages points to is the Self at its most extreme and "emaciated" point, desperate for the light that can transfigure it, a light that is always latent and concealed within blackness.

Finally, for Soulages, blackness is not the end but the starting point for a subtle, almost inexpressible, light. For the alchemist, I believe, this light was the lumen naturae, which, like Jung's scintillae, glows at the heart of matter itself. For Soulages, there remained a primitive and fundamental if not essential split in the psyche between light and dark, which Kuspit feels the painter could never quite resolve. It is as if at the core of the Self there is a primitive divide, a "cut," an irresolvable binary state that has also become a theme for a number of painters. The idea has affected the material basis of painting itself. Artist Lucio Fontana pierced and sliced his canvasses, as if canvas was psyche, in an attempt to show what was going on in the "interior" of a painting.[76] Other artists changed the way canvasses were constructed and the way they used material. The very matter of paintings was alchemically transformed, and, for some, alchemy itself became an inspiration to creative process.

The work of renowned German artist Anselm Kiefer is filled with obvious alchemical allusions. He broke a number of different conventions in the material base of his art, mixing painting, sculpture, and photography as well as using both "visual and verbal languages long considered an impure practice" in the art world. On his huge canvasses, he uses not only paint but also "straw, wax, lead, wood and human hair."[77] In 1984, he painted *The Nigredo,* and in a critical commentary on his work, Jack Flam refers to him as "The Alchemist."[78]

Lopez-Pedraza, a Jungian analyst from Caracas, Venezuela, comments in his book on Kiefer that "the *nigredo* was called the darkness, darker than darkness."[79] However, in the painting by this name, the "*mortificatio* of the Earth transformed suffering into psyche and art."[80] Here as in other paintings Kiefer goes to the margins of the darkest shadows of our history and our personal and cultural life. His art demands a confrontation with taboos, indigestible traumas, and the unhealed wounds of our age.

Such a conscious struggle with wounds affects the soul of the artist and stimulates the individuation process. In "The Starred Heaven" (1980) (figure 3.10), a photograph of Kiefer appears faded out, and a dark, stormy sky is painted all around him.

Standing on a snake, the figure has his hands on his hips. Written on the painting are words taken from Kant, "The starred heavens above [us]: The moral law within us." For Lopez-Pedraza, Kiefer's self-image is an expression of the artist's individuation. He notes, as other commentators have, that in the center of the figure's chest, at the site of his heart, is the artist's pallet, marking the place from which creative expression comes. The starred heaven is then equated by Lopez-Pedraza with the alchemical scintillae, the first appearance of the soul, the

Figure 3.10. The Starred Heaven *(1980), painting by Anselm Kiefer.*
© *Anselm Kiefer. Used by permission.*

sparks of light in the dark sky that for Jung reflected the multiple centers of the psyche in the darkness of the unconscious.

Note that what has been seen as a palette in the heart area of a starred heaven also resembles a black sun—and with Sol niger, individuation leads to dying. If this is so, then it is not surprising that the body image is also fading, perhaps giving a visual register to what philosopher Theodor Adorno has earlier called the "emaciation of the subject."

A second portrait, called "Broken Flowers and Grass" (figure 3.11), lends credence to this view, I believe.

In this image, Kiefer is lying on a bed, appearing to be asleep or dead. The entire picture is painted over with broken black-and-white flowers and grass. For López-Pedraza, this image has a "hermetic, freakish touch, that of rehearsing one's own death."[81] In and through these images, López-Pedraza links depression, death, the body, and feeling to individuation and the creative processes.

From this perspective, the image of dying is perhaps "freakish" in the same way that alchemical images are—in portraying those "ontological pivot points" in which opposites coalesce—life and death, creation and destruction, inner and outer, light and dark, microcosm and macrocosm. From this point of view, "The Starred Heaven" and "Broken Flowers and Grass" might be seen as an imaging of the relation between the Sol niger of the heart and the scintilla of the cosmos. The paradox continues to be a theme for contemporary artists.

Janet Towbin, who did a series of black paintings influenced by alchemists, writes:

[B]lack is the beginning of consciousness—you cannot have light without darkness or darkness without light. The dyad of black and white sets up a diurnal rhythm and the contrast is essential to consciousness. This is the symbol of Tao, the yin and yang.

In alchemy, the color black refers to the *nigredo,* a stage in alchemy where there is an inward turning toward creative and fecund activity. It is this level of the psyche's development that brings with it the beginning awareness of consciousness—a first

Figure 3.11. Broken Flowers and Grass *(1980), paiting by Anselm Kiefer.*
© *Anselm Kiefer. Used by permission.*

glimmer of light after the profound darkness of melancholia.
Pattern and order begin to emerge out of chaos.

It is the paradox of the *nigredo* that I have painted—the conjunction of light and dark, growth and decay, mystery and revelation, the unconscious and conscious. These paintings are

Figure 3.12. The Seduction of Black, *painting by Janet Towbin.*
Used by permission of Janet Towbin.

visualizations of the void—a black abyss which contains everything and nothing.[82]

Figure 3.12 is an example of Towbin's efforts to capture the luminous
paradox at the heart of blackness itself, a blackness that glistens with
light. The image of luminous blackness has appeared over the course
of our reflections—in the black paintings of Rothko and Reinhardt,
the black light of Matisse, the light that dwells in the darkness of
Soulages, the illuminated black sky of Kiefer, the shining blackness of
Kali, and the glowing orbs of alchemy. All of these reveal what Jung
calls the light of darkness itself, an expression of the alchemist's lumen
naturae.

As we have seen, if one explores Sol niger beyond the analysis of defense, one discovers an archetypal "intention" to drive the Self into unthinkable but transformative darkness. This is the darkness many artists have tried to render in their art, a rendering that demands a symbolic death, an egocide that is simultaneously blackness and luminescence, the central mystery of Sol niger. In the next chapter we explore the lumen naturae in order to deepen our understanding of this paradoxical luminescence.

■

CHAPTER 4

Lumen Naturae
The Light of Darkness Itself

*Yet mystery and manifestations arise from the same
source. This source is called darkness . . . Darkness
within darkness, the gateway to all understanding.*

—*Lao-Tzu*

The lumen naturae is an image of light at the core of ancient alchemical ideas. One of the aims of alchemy was to beget this light hidden in
nature, a light very different from the Western association of light as
separate from darkness. In *Alchemical Studies,* Jung writes about the
light of nature (lumen naturae), which he calls "the light of darkness
itself, which illuminates its own darkness, and this light the darkness
comprehends. Therefore it turns blackness into brightness, burns
away 'all superfluities,' and leaves behind nothing but 'faecem et sco-
riam et terram damnatam' (dross and scoriae and the rejected earth)."[1]

The process of burning away the inessential was part of the alchemical phenomenology of fire intended to bring about a purification. The
alchemists called the process *calcinatio.* Edinger dedicates a chapter
of *Anatomy of the Psyche* to this procedure. One aspect of this process
is "cremation," which brings about both the "death and blackness of
mortificatio," as well as drying and "whitening" of the matter undergoing the process.[2] The alchemists refer to this process as the *albedo.*

Figure 4.1. Kali, seventeenth century. From Ajit Mookerjee,
The Feminine Force, *p. 64.*

Abraham notes that "The clear moonlight of the albedo leads the adept
out of the black night of the soul (the nigredo)."[3]

The alchemical procedure *calcinatio* has its parallel in Tantric rites,
in which Kali is worshipped at cemeteries. The goddess copulates with
her consort, Siva, on the body of a corpse, which is burning in a funeral
pyre. These rites symbolically and ritually depict death, out of which a
new spiritual "human being arises shining."[4] Kali's blackness is said to
shine, and in figure 4.1 we see the Kali figure, who reduces the universe
to ashes, the darkness just before the "bright" phase of a reconstituted

self.[5] I believe the idea of the shining that we see here parallels the alchemical idea of the whitening and silvering.

In alchemy, certain passages of text also emphasize a shining or glowing blackness. In one, the black matter is called "the Ethiopian." A text by fifteenth-century alchemist and astrologer Melchior says, "Then will appear in the bottom of the vessel the mighty Ethiopian. . . . He asks to be buried, to be sprinkled with his own moisture and slowly calcined till he shall rise in glowing form from the fierce fire."[6]

As noted, alchemical texts have traditionally spoken of this kind of renewal as a transition from the blackness of the nigredo to the whiteness of the albedo, but I believe we have to be careful not to interpret this white outcome of the alchemical process in terms of literal color since there is a tendency in modern culture to see white and black as opposites. The whiteness of the albedo is simultaneously a developmental step in a series of alchemical processes *and* the illuminating quality intrinsic in the blackness of the nigredo process. The whiteness that the alchemists speak of is not a whiteness separate from blackness. On the contrary, to understand the "renewal" that "follows" the nigredo, one must go beyond simple dichotomies and see into the complexity of the blackness itself.[7]

"'Putrefaction extends and continues even unto whiteness,' says Figulus."[8] Hillman notes that the "shadow is not washed away and gone but is built into the psyche's body," which then exhibits its own kind of lustration and contains both darkness and "light."[9]

It was a light Jung came to know in his alchemical studies. In an Arabic treatise (1541) attributed to Hermes, the *Tractatus Aureus*, Mercurius says: "I beget the light, but the darkness too is of my nature."[10] In alchemy, light and dark and male and female are joined together in the idea of the chemical marriage, and from the marriage (of light and dark) the *filius philosophorum* emerges, and a new light is born: "They embrace and the new light is begotten of them, which is like no other light in the whole world."[11] This light is a central mystery of alchemy.

Jung traces the idea of the filius—the child of the marriage of opposites—to the archetypal image of the Primordial Man of Light, a vision of the Self that is both light and dark, male and female. Jung finds

Figure 4.2. The alchemist and the lumen naturae, *1721.*
From Johannes Fabricius, Alchemy: The Medieval Alchemists
and Their Royal Art, *p. 8.*

amplification for figure 4.2 in the mythic figures of Prajapati or Purasha in India, in Gayomort in Persia—a youth of dazzling whiteness like Mercurius—and in Metatron, who in the kabbalistic text of the Zohar was created together with light. Paracelsus also describes the Man of Light, whose illumination is the result of the integration of opposites, as identical with the "astral" man. The astral, or primordial, man also expresses our own archetypal possibility for illumination and wisdom: "The true man is the star in us. The star desires to drive men towards great wisdom."[12]

It is interesting to see Derrida's reading of solar mythology and the problematics of illumination resonating with Jung's thoughts about the primordial man; both struggle with primary dichotomies and are concerned with going beyond the literal nature of light to a more intrinsic understanding. Derrida's reading of solar mythology is more complex. He agrees with Jung that light should not be simply equated with the light of the sun but also linked to the light of enlightenment. Derrida also alludes to a metaphorical Sun that is associated with alternatives to the light of empiricist and other specular conceptions. He speaks of a light that is a "night light [which is a] supplement to daylight."[13] In his commentary on Derrida, Martin Jay notes: "The sun is also a star, after all, like all the other stars that appear only at night and are invisible during the day. As such it suggests a source of truth or properness that was not available to the eye, at least at certain times."[14]

Derrida was aware that there were two suns, the literal sun and the Platonic sun representing the Good. Derrida notes that, for Plato, the Good was a nocturnal source of all light—"the light of light beyond light." Following Bachelard and intimating a philosophical awareness of Sol niger, Derrida also states that the heart of light is black. Plato's Sun "not only enlighten[s], it engenders. The good is the father of the visible sun which provides living beings with 'creation, growth and nourishment.'"[15]

Jung, like Derrida, mentions two images of light: the great light and the inner light of nature, an innerness that is also an outerness.[16] This dual vision is characteristic of the Primordial Man, whose light is ultimately the *mundus imaginalis*.[17] This, according to twentieth-century

French scholar, philosopher, and mystic Henri Corbin, must not be confused with the "imaginary" in our current understanding of the term.[18]

The double nature of light is itself an archetypal theme along with the invisibility of the so-called inner light. It is a light that is neither simply subjective nor simply found in the outer world, in phenomena, or in our speech, but it "buildeth shapes in sleep from the power of the word" and can be found in dreams.[19] The attainment of this light was, for Paracelsus, his deepest and most secret passion. His whole creative yearning belonged to the lumen naturae, a divine spark buried in the darkness. The divine spark was, according to the alchemists, an animating principle, "a *natura abscondita* (hidden nature) perceived only by the inward man."[20]

What Paracelsus called the "luminous vehicle," neo-Platonic philosophers called the "subtle body," or the *soma pneumatikon*, a paradoxical term referring to an intermediate realm that "may be said without exaggeration to have been what might be called the very soul of astrology and alchemy."[21] This hidden nature is essential in understanding Sol niger.[22]

The Subtle Body

Images of the subtle body have been known throughout history and across cultures and have been discussed and imaged in a variety of contexts. From the Western astrological, kabbalistic, alchemical, hermetic, and magical traditions to Indian, Chinese, Buddhist, and Taoist ones, imagining the subtle body has played an important role in medical, psychological, sexual, and sacred psychologies. For all of these traditions, human beings constitute a microcosm, internally linked with the larger universe, and are reflected in a body that is not simply material but also "subtle" and primordial.[23]

Sanford L. Drob, a philosopher and psychologist who has written extensively on the kabbala, traces the emergence of the symbol of the primordial man in a number of religious and philosophical traditions from the Atman of the Upanishads to the macroanthropos of Plutarch for whom "the sun is at the heart and the moon located between the heart and the belly."[24] He notes that the Primordial Man is also important in Gnosticism: "In the Nag Hammadi text, the *Apocryphon of John*, we learn that this anthropos is the first . . . luminary of the heavens."[25] The idea of the Primordial Man also appeared in the Jewish tradition first in the literature of *"Merkaveh* mysticism." Drob notes that the "clearest example of this is found in a work that he dates as "no later than the sixth century" titled *Shi'ur Koma* (the Measure of [the Divine] Body), "where the author seeks a vision of one 'who sits upon the throne,' a gigantic supernal man who is imprinted with magical letters and names."[26]

The one who sits on the throne was part of the ecstatic vision of Ezekiel's chariot and was considered to be an "image" of God. Ezekiel describes what he "sees" above the firmament: "and the likeness of the throne was a likeness as the appearance of a man upon it above. And I saw as the colour of electrum, as the appearance of fire round about enclosing it, from the appearance of his loins and upward . . . and downward I saw as it were the appearance of fire, and there was brightness round about him."[27]

Imagining the divine in human form presented a problem for some Jewish thinkers. The twelfth-century, Jewish rationalist Maimonides "believed that the Shi'ur Koma was heretical and should be burned,"[28] but other authorities understood these images differently. Scholem, a scholar of Jewish mysticism and a colleague of Jung's at the Eranos circle, held that these images did "not imply that God himself had a body" but that a bodily form could be attributed to God's "glory" or the divine presence or "Shekinah."[29] As Jewish mysticism developed, especially in Lurianic kabbala, the attempt to imagine the divine took shape in the image of the Primordial Man, Adam Kadmon, who began to be imagined in bodily form (figure 4.3a).[30] The body of Adam Kadmon is considered to comprise ten sefirot, a kind of infrastructure of fundamental archetypes linking God, human beings, and the world.[31] Sometimes the configuration of these structures is imagined in the form of a tree and at other times as comprising the structure of primordial humans.

In figure 4.3b, the archetypal structure shows itself in the spheres of wisdom, intelligence, beauty, mercy, justice, foundation, honor, victory, and kingdom, which are laid out according to a traditional pat-

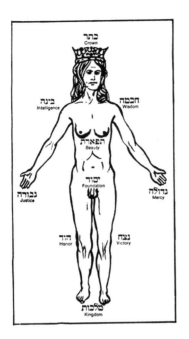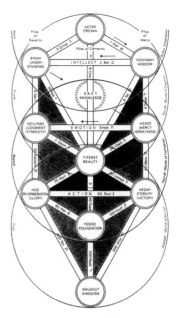

Figure 4.3. *The body of Adam Kadmon (a) as primordial man, from
Charles Poncé,* Kabbalah: An Introduction and Illumination for the
World Today, *p. 141; and (b) as the tree of life, from Z'ev ben Shimon Halevi,*
Kabbalah: Tradition of Hidden Knowledge, *p. 40.*

tern, constituting what has also been referred to as the Tree of Life.
There have been many descriptions of and variations on both Adam
Kadmon and the Tree of Life in kabbalistic literature.[32]

Adam Kadmon as Cosmic Man and an image of the subtle body has
also been taken up in Christian kabbala. In this image of the head of
Adam Kadmon (figure 4.4), the skull is drawn in such a way as to reveal roots as part of the brain structure, linking his subtle body with
the image of the tree.[33] From this head, a white light is said to "illumi-
nate a hundred thousand worlds. . . . The length of His face is three
hundred and seventy thousand worlds. He is called the Long-Face, for
this is the name of the ancient of ancients."[34]

The body of Adam Kadmon is a body of lights, an illuminated body
whose organs are divine lights. The sefirot themselves are a source of

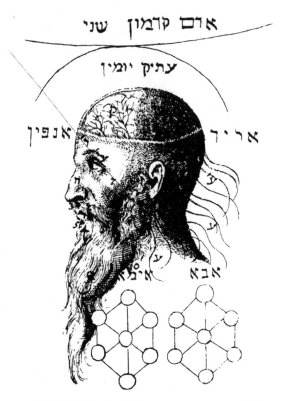

אדם קדמון שני

עתיק יומין

אריך

אנפין

אבא אימא

Figure 4.4. The Head of Adam Kadmon, *1684. From Kurt Seligman,*
The History of Magic, *p. 135.*

lights, colored translucent spheres that serve to modify the infinite ex-
panse of the God, referred to by the kabbalists as Ein-sof.[35] Dramatic
images of the subtle body of Adam Kadmon have been painted by Alex
Grey, a contemporary artist. One of his paintings, titled *Psychic Energy
System* (1980), represents for the artist the kabbalistic Tree of Life
(color plate 7). He writes: "The Kabbalistic Tree, when keyed to the human body is known as the Adam Kadmon or . . . First Man, and de-
notes the emanation of the highest spiritual world from above the head
down through the physical world at the feet. The symbols represent ten
divine attributes, such as wisdom, mercy, judgment, and beauty."[36]

Grey's image links the kabbalistic subtle body with the Chakra system of the Hindu tradition. He considers them to present a "similar

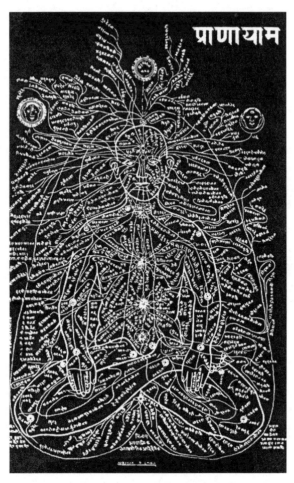

Figure 4.5. A Tantric image of the subtle body. From David V. Tansley,
The Subtle Body: Essence and Shadow, *p. 46. Courtesy of*
Thames and Hudson, London and New York.

spiritual-to-physical spectrum." In both systems, "the body has become a permeable channel for the circulation of the subtle and fine
energies of spiritual consciousness that are ever-present and interpen-
etrate the self and surroundings."[37]

The intensity of such fine energies is also known in Tantric representations of the subtle body, where they are referred to as *nadis*, which
"form an intricate web of subtle energy fibers that permeate the phys-

ical form. Certain texts speak of 350,000 nadis, through which the solar and lunar energies flow" (figure 4.5).[38]

In *Praying* (color plate 8), Grey depicts what he considers "the spiritual core of light which transcends, unites, and manifests in the various religious paths." Here again he blends the subtle body idea into a syncretist "portrait revealing a sun in the heart and mind." "From the inner light in the center of the brain, a halo emanates and surrounds the head. The halo is inscribed with signs of contemplation from six different paths": Taoist, Hindu, Jewish, Tibetan, Christian, and Islamic.[39]

Grey's focus emphasizes the significant overlapping unity between the variety of images of the subtle body. However, just as there are differences in the metapsychologies and individual experiences that produced them, differences in general patterns and particulars also exist with regard to the chakras. Phillip Rawson notes that the "Tibetan Buddhists assert that there is a significant difference between their pattern of the subtle body and the normal Hindu one."[40] These differences are further compounded as we look at the various traditions we are discussing. Yet, Grey is not wrong about the significant archetypal overlap between them.

In color plate 9, which shows a traditional scroll painting from seventeenth-century Nepal, the ajna chakra is placed in a similar position as Grey's sun and is considered the third eye of wisdom. At the very top, not indicated in Grey's image, are the male and female deities pictured in intimate embrace, signifying the interpenetration of opposite forces.

In figure 4.6 we see a full body view of the chakra system. The ajna chakra is again pictured with male and female deities in an intimate relationship, and a number of different deities appear in each chakra. At times, some of these figures become standardized, but in other representations they change according to the individual, inward psychic experience of yoga and Tantric practice.

Rawson describes how, when "the subtle energy (Bodhicitta) becomes united with the void of wisdom, the sky of the mind fills with infinite visions and scenes. Then like sparks, seed-mantras emerge and crystallize gradually into complete and glowing living forms of devatās, beautiful or terrible, which confront the meditator."[41]

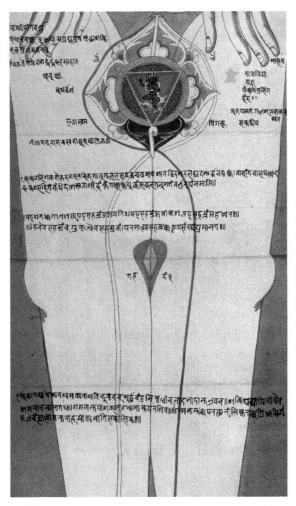

Figure 4.6. View of the Chakra system. From Ajit Mookerjee, Tantra Art: Its
Philosophy and Physics, *p. 128. Courtesy Ravi Kumar, Publisher, Paris.*

These images of the creative imagination can be both personal and
transpersonal to the mediator. Like active imagination in analysis,
these forms can become important reference points and inner powers
that at times extend individual consciousness, while at other times
they challenge and prepare the ego for dissolution and transformation. These images have a personal psycho-spiritual importance, as

well as contributing to the traditions from which they emerge and add to the overall collective representation of the subtle body.

The Subtle Body of Taoist Alchemy

Many years ago I read an impressive article by scholar Erwin Rousselle titled "Spiritual Guidance in Contemporary Taoism."[42] In the article Rousselle describes two alchemical diagrams, a black-and-white rubbing made from a stone tablet he found in the Monastery of the White Clouds near Beijing and a colored scroll "unquestionably based on the stone rubbing." Rousselle comments that both "stone and painting are identical" with some small differences.[43] The rubbing, figure 4.7, is translated as "Illustration of Inner Circulation" and "consists of a diagram of the head and torso, seen from the side. The entire diagram is framed on the right by the spinal cord, which connects the lower torso with the cranial cavity."[44]

Rousselle notes that on closer inspection, the whole image is a symbolic one and is in essence a diagram of the subtle body and a map of the transformation process of Taoist alchemy. The progression is "physical as well as spiritual. For the body must provide the vital force through whose sublimation the spiritual, immortal man is born."[45] Within this subtle body are several images based on alchemical principles. Taoist alchemy, known as inner alchemy (neidam), focuses on visualization and the use of symbols in an effort to achieve purification, spiritual renewal, and union with the Tao.

I particularly remember a section of Rousselle's article dealing with internal alchemy and Chinese medicine, in which he wrote, "In the dark firmament of our inner world the constellations of the microcosm and the genii or gods of our organs appear." He is describing a system of inner, nonliteral physiology, part of the magico-animistic system of old Chinese cosmology, in which the human being is seen as a little cosmos. Here the processes of transformation, circulation, and renewal are symbolically described in great detail as a guide to the initiate's search for eternal rejuvenation and the creation of the immortal Self.

In this "inner world" one comes across the cave of the spirit field, the plowing of the earth, and a place where "the spring takes its

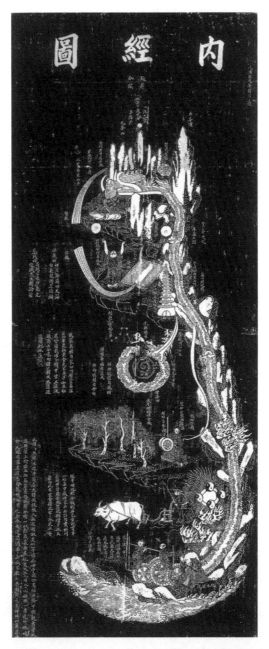

Figure 4.7. Illustration of Inner Circulatio, Qing dynasty, nineteenth century. Subtle body image from Chinese alchemy. Used by permission of The Rosenblum Family Collection.

ambrosian liquid from the 'moon'. . . . In the kidney region we therefore find pictured the Weaving Maiden [who] sets in motion a pulse in the form of a thread [that] can be seen running upward from the spinning wheel to the spinal cord."[46] Down further is the yin-yang gate of the underworld. The text is filled with provocative images of transformational archetypes that have remained with me over the years.

A few years ago I had an opportunity to lecture on Taoist alchemy and Jungian analysis in China. With these images in mind and my current work on Taoist alchemy in hand, I set out to find the monastery, the Taoist monks, and the Chinese doctors who might help to further elaborate this process.

In Beijing I had a fruitful exchange with Li Chun-Yin, professor and doctor in charge of the Institute of Traditional Chinese Medicine. Li elaborated on the complex interrelationships between emotions and "organs" that are reported to have physical, mental, and spiritual functions. She spoke about the process of healing and the use of dreams in her practice and offered examples.

Later I went to the Temple of the White Clouds, where I found a copy of the stone rubbing Rousselle had earlier described. It was a moving experience to arrive there where the work of internal alchemy had been practiced over the centuries. The famous poet Cha Shenxing of the Qing Dynasty (1644–1911) described the temple in the following poem:

> The winter gravel path looks warm,
> At dusk the old temple is shady and cool.
> Falling leaves are crushed under my feet,
> The last sun rays linger in half the court.
> Grave the closed alchemical stove stands.
> Serene the stone ordination altar remains.
> So familiar seem the meritorious pillars.
> A fairy land indeed this is.[47]

These images capture well the mysterious and legendary temple of the white clouds.[48]

While at the temple, I also acquired a book on internal alchemy, which to my knowledge has not yet been translated into English. In it are some of the images that appear in the Jung/Wilhelm version of *The Secret of the Golden Flower,* along with many additional illustrations. The copy I obtained was a little blue paperback. I was told that the writer was an unknown Taoist and a student of Master Yin. The Chinese was extremely difficult to translate even for native Chinese scholars. The title was something like "The Main Purpose of Life" or "The Root of Life." Years later Stephen Little published *Taoism and the Arts of China,* which includes a few of the same drawings contained in the book I obtained at the White Cloud Monastery. It appears that the book is a copy of a 1615 text translated as *Directions for Endowment and Vitality.*

Little's commentary states that the text, which is illustrated with more than fifty diagrams, is a Ming dynasty treatise on inner alchemy. The breadth of the text and illustrations led Joseph Needham to call it "the *Summa* of physiological alchemy (*Neidam*)."[49] The discovery of this book and scroll led me to seek out a number of meetings with Taoist monks, many of whom were surprisingly willing to share something of their esoteric practice and knowledge of this text and scroll.[50]

For our purposes here, I focus on the birth of the spiritual embryo in the solar plexus. I have written about an analytic parallel to this alchemical process in an article titled "The Metaphor of Light and Renewal in Taoist Alchemy and Jungian Analysis."[51] The solar plexus is an important area of subtle body theory and a center of vital force in Taoist alchemy.

In figure 4.8, from the text by Master Yin, one can see the importance of this center and the dynamic energies that are activated in the alchemical process. The center is called the elixir field, and in this center a spiritual embryo is born, representing a newly rejuvenated life. The role of the spiritual embryo is similar to Western alchemy's role of the *filius philosophorum,* which Jung discusses.

In analytic practice as well as in Taoist alchemy, the psyche works to activate this "elixir field." Experiences similar to these images from Taoist alchemy appear in analytic practice, but they do so in a highly individual way. Jung's *Alchemical Studies* references a series of drawings (figure 4.9) that reflect the inner experiences of a patient whose images might well be imagined as parallel to, but highly individual

Figure 4.8 Birth of the spiritual embryo. From *Master Yin,* Directions for Endowment and Vitality, *1615 (Beijing: Chinese Daoist Association).*

expressions of, a subtle body in traditional Taoist alchemy. He briefly comments on these images, noting how in this image, the "black earth" that was previously far below his patient's feet "is now in her body as a black ball, in the region of the *manipūra-chakra,* which coincides with the solar plexus." In a surprising connection, Jung then states that the "alchemical parallel to this is the 'black sun.' This means that the dark principle, or shadow, has been integrated [lifted up] and is now felt as a kind of center in the body."[52]

Interestingly, Rebekah Kenton, who also has written about the subtle body, notes in the same way that the sun continually radiates energy to the planets, the manipura, or third chakra and distributes psychic energy throughout the entire human framework, regulating and energizing the activity of various organ systems and processes of life.[53] She adds that the manipura (or Tiferet) is the self, the midpoint of the psyche, so it is important not only with regard to the physical body but also with regard to psychological and subtle body functioning. It is often compared to the dazzling heat and power of the sun.

As shown in the images Jung presents, the dark sun is linked to earth and shadow and to *caput corvi* and the nigredo. Thus, Sol niger is here lifted to the center of the subtle body. While the dark sphere itself appears inert, the power of Sol niger shows itself in the background and in the flowering tree of life emerging from the head. This is reminis-

Figure 4.9. Figures of the subtle body. From C. G. Jung, Alchemical Studies, *figures 26 and 28. © The Estate of Carl Gustav Jung. Used by permission.*

cent of Adam Kadmon, Grey's halo, the thousand-petaled lotus of Kundalini yoga, and the movement of the spiritual embryo out of the old body and into a sphere of its own, as is illustrated in the Taoist alchemy images of the subtle body in figure 4.10. The subtle body imagery has also shown itself in the clinical material of a patient discussed later in this chapter.

The Appearance of the Subtle Body in Analysis

What follows is material from an analytic patient, part of whose work began with images of the solar plexus and for whom Sol niger played an important role. The idea of a dark energy radiating in the area of the solar plexus was the stimulus for this gifted artist to enter analysis. She represented her dramatic individuation process by producing more than 150 drawings, some of which contain black sun images—a series that culminated in the constellation of what might traditionally be

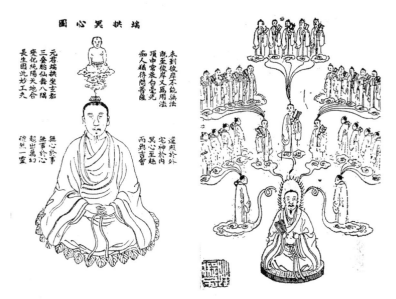

Figure 4.10. Taoist images of the subtle body. From Master Yin, Directions for Endowment and Vitality, *1615 (Beijing: Chinese Daoist Association).*

called a Self figure. I present a small but representative selection of her drawings that are relevant to the themes of darkness, death, renewal, and the black sun. In this case, there are parallels between her analysis and art, myth, literature, and religion that amplify the artistic expression of her individuation process.

As Peter Tatham has noted, for many people something like a "black emptiness (often in the abdominal region) . . . is not necessarily fatal or even immutable."[54] This was clearly the case with this artist. She began her work deeply concerned over a troubled marriage and a profound sense of stasis in her life. She had lost touch with her sexuality and sense of womanhood, and her deeply introverted style had led her into an exploration of deep grief and a profound center of darkness compressed in her solar plexus.

Here the analytic process began with in an image of a "knot" in her stomach. She reported feeling something dead and buried. It was her habit to use the dictionary as a kind of oracle the way one might use

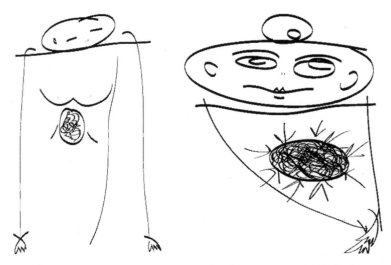

Figure 4.11. Psychic activation in the solar plexus—an internal black orb.
Artwork by analysand. Used by permission.

the *I Ching* or tarot cards. She would open the book randomly, point
to a word, and consider it as a hint for further reflection. Prior to coming into analysis, she remembered pointing to a word and reading
something about the "midnight sun." The experience of a knotlike
feeling in her abdomen became more acute, and she represented it in
a series of drawings (figure 4.11).

As she progressed from the first image to the next, arrows pointed
to this black center from all sides. In her analysis, she began to focus on
these interior feelings. Next, in another drawing not portrayed here,
the dark center expanded, and her body seemed to encircle it. Hands
appeared as if to grasp and reach inside this center. The figure's eyes
were closed as if introvertedly looking down into this expanding darkness. The black-and-white, jesterlike hat on the head had tassels looking like miniature black suns. To the upper right of her drawing there
was an open doorway.

The theme of grabbing hold of this center is continued in the next
image (figure 4.12), in which the interior process is superimposed on a
landscape filled with trees. The picture is divided into upper and lower,
and in each there appears a circular, glowing orb. From the upper one,

*Figure 4.12. Grabbing hold of the lower orb. Artwork by analysand.
Used by permission.*

there is a downward motion, and eventually arms reach down to the
lower sphere, turning black as they extend below ground. These arms
hold onto the sphere as if continuing the process initiated in the previous image.

What followed from this is a series of drawings, one of which is

Figure 4.13. Eruption from the solar plexus. Artwork by analysand.
Used by permission.

shown in figure 4.13, in which what was deeply disturbing to her burst forth out of an empty place in her solar plexus and took the form of a humanized shadow figure.

A similar hole in the solar plexus appears in this Alaskan Inuit image of the body (figure 4.14) of a shaman, or tutelary deity. The idea is that, in religious life, the body is opened up, broken down, and transformed. In terms of Inuit mythology, if we maintain a respectful religious attitude toward our suffering as the price of transformation, then we may hear the crow call in the midst of a cold, arctic darkness: "'qua, qua, qua'—'light, light, light.'"[55]

As my patient engaged this dark form in active imagination as portrayed in figure 4.15a, it became overwhelming and aggressive, and in place of having a knot in her abdomen, she found herself in knots in the belly of a beast (figure 4.15b).

For a considerable period of time her struggle with this dark energy

Figure 4.14. Shaman's Mask. Eskimo, Lower Kuskowin River, nineteenth century. Collection of George Terasaki, New York. Photo by Werner Forman / Art Resource, New York. Used by permission.

felt consuming, but as she actively responded to the issues that emerged, a change in the quality of her relationship to her unconscious began to take place. The image of dancing with the shadow (figure 4.16) took a dynamic form and eventually led toward integration.

The furthering of her assimilation of the shadow is shown in a rather remarkable drawing of the shadow form installed inside a larger, fleshy pink, humanlike shape shown in grayscale in figure 4.17. The pinkish

Figure 4.15. (a): The beginning of active imagination; (b): the belly of the beast. Artwork by analysand. Used by permission.

Figure 4.16. Dancing with the shadow. Artwork by analysand. Used by permission.

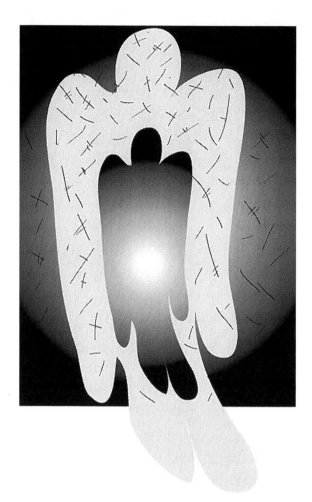

Figure 4.17. Incorporation of the shadow. Artwork by analysand.
Used by permission.

figure stands against a black field, but its feet are outside this dark frame. A dark, effulgent orb emerges from within the solar plexus area of the dark figure, and a similar form surrounds the pink image as well. I consider this deep illumination as the emergence of the shine of Sol niger and an expression of the lumen naturae. It is a kind of shadow light that heralds a developing consciousness of both sexuality and other aspects of what Jung would call the repressed feminine shadow.

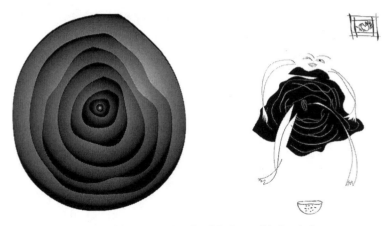

Figure 4.18. (a): Concentric tufts of darkness; (b): female figure. Artwork by analysand. Used by permission.

The theme of pinkness continued to represent these issues and in a subsequent image appeared inside a dark sphere. The issues surrounding her female identity and sexuality remained difficult, imagistically wrapped in vagina-like concentric tufts of darkness (figure 4.18a) and emitting a strange luminescence. Later a female figure emerged; her black dress is mandala-like and reminiscent of the vaginal darkness of the prior image (figure 4.18b).

In these images we see the continuing development of feminine sexuality, which continues its awakening in the next image. In this image, portrayed in grayscale in figure 4.19, a pink deer's tongue moistens the gray face of a woman lying in darkness.

The moisture of tears pours down her face. At the top edge of the picture is a green-and-blue band with what looks like an emerging sun and a small plant growing out of the darkness. The whole image gives one the feeling of a possible awakening, Sleeping-Beauty-like, but here the "prince" appears as a nurturing animal soul. Jungian analyst Von Franz notes the importance of animal instinct in such an awakening.[56]

The awakened female body appears in the next image, in which a black field is covered over by intense red, exploding with images of copulating Asian figures (color plate 10). At the bottom of this image a figure reclines on a pillow, bathed in a golden light representing the

Figure 4.19. Instinctual awakening. Artwork by analysand. Used by permission.

intensity and pleasure of an awakened body and the beginning of the overcoming of the tension of opposites. The rising sun in the earlier animal image is realized in the illuminated body below.

Asian erotic art has produced similar images. For the Chinese, sexuality has a central place in the cosmic scheme of things, and it is useful to place such images against the background of the Taoist vision. As scholars Phillip Rawson and Lazslo Legeza note:

The male and female sexual organs have names whose imagery forms part of the secret language of Taoism. The male is "the red bird," "the jade stalk," "the coral stem," "turtle-head," "the heavenly dragon pillar," "the swelling mushroom." The female is "the peach," "the open peony blossom," "the vermillion gate," "the pink shell." . . . Sexual intercourse itself is referred to as "the bursting of the clouds and the rain." "Plum blossom" is a subject painted tens of thousands of times on beds, screens, and porcelain—is actually a name for sexual pleasure.[57]

For the Taoist, mutual sexual orgasm is the physical or poetic event in which an important exchange takes place; the transference of yin and yang energies creates a valuable harmonization of the soul. This kind of intercourse can be seen as the cultivation of literal sexual acts in the inner realms of the subtle body, as in some forms of Taoist alchemy. Rawson notes that the inner alchemy of Taoism is closely related to both Indian and Buddhist Tantrism. In Tantric Buddhism, sexual images also play an important role in symbolizing the union of opposites. The term *yabyum* refers to the divine ecstatic embrace of male and female figures, which at the highest level are said to link the forces of wisdom and compassion.

In Western esotericism such processes are also known (e.g., in kabbalistic theory and in alchemy). Alchemically, such a process is known as the *coniunctio* and in some contexts is thought to represent the culmination of the alchemical work. However, the alchemists made an important distinction between the lesser and greater coniunctio. The lesser coniunctio reflects a premature union of things that have not yet been thoroughly separated and properly integrated. Such "integrations" do not have the stability of the alchemical goal. Edinger notes that in reality these two aspects are combined with each other. "The experience of the coniunctio is almost always a mixture of the lesser and the greater aspects."[58] However, because of its instability, the lesser coniunctio is always followed by a death or mortificatio process. "The product of the lesser coniunctio is pictured as killed, maimed, or fragmented (an overlap with the *solutio* and *mortificatio* symbolism)."[59]

In the case we have been discussing, the pictured coniunctio of Asian lovers gave way to a mortificatio process. In the face of a troubled marriage, her personal attempt at integrating her feminine sexual identity and vitality was once again blocked and left her feeling trapped, unable to move forward in her life or her psyche. She felt again as if things were falling apart and that she was facing an impenetrable darkness. She found herself once again in the midst of a nigredo. The loss of the previous hopeful experience of awakening was excruciating.

Entering into this darkness required tears of blood and being stripped to the bone, but it was also a process in which she began to see a key that she hoped could unlock her blockages. She began to see what was behind this black door but was unsure whether it was a vision of life or death (figure 4.20).

Such images reflect an archetypal moment when we stand on the threshold of our individuation and wonder whether going forward is going to lead to our demise. As she went more deeply into her uncertainty, the images of life and death appeared together as if they were two faces of the same skeletal body (figure 4.21). The outer garments have been shredded, and four strange monkeylike figures have appeared, one inside and three outside the door. At the bottom of this drawing a dreamer is shown with an illuminated orb around her head, and a butterfly, often an image of psyche, sits on her uplifted knee. In these images, the ambiguity of life and death is strong. One usually imagines dead figures as reclining and living ones as standing up. Here, as if in the underworld, this expectation is reversed. One might also imagine the female figure in deep meditation or dreaming and the scene we see above her as her dream or vision.

The theme of the dreamer and the skeleton repeats in the next image, not included here. This time the pinkness returns in the orb surrounding the dreamer's head and as some kind of shroud over the skeleton. It is hard to say exactly what is going on here, but the pinkness seems to link the deep dream or meditation to death or to being stripped bare.

In figure 4.22, the dream of death theme seems to bear creative fruit. The pink orb has expanded into a large sphere of two concentric circles in which a tree seems to be sprouting from the dreamer's solar plexus. The orb is now outside her body and seems to be resting on it.

Figure 4.20. Tears of blood, a key to darkness. Artwork by analysand.
Used by permission.

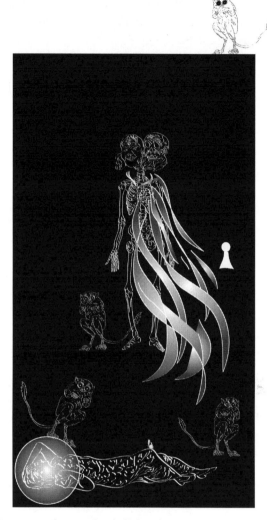

Figure 4.21. The Janus head of life and death. Artwork by analysand. Used by permission.

Four dark birds are flying around inside it, two on the right and two on the left of the tree. As one moves outward into the second sphere, a lone bird appears on the left; on the right, the area is primarily white with a touch of pink and black. The emergence of the tree and of both black-and-white birds are important alchemical themes.[60]

In *Psychology and Alchemy*, Jung quotes the alchemist Khunrath, who states, "I pray you, look with the eyes of the mind at the little tree of the grain of wheat, regarding all its circumstances, so that you may bring us the tree of the philosophers to grow."[61] For Jung, Khunrath seems to be pointing to the activation of the psyche through active imagination. Jung illustrates this using the image of "Adam as *prima materia,* [whose side is] pierced by the arrow of *Mercurius.* [He is wounded and] the *arbor philosphica* is growing out of him" (figure 4.23a). Here, creativity, the flowering philosophical tree, is linked to wounding and the mortificatio. It would appear that what is essential to the creative flowering of the psyche is a wounding and a death of the old self, out of which emerges the new life. In this male version of the process, the tree emerges as a phallus.

Jung also presents what he thinks is a female version of this process, reflected in the image of the mortificatio of Eve (figure 4.23b). In this image, the female's figure points to the skull symbolizing the mortificatio. Here the tree grows out of Eve's head.[62]

In this case and other descriptions, wounding, death and creativity, and darkness and light are linked together. The flowering of the tree is also sometimes linked to the flight of birds and the freeing of the creative spirit (as seen from Jung's *Alchemical Studies,* reproduced as figure 4.9 earlier in this chapter).[63] Birds further amplify this freed energy, and in alchemy they appear as black or white or in some combination of these colors as seen both in my patient's and Jung's representations. Traditionally the transformation of a black to a white bird signifies the alchemical albedo, a whitening process that suggests a movement of the psyche out of its dark and depressive leadened state into a reflective sublimation that lightens the soul and is thought to bring a greater sense of consciousness and freedom. It is a kind of purification process and catalyzes psychic development. A classical

Figure 4.22. The emergence of the philosophical tree and the flight of the spirit.
Artwork by analysand. Used by permission.

Figure 4.23. (a): Adam as prima materia, *pierced by the arrow of Mercurius,
from C. G. Jung,* Psychology and Alchemy, *p. 245;
(b): the skull, symbol of a mortificatio of Eve, the feminine aspect of the* prima
materia. *From C. G. Jung,* Psychology and Alchemy, *p. 257.*

image of this is seen in Solomon Trismosim's *Splendor Solis*, which also
links the birds with the philosophical tree (color plate 11).

The theme of the albedo and philosophical tree are both present in
an interrelated way in my patient's drawings. What is interesting in her
expression of these themes is that the emergence of creative energy
comes neither from the phallus per se nor from the head, as in Jung's
portrayal, but rather from the solar plexus, in between the two positions represented by Jung. This theme, which continues through the
next several images, follows our exploration of the solar plexus in many
sacred traditions. This representation of the philosophical tree devel-
ops into the appearance of what Jung might call a philosophical *animus*
first standing at her feet and subsequently expressing the creative energy of the tree, his head rooted in her solar plexus (figure 4.24a and b).
Along with the tree, the theme of the whitening birds and the albedo is
present, indicating the upward movement of her psychic energy.

My patient identified the figure as the philosopher Foucault, whose
work is in part identified with passion, sexuality, and the politics of lib-
eration and who further expresses the tree's spiritual energy. At the

Figure 4.24. The philosopher Foucault as (a): spiritual animus *and (b): the* arbor philosophica. *Artwork by analysand. Used by permission.*

time she created this image, my analysand was deeply engaged in reading Foucault, who came alive for her, as the image suggests. Red roots emerge at the bottom of the image. The psyche, as represented by the butterfly, is now engaged in a struggle with the deep experience of its unconscious roots, which might traditionally be conceived of as a compensation for the upward spiritual growth of the figure. The theme is dramatically amplified in figure 4.24b. The figure of the philosopher is enlarged, and his head penetrates the solar plexus of a female body reclining on a couch. A similar couch appeared in the earlier coniunctio image, in which the golden woman exhibited a vitalized sexuality.

On the one hand, this couch might traditionally refer to the psychoanalytic couch and to the evolving erotic transference, but here the transference takes on a further dimension. The phallus that penetrates is the head of the philosopher, and this results in a creative flowering up above. One can imagine this as a sublimation in a regressive or defensive sense. On the other hand, I believe it instead represented the development of an eroticized and spiritual unfolding that facilitated rather than retarded her analytic process.

The upside-down figure of the philosopher resembles the image of the hanged man in the tarot, an image that has been given many interpretations by various authors. At times, the tarot image signifies a turning point, linked to sacrifice and death, leading to a reversal of ordinary consciousness; the aspirant becomes grounded in higher truths that come from above. Tarot authority Eden Gray links this reversal to the recognition of "the utter dependency of the human personality on the tree of Cosmic Life."[64]

For Jung, this turning point can be linked with the beginning of the relativization of the ego and the growing awareness of the Self. The image is related to a number of interpenetrating archetypal themes, including the growth of the filius philosophorum and the theme of the inverted tree *(arbor inversa)*.

Filius Philosophorum

We have already discussed Jung's idea that in alchemy, when light and darkness and male and female come together, the filius philosophorum is born. This inner child or immortal fetus, a representation that we have seen in Taoist alchemy, also appeared in the visions of my analysand. In figure 4.25a, a man or rabbi figure is standing on a Star of David, which consists of interlocking triangles symbolizing an integration of opposites, above and below, light and darkness, male and female.

Standing in this place of integration—or where the opposites are unified—implies both the sacred marriage and the birth of the immortal child whom, in this image, the wise old man carries close to his heart. The rabbi's head is covered with what appears to be a yarmulke. The yarmulke in the *Code of Jewish Law* signifies a stance of humility

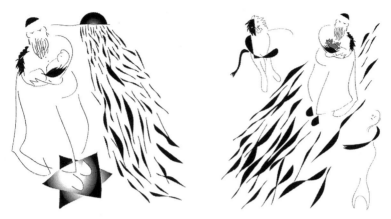

Figure 4.25. (a): Rabbi, child, and the black sun; (b): Rabbi with flaming heart, mermaid, and lion. Artwork by analysand. Used by permission.

or nullification, often a position we are forced into in relation to Sol niger, which appears in the right side of the picture, emitting a shower of black rays. My patient was not Jewish, but her wise old man presented himself in figures 4.25a and 4.25b in the form of a rabbi.

In figure 4.25b, instead of a child we find a flaming heart. Two figures stand on each side of him, a lion on the left and a mermaid on the right. Both figures are black and white and stand erect as if welcoming or calling forth this religious figure. My analysand reported that she felt deeply connected to the mermaid, who is so comfortable in the water and in the depths. For her, the mermaid brought to mind her feelings of fluidity and mystery. It reminded her of an experience long ago in a church, where an old man with a long white beard sat quietly next to her and her child put his head down on his lap. He said nothing to her, but she felt a silent connection of considerable depth with this man.

Her images of the wise old man also resonated with her developing feelings in the transference. As we often sat in silence, she felt as if we too shared an unspoken mystery. Associating to the image, she felt that the old man was bringing her heart to her. The deep feelings of transference were also captured in an important dream in which she found herself giving birth to the moon.

I will not recount the entire complicated dream, but it begins with her lying naked on a high table in the center of a large white room. Three figures are around her, possibly doctors or researchers. She knows she is going to give birth, but she doesn't know to what since she thinks, "I am too old to have a child." She is apprehensive and wonders whether I should be there with her as this happens. Her labor pains begin with small contractions and grow more intense. She cannot think about anything anymore. She feels she has to let go into the pain, and her body takes over.

She is in such pain that she is delirious and hears everyone gasping. As she looks down at her belly, protruding from it is a huge three-to-four-foot flower bud. As everyone is staring, it begins, petal by petal, to unfold. The petals are all a translucent white. When all the petals are open and lying flat, she can see that the center of it is a clear, still lake. Everyone is mesmerized as the petals begin to close. As this happens, she feels darkness and terror enter the room. With her body in unbearable pain, she begins convulsing. She knows she is going to lose consciousness.

When she opens her eyes, they open into my (her analyst's) face a few inches above her. The room is completely still. We just stay in that place for a while. Then I lean and whisper in her ear, "you just gave birth to the moon." She looks down, and her belly has become this gleaming black orb—the substance of which is thick and slippery. As we watch, it seems as if there is a body playfully swimming and diving underneath as we can see the ripples and movements on the surface. It is magical and beautiful beyond description.

My analysand's experience of giving birth to the moon suggests an archetypal identification with the Great Mother, the unconscious. Her proclivity toward diving into the unconscious was linked with her relationship to the mermaid. The mermaid image has many historical associations, including the power of prophecy and granting wishes. It is connected with the muses, but the dark side of this figure is considered dangerous.[65] Listening to a mermaid's song can put one to sleep, seduce one into living under the sea, and, in the worst-case scenario, cause madness, disaster, or death.[66]

My analysand was seduced into the waters of the unconscious, but this required the presence of an additional energy: the lion at the left of the wise old man or rabbi. For Jewish people, the lion has been associated with spiritual strength and the courage to perform God's will and is mentioned more than 150 times in the Old Testament.[67] The great "sixteenth-century Kabbalist Rabbi Issac Luria was known as Ari, the Lion, in recognition of his extraordinary learning and spiritual power."[68] In addition, the name Judah is identified with the lion as in the Davidic monarchy. It is of interest to note that from this royal house a Messiah was expected to emerge, like the filius emerging from the opposites.[69]

For my patient, one might say that such a savior comes in the form of this wise old man bringing her her heart, which he holds in the middle of his chest. He is walking along a middle ground between mermaid and lion, his feet planted on a river of voidness composed of the black rays of Sol niger. It is a path not unlike the mystical middle pillar of the kabbalist that weaves its way between opposites. The middle pillar in kabbalistic thought is also referred to as the Tree of Life and is an essential representation of the unfolding of the soul. A variation on the theme of the tree emphasizing spiritual and psychological development is archetypally portrayed in an inverted position with its roots not in the literal earth but in the heavens, linking it with the forces above.

The Inverted Tree

The theme of the inverted tree has been richly amplified by Jung as well as in an obscure but important article by Indian philosopher Ananda Coomaraswamy called "The Inverted Tree."[70] Jung notes that "the tree [in general] symbolizes a living process as well as a process of enlightenment."[71] It signifies the creative unfolding of the soul, which can be expressed intellectually but is not reducible to the intellect. Jung amplifies the idea of the inverted tree by citing a number of ancient thinkers whose ideas are remarkably similar. Sixteenth-century alchemist Laurentious Ventura comments, "The roots of its ores are in the air and the summits in the earth." The fifteenth-century alchemical text *Gloria mundi* "likewise mentions that the philosophers had said that 'the root of its minerals is in the air and its head in the earth.'"[72] Fifteenth-century alchemist George Ripley also says that "the tree has its roots in the air, and, elsewhere, that it is rooted in the 'glorified earth,' in the earth of paradise, or in the future world."[73]

A rabbi, the son of Josephus Carnitolus, speaks of the inverted tree with regard to a kabbalistic vision noting, "the foundation of every lower structure is affixed above and its summit is here below, like an inverted tree." With regard to the kabbala, we have seen that the mystical tree, as a tree of lights, also signifies man, who in Jewish thought "is implanted in paradise by the roots of his hair, a reference to Song of Songs."[74] Plato's Timaeus notes that "we are not an earthly but a heavenly plant," a "plant" the Hindus see as "pour[ing] down from above."[75] Jung quotes from the *Bhagavad-Gita:*

> *There is a fig tree*
> *In ancient story,*
> *The giant Ashvetha,*
> *The everlasting,*
> *Rooted in heaven,*
> *Its branches earthward;*
> *Each of its leaves*
> *Is a song of the Vedas,*
> *And he who knows it*
> *Knows all the Vedas*[76]

In the preceding passage, the inverted tree refers to finding a sacred ground above. It signifies a reversal and relativization of ordinary consciousness that equates with the activation of what Jung calls the religious function.

In my analysand's next image (figure 4.26), two trees appear, one growing from the ground up and the other growing downward as if rooted in the church above it. Although these two trees reflect an archetypal process of the movement of the opposites, an effort to bring together both instinctual and religious dimensions of her psyche, they also capture the erotic energy of the transference that held both of

*Figure 4.26. Trees: reaching for the unity of instinct and spirit.
Artwork by analysand. Used by permission.*

these dimensions. The rosary window or mandala-like sphere, which often indicates a potential unification between two dimensions, appears as a Sol niger image; it is illuminated and has a black center and a sunlike appearance. Just beneath the mandala, two monkeys suggest the presence of the animal instinct or spirit. Nearer the bottom and deeper down, below the red roots another sun appears. It is as if, below all of the blackness, another sky and another sun exist.

Figure 4.27 seems to be an elaboration of the one just discussed but with several changes. This time, the center of the illuminated mandala bursts into many colors, and a second church, or another vision of it, is shown in the center of the dark field in the middle of the page. The entire church is in blackness. Under an arch at its bottom is a sunlike orb in which we again see the image of the two women seen in the spires of the church of the previous image. Now, however, they are now facing in opposite directions and are joined together at the feet, as if to suggest a connection between them. Rather than merging into a simple unity, they have become connected, yet remain separate. At this point the process moves away from the theme of the inverted tree and toward the work of differentiation and doubling.

In addition to the two women facing in opposing directions, two large butterflies appear, one at the top and one at the bottom. Their size has dramatically increased from earlier images, perhaps corresponding to the growth of the psyche. The theme of doubling—two suns, two trees, two women, and two butterflies—has become prominent, emphasizing the themes of both differentiation and sameness.

Figure 4.28 picks up on this theme by depicting two forces with independent centers. They are beginning to overlap but maintain their separateness. These energies are contained in larger egg-shaped, concentric forms, suggesting the potential for new possibilities. I consider it a dynamic Sol niger image expressing the dynamism of the two forces—as if representing all of the doublings and polarities we have been speaking about: light and dark, up and down, sexual and spiritual. Each of the two dynamisms maintains its own center, and yet they can be seen to be interrelated, the force fields of each center radiating and intermingling with the other. In this image of the coniunctio, the two

Figure 4.27. Dark church with butterflies and mandala.
Artwork by analysand. Used by permission.

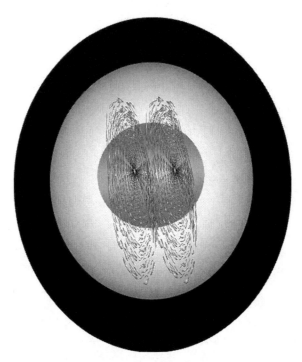

Figure 4.28. Twin spheres. Artwork by analysand. Used by permission.

force fields maintain their connection and their acute difference, thus avoiding any premature collapse into undifferentiated unity. This image continues to portray both the dynamic transferential process in the analysis as well as the beginning of separation and the withdrawal of some projections. As the next image depicts, this withdrawal of projections also prefigures the constellation of an archetypal process reflecting the containment of opposites within. What was projected outward is now contained in the fiery inner heat of a whirling inner sun.

In my analysand's next image (color plate 12), the sphere with the two women joined at the feet, first seen in figure 4.27, forms the center of a dramatic mandala. Two luminescent spheres appear, one above and one below, and a powerful, dynamic, fiery energy appears like a wheel of flames or a strange sun that covers the center of the black field. Jung talked about the tension of the opposites and the transcendent

Figure 4.29. The fusion of opposites, 1617. From Johannes Fabricius,
Alchemy: The Medieval Alchemists and Their Royal Art, *p. 61.*

function, and one might well consider this image as a picture of the Sol niger holding the enormous energy that is present when two arche-typal energies are contained together.

Figure 4.29 shows an alchemical version of this image in the fusion of opposites. The alchemist points to the fiery energy linking above and below: the sun and the moon.

However, are the two energies we are speaking about a pair of op-posites? Traditional theory suggests that this is the case, but it is worth considering that the images we have been discussing seem to reflect the coming together of two independent centers of the "same"—two women, two butterflies, two force fields. The doubling of a single im-age may not always be a tension of opposites but rather the energy of a doubling of mirror images reflecting and interpenetrating one an-other, images joined at the heel, so to speak.

Hillman explores the theme of the union of the sames in his article

"Senex and Puer," where he notes this process at the center of the feminine personality and the mother-daughter mysteries.[77] This theme has been further developed by Jungian analysts Claire Douglas and Lyn Cowan and by psychologist and feminist scholar Claudette Kulkarni.[78] Hillman notes that "Dionysian consciousness understands the conflicts in our stories through dramatic tensions and not through conceptual opposites; we are composed of agonies not polarities."[79]

In the next two images (figures 4.30 and 4.31), a new woman is emerging. Each image once again emits an odd luminescence and a play between light and dark. In the first one are five Sol niger images. Four of them appear on the bottom of the image as black holes with sun images partially illuminating them and the Earth around them. Over three of the illuminated black holes are butterflies and, as if out of the fourth, a masked female figure unfolds from a pale pink-and-green flower. A central dark sun is present in a black sky. One might here imagine that from the midst of Sol niger, a new psychic energy shows itself.

Figure 4.31 is divided. On the left, the field is black, while on the right it is mostly illuminated. It is an undersea image, and a woman is surfacing like an underworld Aphrodite—the initial emergence of her embodiment.

I end this series of images with one that appeared earlier in the analysis but that, I believe, was a prefiguration of what might traditionally be called a Self image that took on a lived form at this point. Figure 4.32 is an image of a more integrated and peaceful woman standing in a pool of water, connected to the unconscious and the psyche. A snail and white flowers are scattered around the pool. It appears that the woman stands on a sphere similar to the one that surrounds her head like a halo. She stands in a dignified pose, bare breasted, and her skin is pink; her sexuality is expressed as a more natural dimension of her stance in the world. The lower part of her body is wrapped in a black tunic. A butterfly, a classic image of the psyche, appears almost as an adornment—pin or buckle—over the solar plexus area. She is decorated with a bejeweled necklace; flowers adorn her hair; and her head is illuminated by a Sol niger sphere. As noted, a similar sphere can be detected within

Figure 4.30. The flowering of psyche in the midst of darkness.
Artwork by analysand. Used by permission.

Figure 4.31. Underworld Aphrodite. Artwork by analysand. Used by permission.

the pool, and so we can see the Sol niger both grounding and illuminating her. Here one might imagine that the shine of Sol niger is also the shine of the Self—one that emits an aura or inner radiance.

The emergence of these figures does not suggest the end of her psychic process but did prefigure the ending of her analysis. I here include a final transference dream:

Figure 4.32. Illuminated female figure. Artwork by analysand.
Used by permission.

It is just before dawn. Stan and I are sitting together in his living room engaged in intimate but relaxed conversation. The room is very large, and two walls are all windows from floor to ceiling. He gives me two gifts. The first is a necklace made of very unusual stones—a mixture of translucent and opaque/dark, subtle colors with veins of alizarin crimson running through. All but the center stone is [sic] square, and on each side is a small, round glass bead. The center stone is a perfect sphere and a beautiful, transparent greenish color (reminding me of sea glass). Covering this stone are as many black glass beads in a mysterious pattern. The necklace is exquisite.

Next, he hands me a shoe box. Inside, I immediately recognize shoes that had been lost a lifetime before. They had always been my favorite shoes and, although worn, were not worn out. I am so happy to have them back and am amazed not only that he found them but that he even knew of them in the first place.

I wonder what my gift is to him. As soon as I have the thought, I feel a burning in my chest over my heart. When I look down, there is a visible energy emanating from it. At first, it just flows between us; then it slowly begins to fill the room in waves. We sit immersed in this energy, appreciating its warmth and uniqueness.

As the sun just barely begins to fill the room, I hear movement behind and above us. I look around and notice that this very large house is populated by many others. Those around begin coming down the stairs, go into the kitchen for coffee, then appear at the doorway and either ask something of Stan or remind him of something he has to do. I sit and watch him interact with these people . . . thinking he has a very professional manner but looks drained and tired.

I do not want this night to end. Yet, I feel it is time to leave when his wife comes to the door and stares at him. I gather my gifts as his wife tries to usher me out of the door. I turn around and look at Stan before leaving—the feeling between us is close, heavy, and intense. I think "well, choice is the proof of love and he has chosen this." I feel, however, that this is not really the end of the relationship.

The ending of our work was marked by the recognition of both eros and limit—the recognition that this was a professional relationship and that the analyst had an independent life. With this, the analysis moved toward ending. My analysand's last statement remained unclear; the feeling that this was not the end of the relationship seemed at the time to refer to her feeling that the inner work with the analyst would not stop with termination, but it also concerned me that the transference aspect was not adequately resolved or the analyst figure integrated. However, it was clear that she felt she had recovered something that had been long lost, a comfortable stance in the world that included her sexuality, eros, and sense of feminine being and that her work would go on independently of formal analysis.

In this chapter we have explored the alchemical idea of the lumen naturae—the light of darkness itself—and amplified it by considering traditional images of the subtle body. We have shown how these archetypal images continue to have dramatic resonances with the images that emerge in contemporary analysis. The black sun is one such image that plays an important role in the transformation of psychic life. Although this chapter ends in a manner coherent with a traditional conception of the Self, I have come to consider the black sun as an image of a non-Self that has helped me to reimagine my understanding of the Self as Jung has described it.

■

CHAPTER 5

The Black Sun
Archetypal Image of
the Non-Self

What is Divine Darkness?
> —*Pseudo-Dionysus*, The Mystical Theology

I begin with nothingness. Nothingness is the same as
fullness.
> —C. G. *Jung*, The Seven Sermons to the Dead

Up to this point we have been considering the Sol niger, the black sun, as a powerful and important image of the unconscious and have been tracing its appearance in a wide variety of contexts from the alchemical mortificatio, in literal and symbolic experiences of death and dying, to the paradoxical shine and luminescence of the lumen naturae in images of regeneration. Like Jung's idea of the Self, Sol niger also expresses a *coincidentia oppositorum*—a black sun that shines contains the paradoxical play of light and dark, life and death, and spirit and matter. For Jung, the sun was a "symbol of the source of life and the ultimate wholeness of man" as indicated in the alchemical image of the *solificatio,* a process that corresponds to enlightenment or illumination.[1] In color plate 13, a seventeenth-century miniature, the solificatio is represented as an alchemist whose body is "filled with light," portraying the ultimate goal of alchemy.[2]

This represents one of the many important symbols of the Self.[3] However, for the sun to adequately express human wholeness, it cannot be only an ultimate image of light; it also must include darkness as an essential aspect of its nature. The black sun might well be considered to express this paradoxical dimension of light and darkness and might ultimately be understood as an archetype of the non-Self. This non-Self should not be considered antithetical to the Self or as an independent entity of any kind. Instead, it expresses a mysterious and paradoxical unknowing that was at the core of Jung's original attempt to describe the ungraspable wholeness of the psyche.

Like the sun, the Christ image represented the Self for Jung. He chose the Christ figure because it is "the still living myth of our culture," and many significant images surround it.[4] Also like the sun, the Christ image became identified primarily with the "light." In fact, the early Christians had some difficulty in distinguishing the rising sun from Christ.[5] Jung states that Christ represents the "totality of a divine or heavenly kind, a glorified man, a son of God . . . unspotted of sin."[6] Yet for him, this concept lacks wholeness in the psychological sense. "As the Gnostics said, [he] has put aside his shadow, and thus leads a separate existence which manifests itself in the coming of the antichrist."[7] In other words, the principle of darkness has to manifest itself in some form.

Jung realized this, as indicated in this statement concerning the Self. We cannot ignore the shadow that belongs to this figure of light and without which it lacks a body and therewith humanity. "Light and shadow form a paradoxical unity within the empirical self."[8]

For Jung, ultimately, the Christian concept becomes "hopelessly split into two irreconcilable halves: the last days bring about a metaphysical dualism, namely a final separation of the kingdom of heaven from the flaming world of damnation."[9] An ideal spirituality striving for the heights is sure to clash with the materialistic earth-bound passion of the modern world. In short, the Christ figure as an image of the Self "lacks the shadow, which belongs to it."[10]

For Jung, the Self can neither be limited to images of light nor split off from its shadow. The Self is a "transcendent concept . . . that . . . expresses the sum of the conscious and unconscious contents" and as such "can be described only in the form of antimony."[11] "For this reason, [the process of] individuation is a *mysterium coniunctionis* [a mysterious conjunction of opposites], in that the Self is experienced in a nuptial union of opposite halves."[12] The emergence of the Christ figure embodied the need to achieve this union, but for Jung the figure falls short of the goal.[13]

Jung's last work, the *Mysterium Coniunctionis: An Inquiry into the Separation and Synthesis of Psychic Opposites in Alchemy*, is dedicated to the task of describing his idea of a mystical union. The union of opposites is an attractive idea because it implies psychological wholeness, but the enormity of the struggle involved in any engagement with otherness and with the darkness of the unconscious has become lost as Jung's theories become assimilated and taken for granted. This point of view has been expressed by Jungian analyst Neil Micklem, who emphasizes the importance of paradox rather than unity and notes that paradox usually gets glossed over as our attention moves toward the more attractive idea of the union of opposites.[14] The theme of the unity of opposites catches the attention of people because it "points in the direction of wholeness,"[15] and the idea of wholeness can easily become a shorthand way to pass over significant tensions. When this happens, the ideal of wholeness can lose its mystery and power and become a cliché or caricature. Micklem writes, "As long as we are fixed on making whole we are likely to miss that paradox."[16]

Yet, mystery and paradox are essential to understanding what Jung calls the Self. For Jung, "paradox is characteristic of all transcendental situations."[17] This is "because it alone gives adequate expression to their indescribable nature."[18] Wherever the archetype of the Self predominates, there are always conflicting truths, and the history of reflective philosophical and religious thought is filled with diverse attempts to reconcile such differences. Just a few of these attempts include Buddhism's middle way, Aristotle's golden mean, the rational antinomies of Kant, Hegel's dialectic, Marx's dialectical materialism, Freud's eros and thanatos, Ricouer's tension between suspicion and belief, and Derrida's différance, all of which struggle with the problem in their characteristically different ways. For most of these, a simple rational mastery is not an adequate resolution to the problem of opposites, which seems to require a continuing attempt to express the complexity of the soul. Micklem writes that "Paradox enriches, because only paradox comes near to comprehending the fullness of life, and without it we are inwardly impoverished. . . . When we talk of paradox, we mean the presence of any two conflicting truths present at the same time in consciousness."[19]

To hold two conflicting truths in consciousness at the same time creates an enormous tension. When confronted with such a situation, most people try to alleviate the tension by merging the paradox into a unity of the same, but in fact each truth must be preserved and is in need of careful differentiation until the transcendent function truly produces a symbolic solution. Symbols too easily become intellectual idealizations. To further illustrate the critique, Micklem points to the image of the hermaphrodite in the last print of the *Rosarium Philosophorum* in Jung's essay "The Psychology of Transference" and notes that most people simply see it as a symbol representing an integrated wholeness without really letting themselves experience its grotesque and monstrous character.[20] In short, for Micklem, the *coniunctio*, or reconciliation of opposites, is a monstrosity almost unbearable for the ego to tolerate.[21] Yet it is important to confront such an experience if we are to have any genuine recognition of the Self. The tensions we are speaking about "destroy us, but they also make us," and so we are caught in a strange paradox.[22] Such a monstrosity is present in our illnesses and symptoms, and it is important not to turn away from it because it is essential for any differentiated sense of wholeness beyond any idealized ego fantasy. As we have noted, for Jung even the Christ figure could not contain the darkest dimensions of psyche, and, at least for some Christian thinkers, the thought of linking Christ and anti-Christ in intimate connection is indeed a monstrous idea.

The issue of monstrosity and the Christian psyche is also discussed by Edinger, who takes up the issue of what was left out of Christian symbolism as it developed over the past two thousand years.[23] He turns to the Reusner's picture *Pandora*, which he believes contains the essence of alchemy and which, for Jung, was the carrier of those psychological elements elided by Christianity and that served as a counter-balance to it.

In figure 5.1 we see the assumption of Mary into heaven and her coronation. In the lower part of the picture one can see what Edinger calls the birth of a monster. What is so shocking for Edinger is the juxtaposition of the spiritual image of the assumption with "the image of the birth of a monster out of a lump of matter."[24] The whole image reflects the struggle to integrate both the feminine and the principle of materiality into the Christian vision. The image is monstrous to the Christian eye, and for Edinger the lower image of a birth from matter is "like a cuckoo's egg that's been laid in someone else's nest." The egg has been laid in the nest of the Christian vision, and "something unexpected is going to hatch out of it!"[25]

Color plate 14 is an image of the unconscious reproduced from Jung's *Alchemical Studies* in the form of Mercurius, whose three extra heads represent Luna, Sol, and a coniunctio of Sol and Luna on the far right.[26] The unity of the three is symbolized by Hermes, who represents the quaternity "in which the fourth is at the same time the unity of the three."[27] This image captures the quality of paradox and monstrosity stressed by Jung, Micklem, and Edinger. It is a symbolic unification but one not easily assimilable by the ego. This image may well be considered an example of a transformation going on in the God image of the Western psyche by virtue of the alchemical process that has been inserted into it, a process that gives birth to new possibilities. The new God image heralds the importance not only of incorporating the feminine and matter into our vision of spirit but also of "the discovery of the unconscious and the process of individuation."[28]

On a personal level, it also signifies all of the struggles of incarnated existence: "every hard disagreeable fact" of ordinary life. Edinger uses the eloquence of Shakespeare to describe the painful facts: "The slings and arrows of outrageous fortune, . . . the whips and scorns of time, Th' oppressor's wrong, the proud man's contumely, the pangs of dispriz'd love, the law's delay, the insolence of office, and the spurns that patient merit of th' unworthy takes, [leaving us] to grunt and sweat under a weary life."[29]

If one is honest, these insults of life cannot simply be passed over in

Figure 5.1. Extraction of Mercurius and the coronation of the virgin, 1582.
From Edward Edinger, The Mysterium Lectures: A Journey through
C. G. Jung's Mysterium Coniunctionis, *p. 133.*

any idealized transcendence. Such experiences hurt, sting, enrage, and
sometimes depress and kill us, and yet they must be acknowledged, ne-
gotiated, and made conscious if any real awareness of the Self is to take
place.

Edinger notes, as Jung and Micklem have, that "the living experience of the Self is a monstrosity. It's a coming together of opposites that
appalls the ego and exposes it to anguish, demoralization, and violation of all reasonable consideration."[30] It is a violation of everything we
have come to expect as natural, reasonable, and normal. In figure 5.2,
Edinger gives us a feeling for this in this image of the unity of opposites. In alchemy, the monstrous aspect of the conjunction is particularly emphasized when the opposites that are brought together are not

Figure 5.2. Union of opposites as monstrosity, 1509. From Edward Edinger, The Mysterium Lectures: A Journey Through C. G. Jung's Mysterium Coniunctionis, *p. 137.*

at first well differentiated. This situation is referred to as a *monstrum*, or premature unity, that is, any unity which does not differentiate itself into distinct realities.[31]

This premature quality of vision can hold true even for those rarified spiritual states described in the "images" of "pure light," the "void," or "merging bliss."[32] As Hillman states:

To go through the world seeing its one underlying truth in synchronistic revelations, its pre-established harmony, that God is becoming man and man becoming God, that inner and outer are one, that mother is daughter and daughter mother, puer is senex, senex puer, that nature and spirit, body and mind, are two aspects of the same invisible energy or implicate order, thereby neglects the acute distinctions joined by these conjunctions, so that our consciousness, no matter how wise and wondrous, is therefore both premature and monstrous. And by monstrous, alchemy means fruitless, barren, without issue.[33]

To have a productive conjunction requires that, even when the bringing together of opposites is not dramatically monstrous, each figure of the pairing remains stubbornly different. Hillman thus describes what a conjunction is not: "It is not a balanced mixture, a composite adding this to that; it is not a blending of substantial differences into a compromise, an arrangement; it is not a symbolic putting together of two halves or two things into a third."[34]

Here Hillman pushes forward our traditional Jungian idea of the symbolic outcome of the transcendent function. He emphasizes that the stubborn resistance of differences and incommensurabilities may mean that paradox, absurdity, and overt enormity are more characteristic of a union than is androgynous wholeness or the harmony of the *unus mundus,* or unitary world. The alchemical conjunction beyond these simple monstrums is more like an absurd pun or the joy of a joke than the bliss of opposites transcended. As a psychological event it takes place in the soul as a recognition, an insight, and an astonishment. "It is not the reconciliation of two differences, but the realization that *differences are each images* which do not deny each other, oppose each other, or even require each other."[35]

The quality of the conjunction that Hillman describes is captured in the following poems, the first of which is said to summarize the operations of Taoist alchemy:

> *Jadelike purity has left a secret of freedom*
> *In the lower world:*
> *Congeal the Spirit in the lair of energy,*
> *And you'll suddenly see*

White snow flying in mid summer.
The sun blazing in the water at midnight.
Going along harmoniously,
You roam in the heavens
Then return to absorb
The virtues of the receptive.[36]

In this image there is a harmony but also the jolting confrontation of differences: "white snow flying in mid Summer." The second poem is an obscure haiku that humorously captures the subtlety of "the conjunction":

On how to sing
the frog school and the skylark school
are arguing.[37]

In this instance, the frog and the skylark at one level are far apart, yet they are both creatures that have a song, and from a certain perspective they express the harmony of the universe.

An even more enigmatic description is given by a female adept of the Complete Reality School (CRS) of Tao, Sun Bu-er, in her poem:

At the right time, just out of the valley
You rise lightly into the spiritual firmament.
The jade girl rides a blue phoenix,
The gold boy offers a scarlet peach.
One strums a brocade lute amidst the flowers,
One plays jewel pipes under the moon.
One day immortal and mortal are separated,
And you coolly cross the ocean.[38]

In this enigmatic poem are many strange juxtapositions and hints of a transcendence that do not reconcile the differences but allow them to stand together and nonetheless express an invisible alchemical conjunction that is quite astonishing. Though Micklem, Edinger, and Hillman emphasize the monstrous and/or astonishing aspects of the coniunctio, not every genuine experience of conjunction has this quality. Consider this description in Cleary's recent translation of the classic Chinese alchemical text and meditation manual, *The Secret of the Golden Flower*:

> [O]nce the two things meet, they join inextricably, the living movement of creative energy now coming, now going, now floating, now sinking. In the basic chamber in oneself there is an ungraspable sense of vast space, beyond measure; and the whole body feels wondrously light and buoyant. This is what is called 'clouds filling the thousand mountains.' . . . [T]he coming and going is traceless, the floating and sinking are indiscernible. The channels are stilled, energy stops: this is the true intercourse. This is what is called 'the moon steeped in myriad waters.'[39]

Here is another description emphasizing the vital pleasures of union: "The pores are like after a bath, the bones and circulatory system are like when fast asleep, the vitality and spirit are like husband and wife in blissful embrace, the earthly and heavenly souls are like child and mother remembering their love."[40]

A humorous example of seeking an invisible harmony in learning how to paint occurs in a book by Oscar Mandel.[41] The author creates a scene in which young Chi Po—the main character—approaches his teacher, Bu Fu, for his first lesson. The fictional character of Chi Po is based on one of China's great painters, Chi Po Shih. The account goes as follows:

> "Young one," said Bu Fu at the beginning of the first lesson, "though I am a sorcerer, we must begin at the beginning." "And what's the beginning?" said Chi Po. "Tell me, my foolish piece of youth, if your mother and father could give you anything you desired, what things would you ask them for?" That was a question Chi Po had often dreamed of himself, and had answered, too, in his dreams. So he replied without hesitation: "A new hoop, a dog from Peking, strawberries and whipped cream every afternoon, and two rocking chairs, one for Father and one for Mother, be-

The Black Sun (157)

cause they have always wanted rocking chairs." "Now sit at the door of my cave," said Bu Fu, "and watch the sky and the trees, and watch above all the wind and the destruction of the clouds, and watch the squirrels and the conies, and dream of the brush and of your hand which will sweep over the silk of your next painting." With this, Bu Fu pronounced several frightful incantations, and abandoning Chi Po at the mouth of the cave, he went gathering acorns. Only the bulbul remained with Chi. He sat on a branch where he could watch the newcomer, and you could see by the tilt of his head and the angle of his beak that he doubted whether Chi could *do* it. And it wasn't easy. Now that Bu Fu had reminded him of the new hoop and the strawberries, Chi Po found it hard to send his thoughts into the trees and to keep his eye on the destruction of the clouds. But the afternoon was warm, and Chi settled drowsily with his back to the cave, chewing on a pine needle as he sat. He watched a cloud leave the top of a cedar and edge cautiously over to the top of another cedar. "Like a tightrope walker," thought Chi. And then he heard the wind: well now, it ooooed against the rocks, and frushled among the leaves, and tickled in the pines, and it just went loose above the earth. And on top of the wind went the snitting of the sparrows, the wild geese, the magpies, and above all, the lilling of the scarlet throated winch, and "Oh," thought Chi Po, "the treble of the birds and the bass of the wind—the high of the mountain and the low of the river—the king and the slave—father and boy—above and below—spring and winter," and on he went in this way, delighted with his discovery and getting drowsy indeed, while the bulbul watched him out of his single eye. "Young one," said Bu Fu, returning with acorns, "what is on your mind?" "Oh," said Chi Po, a little ashamed, "nothing." "Excellent, supreme," cried Bu Fu, his beard quivering. "You have had your first lesson. Now go home, because I have work in hand. Come back tomorrow. If your mind is still free of that clutter of strawberries and rocking chairs, I will allow you to paint a single dragonfly on a single lotus flower. Off then!" . . . "So," said Bu Fu the next day, when Chi Po came puffing up to the cave, "what of the

clutter?" "I hope it is still gone, sir," answered Chi Po. "May I try
the dragonfly, please?" "And the lotus blossom. Yes you may."
And Bu Fu told Chi Po why a dragonfly needs a flower, and why
a flower needs a dragonfly, for the one stays in the ground and
rises from the ground upward, while the other moves about and
descends from the sky downward. "Therefore" said Chi Po, "I
must paint them where they meet, where down flows into up and
up flows into down."[42]

Engaging the Monstrous

We have been looking at poems and stories that portray the subtlest
levels of the coniunctio as a traceless union referring to a seamless oneness. However, it is also vital that we not fall into an intellectual idealism and that we keep in mind the astute observations of Micklem,
Edinger, and Hillman so that we do not bypass the more beastly aspects
of the unconscious, of which clinical material is a constant reminder.

The strangeness and difficulty of engaging the monstrous comes in
many different forms. Working with the darkness of the unconscious
is exemplified in two very different but related examples; the first is of
a psychologist who, in remarkable dreams, discovers an image of Sol
niger:

I am home sitting in an armchair. I realize there's a pimple on the
sole of my left foot. I flip my foot over in such a way that I can
take a closer look at the pimple. I turn my sight away on my
right-hand side to fetch a tissue to clean my foot, and when I look
back again, the black liquid has gone back into the pimple. I'm
thinking "Oh, that's odd," so I press again and this time three
black liquid traces come out of the pimple. . . . I quickly grab
them; they have an elastic texture. I try to pull them out, but they
are more deeply and firmly rooted than I thought. I don't understand, so I look closer, bending my head as close as I can to my
foot. The pimple is not a pimple anymore; it's a hole through
which something is breathing, and there are several holes I had
not noticed before. As I look closer at my foot, trying to under-

stand where it goes, and as I follow the black web, my leg becomes transparent, it's in my whole leg too! I follow my leg and my whole body becomes transparent. I look at my hand, my arms, it has spread its thin web-tentacles everywhere inside me, like a thin wired network. I'm getting scared; I try to find the starting point of this spider-web. As I do this, the trunk of my body also becomes transparent. Now I can see it. The central starting point is in the middle of the trunk, on the plexus. It's a black head that looks like one of my childhood licorice sweets. I bend my head over my trunk to take an even closer look and realize that "thing" has eyes and it talks! I ask it "What are you doing here?"

"You called me," he/she says. "I serve you (tu in French), and I don't serve you (vous in French)." He/she smiles at me and his/her eyes blink calmly, sweetly and gently. He/she falls asleep as I slowly put my head back in a straight position.

I'm both scared and also tell myself that there's no reason for being scared, for if it was dangerous, I'd already be dead since it's been there forever anyway.

Nevertheless, I'd better show this to a physician. I go to the general hospital, where I'm told by a doctor that he's not competent in this matter, and he gives me a tiny piece of paper with an address written on it where I shall find someone competent.

I go there, and it's the office of my analyst. As I walk up the outside steps, I realize the plaque does not bear his name anymore. In fact, it says "Alchemist" instead. A man opens the door, and I recognize him. He really is The Alchemist, the one who once in my life introduced me to the "Black Land" and who died several years ago. I feel very touched seeing him again, and full of respect towards him. "What am I doing here?" I ask. "Well," he says, "Don't you know? There are billions of human beings on this planet and yet only twelve will succeed in their journey and make it here to my place. You are here to see the silence."

He leads me down a corridor. (At this point, and even when I write this dream, I have tears falling from my eyes in a form of ecstatic contentment/grace and joy. I feel like thanking God for this.)

He opens a door to a room in which from the ceiling hangs a mobile with two branches. Above the two branches stand two luminaries. On the left a sun; below the sun a double headed solar axe. On the right, a moon, and below it a Foucault pendulum.

The dream is complex, and it would take too much time to explore it fully. Still I would like to emphasize some of the dream narrative and language. In so doing, I stay close to the images as they present themselves in order to hear them speak in a phenomenological way, leaving aside most of the dreamer's personal associations.

The dreamer begins in an armchair in a somewhat relaxed and casual position. What at first appears to him is a little blemish on the sole/soul of his foot. The sound connection of sole and soul is often useful in entering into the inner meaning and site of the dream. What is going on is not simply in his literal foot but also in his dream or subtle body. Something is appearing in a critical place in the soul, a place that grounds and links him to Earth, to the place he stands on, his foundation. Although what's going on at this site seems just a small thing, the dream ego flips itself over to take a closer look. This gesture in dreams is quite common; a second look reflects a movement toward consciousness and shows something more to the dreamer than is available at a causal first glance. The dream ego applies some pressure to this blemish as if to squeeze out something that is under the surface. From this point, a black liquid like a filament starts to flow out. When the dream ego turns away with the intent of just wiping it away, the blackness disappears under the surface as is often the case when dealing with unconscious contents. This dreamer remains curious and presses forward again. As he does so, the blackness reappears and multiplies threefold. He now tries to grab hold of it, and as he does so, it becomes more solid and has an elastic texture.

He then tries to eliminate it by pulling it out of his body but discovers that it is more deeply and firmly rooted than he had thought. Once again, this kind of image is not uncommon in dreams. I have seen it on a number of occasions in which dreamers are trying to pull something out of their mouth, only to discover that it is fastened deeply within the body and cannot be pulled out. Sometimes this refers to an inability to say something that one is having a hard time expressing. The intensity of a conflict keeps it deeply connected to the body and the unconscious. For this dreamer, there seems to be a continuing desire to be rid of this black stuff but a more than equal desire to understand something about the darkness within.

He brings his head down to his foot, signifying a change in perspective, a descent of the head to the lowest part of the body, a coming down of consciousness to see what is going on at the place of the soul/sole and of blackness. As he does so, he discovers something that he had not seen before: The pimple is not just a pimple any longer but has become a hole, actually several holes, through which he discovers something alive and breathing. The dreamer's persistent desire to see what is going on is met by the subtle body becoming transparent. He can now see inside. Black filaments are everywhere, and he sees a black beast living inside himself.

As one might imagine, to discover this kind of unknown Otherness inside of oneself, as part of oneself, is terrifying and monstrous. Yet the dreamer continues to try to determine where all this is leading. He follows the blackness in its spiderlike intricacy throughout his whole body, which is now transparent. This web of tentacles has spread everywhere inside him. The change from casual curiosity to existential fear provokes a desire to get to the bottom of things, to the origin and source of the blackness itself. The source is discovered in the solar plexus, a place where, in literal physiology, a large network of sympathetic nerves and ganglia meet behind the stomach and form a hard, sunlike center. In our dreamer these nerves appear as black tentacles, creating what one might possibly imagine as a black sun center in the pit of the stomach. Here an important vision occurs; the dark center appears as a black head that has eyes and can see and speak to him. For the first time he addresses this darkness and meets it head to head as if engaged in a spontaneous active imagination.

There is a long tradition of head symbolism in alchemy and early literature, linking it both to the nigredo experience and to our human potential for transformation. Edinger believes that "one reason seems to be the connection between the term 'head' and top or beginning. Blackness was considered to be the starting point of the [alchemical] work."[43] Edinger notes that the head also symbolizes the *rotundum*, the round, complete man. The separated head and symbolism of beheading reflect this wholeness as extracted from the empirical man. "The head or skull becomes the round vessel of transformation. In one text it was the head of the black Osiris or Ethiopian that, when boiled, turned into gold."[44]

For our dreamer, the head takes on a less fearsome quality and stimulates sweet memories of childhood, but it also becomes a paradoxical interlocutor. The dreamer asks, "What are you doing here?" "You called me," he/she answers, "I serve you and I don't serve you." These paradoxical responses make clear that the black head is duplex and mercurial and reflects the complexity of the unconscious psyche, which is both trickster and guide. It is both male and female; it serves the ego and yet doesn't serve the ego. In this sense one might imagine this head as a prefiguration of the Self or of the whole man, which is never simply a sweet experience.

What can it mean that the head "serves and doesn't serve"? Jung poignantly expresses this paradox when he says, "The experience of the Self is always a defeat for the ego."[45] Moreover, the oracular head symbolizes the consulting of one's wholeness for information beyond the ego.[46] In this sense the black head and/or skull is a signifier of the memento mori, the existential knowledge of our own death. Edinger states that it is "an emblem for the operation of *mortificatio*. It generates reflections on one's personal mortality and serves as a touchstone for true and false values. To reflect on death can lead one to view life under the aspect of eternity, and thus, the black death head can turn to gold."[47]

In confrontation with the life of the psyche, the paradoxical truth is that such engagement brings both defeat and transformation, death and new life. This 'truth' is difficult to assimilate, if it can be said to be "assimilable" at all. Perhaps it is better to say it is the ego that is assimilated, not into the unconscious but into the larger life of the soul, a move that, as Hillman has said, "places man within psyche (rather than psyche within man)."[48]

Such a process feels like a great danger to the ego, as if it is in danger of dying. This anxiety leads the dreamer to a medical doctor who indicates that in these matters he is not competent. So one might imagine that what the dreamer is dealing with is not in the realm of the "medical body." Next, the dreamer goes to see his analyst, but the analyst no longer occupies the same place as he once did; his space has become occupied by an alchemist. For the dreamer, it appears that the psyche is suggesting that help is not to be found in the realm of either medicine or psychoanalysis.

So, the psyche places the dreamer into connection with an alchemist, with memory, image, and death within his own soul as he recalls the man who had introduced him to the "black land" and who died several years ago.[49] The dreamer feels touched and full of respect and now asks an important question, "What am I doing here?" With this, a deeper dialogue is initiated with the alchemist, who calls him by name and tells him that he is here to see the silence. This is a statement of the phenomenon of *synaesthesia*. *Synaesthesia* is traditionally understood as a condition in which "one type of stimulation evokes the stimulation of another."[50] It takes the dreamer out of his experience of the ordinary, empirical world and returns him to one in which silence is not simply heard, but also seen.

Merleau-Ponty notes that from this perspective, the "objective world . . . and the objective body with its separate organs . . . is [often felt to be] paradoxical."[51] The phenomenon of synaesthetic experience is rather common, but we have lost sight of it because immersion in a scientific Weltanschauung has "shift[ed] the center of gravity of experience so that we have unlearned how to see, hear, and generally speaking, feel."[52] We have left our "natural lived bodies" and deduced from our bodily organization a way of experiencing that is modeled on the physicist's conception of the world of perception.

If Merleau-Ponty is correct, it is not surprising why knowledge of the objective medical body is inadequate to understand the dreamer's experiences. From this perspective, sight and hearing in our everyday constructed mode are not fundamental in our experience. Might we imagine, then, that the alchemist is pointing our dreamer toward a return to both a more primordial way of seeing and to the lived rather than the objectified body?

For Merleau-Ponty, the "lived body" refers to something quite different from the "body" seen as an object of mechanistic physiology or of classical psychology. For him, as for our dreamer, biology and psychology are not the sources of the deepest understanding of our human existence. Rather, Merleau-Ponty speaks of a reawakening of our fundamental ground and of the strangeness and miracle of perception. Such a strange "perception" occurs in our dreamer. As the alchemist leads him down a corridor, he is ecstatic and has a feeling of contentment, grace, and joy. He feels like thanking God. The dream ends with the alchemist opening the door to a final complex, luminous, and mysterious vision—a mobile of the sun and moon.

The theme of the juxtaposed sun and the moon is common in alchemy and psychologically represents the tension and/or play of the opposites—of day and night, rational and irrational, conscious and unconscious. In figure 5.3, opposite flames are held by the male and the female and merge in the alchemist's flask. The sun and the moon appear above the flask. Fabricius writes below the image, "Lighting the fire of oneness in a furrow between two waves of the mercurial sea."[53]

Thus, we might imagine that part of our dreamer's vision has to do with the bringing together of the so-called opposites reflected in the dual snakes entwined around the caduceus near the right knee of the kneeling figure. The sun and moon perspectives are further differentiated by the images of the solar ax and Foucault's pendulum in the dream. The individual symbolism of the dreamer complicates the traditional images of the sun and the moon and gives them further articulation, truly creating a *complexio oppositorum,* similar to the tension in the alchemical engravings reproduced earlier.

The alchemist here opens a way for the dreamer to contemplate a vision of the "opposites" suspended on a mobile, which holds a coincidence of sun and moon, light and darkness. These images hang together in a mysterious suspension, appearing at the end of the dreamer's journey as if responding to the unanswered questioning at the core of blackness itself. The images of the solar ax and Foucault's pendulum add to the mystery of this final image, but here I comment only on the notion of the mobile itself.

The mobile is a term said to be coined by artist Marcel Duchamp in 1932 to describe the kinetic sculptures of Alexander Calder, who was

Figure 5.3. Lighting the fire of oneness, from Nicolas de Locques, 1665. From Johannes Fabricius, Alchemy: The Medieval Alchemists and Their Royal Art, *p. 60*

also a painter of a black sun. Jean-Paul Sartre, the existentialist philosopher and writer, wrote the following of Calder's invention:

> A mobile does not suggest anything: it captures genuine living movement and shapes them [sic]. Mobiles have no meaning, make you think of nothing but themselves. They are, that is all. . . . There is more of the unpredictable about them than in any other human creation. . . . They are nevertheless at once lyrical inventions, technical contributions of an almost mathematical quality and sensitive symbols of nature.[54]

The mobile might well be imagined as another provocative model of the Self. Sun and moon are not joined into any fusion, but each image has its distinctive place. They hang together in a strange balance, turning according to the movement of the universe, suspended as if from some transcendental and invisible point above, as reflected in the patient's dream.

Many of the themes that we have been discussing are expressed in this single dream. In it we find examples of the subtle-body process, the monstrous dark sun, the solar plexus, alchemical transformation, the nigredo, the mortificatio, and the Self. We see the process of psychic transformation expressed as the dream ego engages the darkness of the psyche and leads toward an enigmatic and symbolic vision that deepens his psychic life.

Now we look at a more extensive case vignette, in which the black sun plays a prominent role. In it a pastoral counselor struggles with this image and is thrown into an encounter with psychic realities that challenge his worldview. The pastor whose work I am about to describe became aware of my research and offered to tell me about his experiences. We corresponded for a little more than three months, during which time he elaborated his struggle with Sol niger and his developing understanding of the image. His first experience with the black sun was in the context of his ongoing Jungian analysis. The image of Sol niger emerged in an active imagination. He drew a picture of it (figure 5.4). In the drawing, there are two human figures; he is on the left, and a slightly larger figure of a cowboy is on right. The cowboy

Figure 5.4. Black sun image. Artwork by analysand. Used by permission.

had appeared in other active imaginations and played the role of a guide. The figures are looking out into the desert where there is a large golden pyramid with a bright yellow color surrounding it. Up above is a large black sun.

It is important to note that the image in figure 5.4 appeared roughly six months before he began to experience a deepening depression, which lasted for about three years. He felt that there was some link between his depression and the image of the black sun that appeared in his vision. Shortly after he had the experience of the image, things began to shift in his life.

He left the institution where he was doing chaplaincy work. He separated from his wife of seventeen years (a marriage that had long-standing problems) and was soon to leave his analysis as well. He was working and living alone for the first time in his life, and his depression continued to worsen. When he told this to his analyst, the analyst said, "No, you aren't getting worse; you're getting better." Because he didn't believe that the analyst understood his angst over his depression, he left analysis. He felt that he had to get away from the analyst to literally save his life.

He struggled with the depression for another year and a half with help from another therapist, medication, and a group he was in but finally reached the point where he was simply not functioning. He went into a hospital during the next year for a total of eight months, was discharged, and gradually began to put his life back in order. Following his hospitalization, he struggled with many aspects of Sol niger including a masculine-feminine split and issues of the heart, death, suicide, and obsessionality as well as with what he called a black hole and spiritual transformation.

One of the first things he did upon visualizing the image of the black sun was to look through Jung's works for references. One particular passage impressed him immediately, though it was not until a good deal later that he started to experience what his intuition told him was important. This is the passage he found:

Despite all attempts at denial and obfuscation there is an unconscious factor, a black sun, which is responsible for the surprisingly common phenomenon of masculine split-mindedness, when the right hand mustn't know what the left is doing. The split in the masculine psyche and the regular darkening of the moon in woman together explain the remarkable fact that the woman is accused of all darkness in a man, while he himself basks in the thought that he is a veritable fount of vitality and illumination for all the females in his environment. Actually, he would be better advised to shroud the brilliance of his mind in the profoundest doubt.[55]

His personal experience strongly resonated with Jung's description, and he wrote in a letter:

My relationships with women have never been particularly satisfactory. I like women and get along well as friends and colleagues, but intimacy has been difficult. This was the case in my marriage, and in the couple of relationships I have been involved with since then. Since dealing with the black sun, I have recognized a lot in myself that the Jung passage implies, and have come to see that this has been at least part of what has been at the heart of my difficulties with women.

There were several things that the pastor was almost entirely unaware of before his experience of the black sun. One was his tendency to blame women for his problems. He had done this for years, and even though women, including his former wife, complained about the kind of superiority, hostility, and condescension that can come from such an attitude, he simply could never see it. He always felt himself to be in the right and usually wondered what in the world was wrong with them that they could not see it the way he did. However, he did have the insight that a lot of his feeling life had been deeply buried for a long time. He began to sense that the feelings of which he was unaware were manifested in the ways he experienced and dealt with women. For example, he writes that he had been guilty sometimes of falling into an automatic teaching/lecturing posture with women. He then became aware that this was set off when women expressed their ideas through feelings. It was as if he then had to counter this with his "superior" intellect because he could not deal with it on the feeling level. He realized that he believed that a woman's feelings were inferior and that she needed his bright intellect to enlighten her. For him, feeling was part of the unknown and thus part of the black sun, which he feared.

The pastor reflected that in relation to the black sun, whatever its ultimate significance, a man needs somehow to come to terms with these feelings of superiority in order to also be aware of the duality in himself. If a man can do this, then he might not have to project the unseen aspect onto a woman, a displacement that had occurred not only for himself but also for other men with whom he had worked professionally or who were his friends and colleagues. While he knew this kind of attitude could be very hard to make conscious, he never really believed that it was buried in him. According to Jung, men often prefer to see their thinking associated with the light of consciousness, and thus it is very easy for them to project their own dark moods and thoughts upon women.

Although the pastor did not think of it in this context, after writing to me about the preceding observations, he recalled an earlier encounter with the theme of Sol niger and the heart. One day he had developed a pain around his heart and had gone to the emergency room at a hospital, but the doctors found nothing physically wrong. One week from that day, the same thing happened, and he went back to the hospital, and again nothing was found. When he next went to see his analyst and told him what had happened, the analyst suggested that since nothing physical was found, the problem must lie elsewhere. He suggested that the pastor do some active imagination in relationship to the heart to see what might happen. For fourteen days in a row, he actively imagined what was going on in his heart, and each time he drew a picture of what he had "seen."

He came to relate what he had considered his masculine-feminine split to problems of the heart that he traced back to wounds associated with his father. As he meditated and actively imagined what was going on inside his heart, he saw an angry fist, a crowbar, a large black stake piercing his heart, and later a large black iron ball that later he had identified with the black sun. He speculated on the relationship between depression and heart disease and commented that it cannot be healthy to carry around a twenty-four-pound ball of iron in your heart.

The work with active imagination eventually led him to a healing process: images of a surgical procedure and the extraction of the iron ball, a black snake with green vegetation leading the way to the emergence of blue waters and a dolphin accompanying a small sailboat in the final picture of the series. The image that most struck him, however, was the black iron ball that had emerged and was now outside. Although there was a healing of the heart, this image pointed to something outside of himself and outside the realm of consciousness. For him it was some darker expression of the soul—instinctual, emotional, symbolic, and archetypal. At its core the darkness of this other was uncanny and strange and perhaps even unknowable, he thought. It could have devastating consequences, physiologically and in his relationships, and it was as unrecognized as a black hole.

The theme of a black hole became important to him as an "outer image" that helped him to grapple with his inner darkness. Just becoming aware that such things exist in the universe helped him when

The Black Sun (171)

he felt he was losing his sanity or even "becoming a bit psychotic." He began to do some spontaneous active imagination on the model of a black hole. He writes that when he was in the throes of the depression, he would draw a blackened circle on a piece of paper. Then, when he looked at it and realized what he had drawn, he was horrified by it. It was as if it was able to draw attention and consciousness right down into it. As he thought more about what black holes are, he was able to see that they did exactly the same thing in the outer universe that the inner image had been doing to him. Black holes are so dense that no light escapes them. There were times when his depression felt exactly like that. In addition he had the sense that he could literally be pulled down into this thing and lost, in just the way things do not come out of black holes, at least not where they went in.

At one point, the pastor's concerns turned toward death, and he reflected on it as it appeared in his depressive states. He connected death with the black sun. He noted that the primary way that thoughts about death entered in was with the preoccupation that he was going to die. The pattern was that the death thought would be most prominent from the morning into the early evening, but through the late evening it would subside completely. He would then go to bed somewhat peacefully, and then in the morning, it would start again. This continued over a three-year period. Every morning for three years, he woke with the same concern about death. During that whole time, not once did it make any difference on any of those mornings that he knew the fear had subsided the night before and had done so every time. Every single day was a repeat of the identical pattern, seemingly disconnected from the day before.

Although he felt that the ultimate significance of his death thoughts was symbolic, for a long time he experienced the thought on a literal level. It took the form of preoccupation with his actual death. "I don't know when that awareness [of the literal quality of these thoughts] began to change, but it did. I think it changed a good deal in relationship to the spiritual changes which eventually came" through a kind of death/rebirth process. In studying the material on the tomb of Ramses VI, he was struck by the following phrase: "the rebirth of the sun at dawn after its night-time netherworld journey, the resurrection of the king after his dark and difficult passage through the underworld following his death, and the emergence of a higher level of consciousness after the arduous and often terrifying examination." He felt this well described what he went through: "I think I have had to live with the black sun for these past years to get ready to deal with the further meaning. . . . There is work to be done, though. I think part of it will be more precise thinking and amplifications regarding the black sun. In other words, there is still unanswered somewhat the question, 'Why the black sun?' 'Why a black sun?'"

It was a question the pastor knew could never be fully answered through analysis or therapy. He noted that his dark experiences, like the sun, had an incredible, seemingly inexhaustible energy. Probably the most significant thing for him with regard to the whole experience is that it eventually led him to convert to the Russian Orthodox Church. He had previously been ordained as a Protestant minister for twenty-three years. He felt that because of the depth to which the whole experience of the depression and the black sun took him, it ultimately resulted in a spiritual revolution. Since becoming Russian Orthodox seven years ago, he has continued to understand some things through the spirituality of that tradition that continued the theme of the black sun. He began to offer a number of reflections on the relationship of the black sun and the dark side of God. He stated that,

In Orthodoxy, it is common to think about God both in terms of "positive" and "negative" theology. This is not unique to Orthodoxy either. The positive theology involves those clear affirmations we are willing to make about God; that God is love, that God is omnipresent, etc. The negative theology proceeds in a different way and basically is the encounter with God through the experience of being stripped of our delusions and illusions about God and ourselves. My sense is that this corresponds more to the idea of the "essence" of God.

Now, with all said, the place I am coming to in regard to Sol niger is to say that what it has of God in it is close to this dark, mysterious aspect of God. One way that I have seen that has been in terms of the change which I experienced in relation to the image. Initially, it was terrifying and something that I wanted to flee but could not.

Sol niger and the depression made him aware of things that had to be faced and dealt with on the psychological level. At the same time, however, he had come to see that all of these factors needed spiritual work as well. In other words, what Sol niger and the depression revealed to him about his soul, he had come to see in his relationship to God as well. While this might sound strange, if the psychological and the spiritual are different but intimately related dimensions, then each will need its own kind of work.

The pastor found that Orthodoxy offers a form of meditative prayer known as *hesycham,* a term that means solitude or quietness and that was first used by St. Gregory Palamas in the fourteenth century. It has to do with what was described as an "uncreated light." This form of prayer uses the "Jesus Prayer," which leads to the "direct perception" of God and the things of God. The uncreated light is also called the "Taborian light" because it is the light that shone forth from Christ at his transfiguration on Mount Tabor. It is a light that comes from God and is not a created light like other light, such as that from the daytime sun. Other saints have reportedly actually shone forth with this light, which is exceedingly brilliant. He sometimes wondered whether that uncreated light might not in some way be connected with the dazzling light that proceeds from Sol niger.

The pastor and I had discussed the work of Julia Kristeva, and he felt that his idea is amplified in her work when she says, "The 'black sun' again takes up the semantic field of 'saturnine,' but pulls it inside out, like a glove: darkness flashes as a solar light, which nevertheless remains dazzling with black invisibility."[56] However, for Kristeva, Sol niger seems to remain tied to states of depression. The pastor reflected, "In this is seen again the paradoxical notion of light ('dazzling,' 'flashes') in the black darkness ('black invisibility'). Ever since the Sol niger began to take on some positive characteristics, this has been my intuition about it—that it is dark but light giving."

For the pastor, the reconciliation of light and darkness is captured in *The Orthodox Way* by Kallistos Ware, who talks about negative theology:

> And so it proves to be for each one who follows the spiritual Way. We go out from the known into the unknown, we *advance* from light into darkness. *We do not simply proceed from the darkness of ignorance to the light of knowledge, but we go forward from the light of partial knowledge into a greater knowledge which is so much more profound that it can only be described as the "darkness of unknowing."* (emphasis added by the pastor)[57]

Though this is clearly a statement about spiritual awareness, it is interesting that the darkness is actually seen as an "advance" over light and a "greater knowledge" than the light of "partial knowledge."

In reflecting on the pastor's experience, one might imagine an individuation process and the spiritual telos of his depression, leading to an integration of both his personal and archetypal shadow. Such an integration might be said to have constellated a well-integrated Self, healing a split in his masculine consciousness and ultimately opening him to an experience of a numinous, dark God image at the core of his new faith. His process "ends" with the creation of an important image relevant to our experience of Sol niger, with a darkness of unknowing, which is strangely described as an advance over light and as a blinding, divine darkness. This "image" of divine darkness is a well-known aspect of mystical theology.

Mystical Theology

The theology of the fifth- or sixth-century mystical philosopher Pseudo-Dionysius further amplifies Sol niger in its luminescent aspect. Many have come to discern in his writing the hand of a brilliant epistemologist, an early philosopher of language, a Socrates-like teacher, and a mystical theologian. Perhaps the best designation of Pseudo-Dionysius is the one underlined by twentieth-century philosopher and theologian Edith Stein: "Father of Mysticism." For Stein, his theology represents the highest stage of "secret revelation," and she notes that "the higher the knowledge, the darker and more mysterious it is, the less it can be put into words." In short, "the ascent to God is an ascent into darkness and silence."[58]

In his letters, Pseudo-Dionysius writes "The divine darkness is that 'unapproachable light' where God is said to live."[59]

In another place he writes, "The pure, absolute and immutable mysteries of theology are veiled in the dazzling obscurity of the secret Silence, outshining all brilliance with the intensity of their Darkness."[60] His *Mystical Theology* has been considered to exemplify the Dionysian method and to be a key to the structure of the entire corpus.[61] Pseudo-Dionysius begins with the question What is Divine darkness? and responds that Divine darkness "is made manifest only to those who travel through foul and fair, who pass beyond the summit of every holy ascent, who leave behind them every divine light, every voice, every word from heaven, and who plunge into the darkness where . . . there dwells the One who is beyond all things."[62]

According to the mystical theology of Pseudo-Dionysius, what remains of what can be known

is not soul or mind, nor does it possess imagination, conviction, speech, or understanding. Nor is it speech per se. It cannot be spoken of and it cannot be grasped by understanding. It is not number or order, greatness or smallness, equality or inequality, similarity or dissimilarity. It is not immovable, moving, or at rest. It has no power, it is not power, nor is it light. It does not live nor is it life. It is not a substance, nor is it eternity or time. It cannot be grasped by the understanding since it is neither knowledge nor truth. It is not kingship. It is not wisdom. It is neither one nor oneness, divinity nor goodness. Nor is it a spirit, in the sense in which we understand that term. It is not sonship or fatherhood and it is nothing known to us or to any other being. It falls neither within the predicate of nonbeing nor of being. Existing beings do not know it as it actually is and it does not know them as they are. There is no speaking of it, nor name nor knowledge of it. Darkness and light, error and truth—it is none of these. It is beyond assertion and denial.[63]

In such a litany, one gets the experience of the process of negative theology, which has a tendency to reduce one both to silence and to a darkness that one cannot even call darkness. So, in an attempt to continue to express what the author is referring to, the image of Divine Darkness stands in the place of having nothing left to say. Throughout his text, we find the metaphors of a darkness of unknowing that is higher than knowledge: a cloud of unknowing; he who has made the shadow his hiding place; a darkness hidden by light; a nakedness that exceeds light; a brilliant darkness resplendent; a dazzling obscurity of secret silence; a ray of Divine shadow that exceeds all existence; an outshining of all brilliance with the intensity of darkness; a supraessential Divine Darkness, beyond affirmation and negation; mystical ecstasy; a transcendent energy that lifts up, beyond sense and intellect; and an eclipse of consciousness that drives one out of one's mind and leaves one in silence.[64]

For Jung, such images are mad and monstrous, the height of paradox, linking and transcending what we think of as opposites in such a way that ordinary consciousness is radically challenged and subverted. In "Silver and White Earth," Hillman speaks of such madness alchemically as a process in which Solar brilliance and Moon madness are marvelously conjoined. The mysterium coniunctionis then is illumined lunacy.[65] However, if, with Hillman, we have ended in being out of our minds with lunacy, it is only fair to say that it is a higher kind of lunacy, a lunacy that is not simply deprivation and solely associated with the moon, depression, or castration, but a lunacy of transcendence, perhaps better associated with art and poetry than literal madness.

In Theodore Roethke's poem "In a Dark Time," he writes that "the eye begins to see;" and in this darkness, he meets his shadow and the darkness deepens. Here, in the dark, he finds both madness and "nobility of soul," an odd correspondence of opposites. Roethke also documents the *via longissama* that leads to the death of the self, set in a "blazing unnatural light," the point where the "I" no longer recognizes itself but finds the mind of God and a sense of freedom in the pain of loss.[66] Indeed, the poem contains several images associated with Sol niger: pure despair, death of the Self, dark light, the nobility of the soul, and madness, all of which form a complex web that may well constitute a kind of lunacy.

Nothingness and the No-Self

It was such a higher lunacy that laid the ground for Jung's more rational, intellectual, and scientific ideas about the Self. Jungian analyst Murray Stein, in *Jung's Map of the Soul*, does a nice job of tracing Jung's primordial experience of the Self, and I quote only a small part that is relevant to our reflections here. He describes a point in Jung's life in 1916, when Jung had a strange visionary experience that led to his writing a Gnostic-like text called the "Seven Sermons to the Dead." Jung heard the following words, which he transcribed: "Harken: I begin with nothingness. Nothingness is the same as fullness. In infinity full is no better than empty. Nothingness is both empty and full. As well might ye say anything else of nothingness, as for instance white is it, or black, or again, it is not, or is it. This nothingness or fullness let us name the Pleroma."[67]

This pleroma was a Gnostic name given to Jung's experiential prefiguration of what later became his hypothesis of the Self. This concept was elaborated throughout many of the *Collected Works* but most fully expressed in *Aion: Researches into the Phenomenology of the Self*.[68] According to Jung, the Self was a concept difficult to define, and, in spite of all of his warnings, it is often taken as a substantialized entity. Perhaps it would be of use to remind ourselves that Jung's Self is not a metaphysical entity. Psychologist and scholar Roger Brooke makes a useful contribution by asserting that to think of the Self as a "something" is less accurate than to understand it as a "no-thing," "a fertile and hospitable emptiness within which the things of the world could shine forth."[69]

In an article that has received too little attention, "Nothing Almost Sees Miracles!: Self and No-Self in Psychology and Religion," scholar of religion and Jungian psychology David Miller writes what amounts to a deconstructive reading of Jung's idea of the Self. He claims that even though Jung ultimately rejects the idea of a No-Self doctrine, in essence what he means by the idea of the "Self" "has the same ontological status as the desubstantialized and deconstructed notion of the 'no-self' in the apophatic religious traditions. 'Self' is no-self.'"[70]

Turning to the margins of Jung's ideas, beyond the formulations of his ideas as an empirical scientist, Miller recalls Jung's comment:

> If you will contemplate [your nothingness,] your lack of fantasy, [lack] of inspiration, and [lack] of inner aliveness which you feel as sheer stagnation and a barren wilderness, and impregnate it with the interest born of alarm at your inner death, then something can take shape in you, for your inner emptiness conceals just as great a fullness, if you allow it to penetrate into you.[71]

An emptiness that is also a fullness resonates with figures such as Pseudo-Dionysius, Meister Eckhart, Lao Tzu, and other masters of Asian or Western philosophies and religions that hold the concept of Nothingness at the core of psychological and religious life. In essence, this is true for Jung, too. For, beyond the scientific Jung, is the alchemical Jung, for whom the so-called Self is "in principle unknown and unknowable."[72] This Jung follows the alchemical dictum *ignotium per ignotius* (the unknown [is explained] by the more unknown). In short, for Jung the Self "is tantamount to religion's no-self."[73]

The paradoxical tension between Self and No-Self that Miller describes is a point of philosophical debate and doctrinal complexity that reaches a high point in Asian philosophy and religion—in the dialogue between Hindu and Buddhist perspectives. The debate is relevant for understanding Jung's idea of the Self since this idea was modeled in part on the ancient Hindu notion of Atman/Brahman.

The Upanishadic perspective holds that beneath and/or above the flux of the empirical world is an unchanging and eternal Self at the core of the universe. Buddhist philosophy, on the other hand, rejects such an idea of an unchanging Self and considers any idea of the Self to be an impermanent construction that must be seen through. In the place of the Self/Atman, the Buddhists see Anatman (or No-Self) and Sunyata (Nothingness or Voidness) as a mark of the "real."

The theme of this debate has been taken up by transpersonal psychologist Sean Kelly.[74] He contributes to this debate, positing what he calls "complex holism," a view in part influenced by Hegel's, Jung's, and Morin's idea of a dialectic that is a "symbiotic combination of two [or more] logics in a manner that is at once complementary *and* antagonistic."[75] What's important in Kelly's position is not just the idea of bringing the two perspectives together in unity but also giving importance to their differences. This gives his vision nuance and complexity. In other words, the doctrine that holds the Self (the Hindu Atman/Brahman) as the supreme principle and the doctrine that holds the No-Self (The Buddhist Annata) as a supreme principle are complementary while *at the same time* remaining antagonistic. Kelly relativizes each fundamental idea by noting that both principles "must negate the truth of the other in order to point out its onesidedness and its missing complement."[76]

It appears that Kelly's idea is parallel to Jung's. Jung's psychology was originally called complex psychology, and later, as it developed, an important component of it was the idea that the unconscious compensates for the one-sided attitudes of the conscious mind with the intent of achieving balance and wholeness. For Jung, the "Self" was also a complex (w)holism, a self-regulating and balancing principle, but what is interesting in Kelly's argument is that he applies the idea of complementarity to the idea of the Self itself.[77] He observes that the concept of the Self as Atman is prone to the kind of sterile hypostatization that impedes rather than facilitates psychic life. On the other hand, without the stability of the atmanic Self, the No-Self Annata doctrine is also prone to a sterile nihilism that leaves psychic life adrift.

It is worth noting here that for each perspective, Hindu or Buddhist, the idea of a complementarity principle can be accounted for from within. The Atman/Brahman perspective has its own way of understanding the flux of the No-Self, just as the No-Self perspective of the Buddhists has its own way of understanding stability. Those who are committed to one perspective or another are likely to feel that the antagonistic other does not *really* understand its perspective, which from within its own point of view the ideas of its critics are already addressed. Those who hold to their own perspectives alone are traditionally considered orthodox, whereas those who seek to break with tradition may be seen as iconoclastic or even heretical, like Jung himself. The history of ideas and cultures seems to move by virtue of such a dialectic, though ultimately this may be a too-limited way to imagine the complexity of history.

Kelly's perspective of complex holism embraces both perspectives, Self and No-Self. To this dialogical complementarity he adds the either/ or of dialogic antagonism, which gives the debate a dynamic thrust that both affirms and relativizes at the same time. If we then imagine Jung's idea of the Self as being subject to a similar critique, the Self would call for the complementarity principle of No-Self to keep it from stagnating into an hypostasized and fixed idea of order, as Hillman has observed.

For Jung as well as Hillman, the Self as the archetype of meaning requires the anima or archetype of life to keep it from stagnation. Hillman, however, prefers not to speak of the Self at all because of its tendency as a transcendental concept to lose connection with the body. For him, the problem with Jung's idea of the Self is that it moves toward transcendence, both mathematical and geometric. Its analogies tend to be drawn from the realm of spirit, abstract philosophy, and mystical theology. Its principles tend to be expressed in terms such as self-actualization, entelechy, the principle of individuation, the monad, the totality, Atman, Brahman, and the Tao.[78]

For Hillman, all of this points to a vision of Self that is removed from life, and so it enters psychology "through the back door, disguised as synchronicity, magic, oracles, science fiction, self-symbolism, mandalas, tarot, astrology and other indiscriminations, equally prophetic, ahistorical and humorless."[79] Here Hillman brings together a variety of ideas and images sacred to the orthodox Jungians, which, while not well differentiated, serves the purpose of painting a vision of the Self as an unconscious, abstract structure that has lost touch with the dynamics of the soul. This is a view of the Self that is not acceptable to the orthodox Jungian, for whom the Self is both structural, dynamic, and deeply connected to life.

It is not surprising to find that fundamental concepts such as the Self are open to multiple interpretations. As noted, there are those who regard Jung's Self as anything but static and others for whom it too easily loses itself in a hypostasized, outmoded, out of touch, and abstract conception that calls out for revision. As I interpret Kelly's perspective of "complex holism," the importance of the tension is to reveal how every fundamental concept has a shadow even when the concept is as wide ranging as the Self. In this sense, the complementary/antagonistic idea of the No-Self reveals the Self's shadow as an esoteric and invisible other that is necessary to the animation of psychic life. Traditionally the shadow is considered to be the counterpart of consciousness, but the Self is said to embrace both the conscious and the unconscious dimensions of psychic life.

However, if one follows Jung in the most radical sense while simultaneously giving credence to the perspectives of Miller and Kelly and to the importance of the idea of the No-Self as being both complementary and antagonistic to Jung's idea of the Self, then it is reasonable to imagine the Self as having a shadow, a dynamic and invisible Otherness that is essential to it.

Often for alchemy, Sol is the most precious thing, while Sol niger as its shadow is like Lacan's "petite a."[80] This petite a is "more worthless than seaweed."[81] Yet without Sol niger there is no ring to consciousness, no dynamic Other that taints and tinctures the brilliance of the Sun. Following the alchemical tradition, Jung writes that "Consciousness requires as its necessary counterpart a dark, latent, non-manifest side. . . . So much did the alchemists sense the duality of his unconscious assumptions that, in the face of all astronomical evidence, he equipped the sun with a shadow [and stated]: 'The sun and its shadow bring the work to perfection.'"[82]

Ultimately, I believe the notion of a shadow of the Self is supported by the paradoxical play of opposites in alchemy.

Sous Rapture, Depth Psychology, and the Soul

From the beginning of this chapter, we have been grappling with the idea of antinomies, with the paradoxical play of light and dark, life and death, spirit and matter. The coincidentia oppositorum and mysterium coniunctionis are expressions of paradox and monstrosity, maddening negations and attempts at unifications or transcendence. In an attempt to understand Sol niger, we have explored the Divine Darkness of mystical theology, the tension between Hindu and Buddhist visions, and the idea of a complex holism that lends itself to a new way of imagining both the Jungian idea of the Self as well as of Sol niger.

As we have seen, the problem is how can we speak about whatever it is that is referred to in the preceding? How can we address that invisible or absent presence that we call the Self or no-Self, Divine Darkness, or Sol niger? It has been challenging for the ancient philosophers, religious mystics, and alchemists, as well as for contemporary poststructuralist philosophers and psychoanalysts to grapple with expressing what is often felt to be inexpressable.

For poststructuralist sensibilities, one difficulty that is often expressed is that in every attempt to name that absent presence, there remains a vestige of metaphysical speculation, a transcendental signified (for our purposes read as Self) that is not deconstructed.

The French poststructuralist philosopher Jacques Derrida, for example, finds this to be the case with regard to negative theology, which his thought resembles but from which he insists it differs. In his "How to Avoid Speaking: Denials," he takes up his relationship with negative theology:

> This which is called X . . . "is" neither this nor that, neither sensible nor intelligible, neither positive nor negative, neither inside nor outside, neither superior nor inferior, neither active nor passive, neither present nor absent, not even neutral, not even subject to a dialectic with a third movement, without any possible sublation ("Aufhebung"). Despite appearances, then, this X is neither a concept nor even a name; it does lend itself to a series of names, but calls for another syntax, and exceeds even the order and the structure of predictive discourse. It "is" not and does not say what "is." It is written completely otherwise.[83]

While mimicking Pseudo-Dionysius, Derrida might be said to write negative theology "otherwise," in a way that does not assume a supreme being beyond the categories of being. Following Heidegger, he elaborates the postmodern practice of *sous rapture*, which has been translated as "under erasure," to mark the paradoxical play of "the absence of a presence, an always already absent present, of the lack at the origin that is the condition of thought and experience."[84]

In Jungian terms, one might think of this with regard to the mysterious core of an "archetype itself," which can never be made fully present or conscious. When we speak of God or Self, we are naming something whose Being is never fully present and cannot be captured in any signification. Even to speak of it as having a core or as being something is problematic. In Jungian language, we speak of images of the Self, but what does it mean to speak of this Self as if it existed as a kind of independent presence or transcendentally signified object or being? We have seen that, in negative theology, trying to name such transcendental "objects" always falls short and that they can be referred to only in terms such as Divine Darkness, which does not seem to refer to any "thing" at all. If no word or sign can capture the transcendental notion of God or Being or the Self and so on, then the words or signs that refer to it must be put under erasure—or crossed out—since the word is inaccurate. However, since all signs or words are necessary but also share the same lack, the convention has been to print both the word or sign and its deletion. Derrida gives this example: "[T]he sign ~~is~~ that ill-named ~~thing~~ . . . that escapes the instituting question of philosophy."[85]

Likewise, if we speak of God, Being, or Self, the convention would dictate that we express such ideas under erasure as ~~God~~, ~~Being~~, and ~~Self~~. That which is the absence of the signified, Derrida calls a trace, an invisible, marked by a sign under erasure. For Derrida, this is an experimental strategy of philosophizing in which what is being referred to as the transcendental arche (origin) must make its necessity felt before letting itself be erased (p. xviii, translator's preface). This is very important from an analytic point of view because if erasure takes place before there is any emotional connection with the other, erasure would remain an intellectual game without analytic gravity.

It is interesting that Derrida uses the notion of arche-trace, which I imagine as a philosophically sophisticated expression of what Jung tried to express by archetype—a notion reflective of Jung's Kantian vision. I cannot here elaborate the complexity of this notion except to say that to follow Derrida's intent is to "change certain habits of mind, rooted in our traditional metaphysics, in language, representation, ideas of the origin and in our binary logic." Using Derrida's strategy of sous rapture, the notion of the S̶e̶l̶f̶ under erasure, rather than being seen as a transcendental idea, essence, or substance, comes even closer to Jung's recognition of its mystery and unknown quality. Seen as a trace, the S̶e̶l̶f̶'s invisible presence is both marked yet effaced, and its shadow Otherness, seen otherwise, is both paradoxical and mysterious, both light and dark, yet neither.

I believe Derrida's sous rapture gets at the intention of Jung's idea in a new and highly original way. It also penetrates into the idea of Nothingness beyond its literal and binary designations. Applying his notion to Jung's concept of the Self adds a perspective that renews our understanding of the *Mysterium Coniunctionis* and helps us resist turning it into a simple conceptual unity or idealism, a danger pointed out by Micklem, who emphasized the *Mysterium Coniunctionis* as a *complexio oppositorum* of paradoxical and monstrous proportions. As we have seen, Edinger also emphasizes the mysterious nature of the opposites and traces it culturally in the development of science and materialism placed like a cuckoo's egg in the nest of the Christian vision.

Imagine Derrida's sous rapture as another such cuckoo's egg placed in the nest of modernism and Jungian psychology. It is paradoxical; it is monstrous, a foreign body that like the egg Edinger describes is also likely to hatch something new. I imagine it as a complexio oppositorum, continually hatching at the core of the mysterium coniunctionis, now bringing into our science and materialism an original, philosophical sensitivity to the paradox of language and continually deconstructing our tendencies to logocentrism.

Applying Derrida's idea of sous rapture to the notion of the Self in Jung's psychology opens a way of imagining the S̶e̶l̶f̶ as under erasure. Imagining such a S̶e̶l̶f̶ psychologically is an attempt to think about something that can never be simply identified with any one side of a binary pair—light or dark, black or white, spirit or matter, masculine or feminine, imaginary or real, conscious or unconscious—or with any hypothesized, transcendental notion that attempts to supersede or lift itself up above these oppositions as if language referred in some nominalist or substantialist way to some literal "thing" or entity.

As we have seen, terms such as Self, Being, and God cannot be privileged or given status outside the language system from which they have been drawn. For Derrida, following twentieth-century linguist Ferdinand de Saussure, these terms derive their meaning in a diacritical way, each making sense only in relation to other signs in a synchronic system of signifiers and having meaning only in relationship to other signs among which none is privileged. Nevertheless, philosophy, psychology, and religion all have a long history of master tropes or metaphors that appear and attempt to refer to something beyond the ordinary images of familiar words, such as Being, God, and Self. These "words" are like arche-traces that refer more to mystical than to literal reality and, like Hermes, stand at the crossroads of "différance," a neologism that Derrida coined from the French word for "difference" and which carries the meaning of both difference and deferral.[86] What is continually deferred is the idea that a word arrives at a literal destination, indicating a one-to-one correspondence and representation of reality.

So, for example, the idea of the Self can never be separated from its invisible counterpart, the No-Self, against which it derives its meaning. Since an insight is marked by placing it under erasure, the line drawn through the word S̶e̶l̶f̶ indicates its negation, its shadow. This ensures that an idea will not be taken literally and reminds us that ideas will continue to disseminate throughout time and culture. No concept, master trope, or metaphor can ever finally complete the play or totality of psyche, which, like Mercurius, always escapes our grasp. The S̶e̶l̶f̶ under erasure is always in a process of continual deconstruction, and, like the philosopher's stone of alchemy, it slips "that grip of *Begriffe* that would capture it."[87] Hillman's reading of alchemy imagines the philosopher's stone as soft and oily, countering both those images that point to its strength, solidity, and unity and also our tendency to crystallize the goal in terms of fixed positions and doctrinal truth. For him, the philosopher's stone is waxy and can "receive endless literalizations without being permanently impressed."[88] Perhaps it is useful to imagine the S̶e̶l̶f̶ under erasure as a kind of contemporary philoso-

pher's stone marking a mystery that has long been sought and continues to remain elusive.

The Philosopher's Stone : Self, Subject, and Soul

Contemporary poststructuralist thought has proceeded toward "if not
a liquidation [or *solutio*], then at least a displacement of the subject
from the center of philosophical and theoretical activity."[89] Lacan and
philosopher Paul Ricœur speak of decentering the subject and Foucault of the "erasure of man like a figure drawn in sand at the edge of
the sea."[90] The removal of the subject from the center of psychic life
also resonates with Jung's displacement and relativization of the ego.
For Jung, the structures of the Self likewise transcend the individual,
and its essence "lies beyond the subjective realm."[91]

Just as for Derrida the subject is an effect of language, so for Jung the
ego is the product of an all-embracing totality. In short, the "Self is
paradoxically *not* oneself."[92] However, insofar as Jung's Self as a totality
rises above and beyond the psychic and subjective realm and is seen as
constituted by impersonal, collective forces, it is consistent with the
poststructuralist contention that the subject is likewise primarily an
effect of larger collective forces: historic, economic, or linguistic.[93] The
poststructuralist view of such forces is quite different from the more
mysterious idea about archetypes and the collective unconscious, but
for some philosophers (e.g., Lévinas) and some post-Jungian psychoanalysts (e.g., Hillman), the distancing from subjectivity has become
problematic. The question remains as to what extent such a subject is
dissolved in structure and function, with a loss of body and ethical
sensibility. In both Lévinas and Hillman, the problem of the body/
sensibility and ethics becomes an important theme in the constitution
of the Self/soul, which resists abstraction.[94] Both Hillman and Lévinas
attempt to maintain a subject that is both fleshy and human while, at
the same time, paradoxically, it moves beyond the idea of a reified subject and/or an abstract transcendence.

The "subject" Hillman describes is an outcome of having under-
gone an alchemical process and/or the successful termination of an
analysis. The transformation of subjectivity is bodily a difficult and

painful process in which the preanalytic or pre-deconstructive subject must undergo both change and erasure. This erasure is not a simple abstract process of thought but rather a powerful experience of negation and mortification that wounds our narcissism and uncovers our relationship with the Other and the world, which was the precondition of any subjectivity to begin with. The negation and mortification of the Self is symbolically expressed by the black sun and has been indicated here by the crossing out of the ~~Self~~. The blackness of the sun crosses out the simple Western metaphysical notions of light and consciousness. The ~~Self~~ under erasure is shorthand for a complex transformation that has been described in different ways, including as an alchemical process of deconstruction and/or as an analysis.

Archetypal Alchemy

In alchemy as in the literatures of deconstruction and analysis, the shorthand of erasure is richly expanded and amplified. It is part of a series of complex and subtle processes of dissolutions and coagulations *(solve et coagula)*, negation and conjunction, and mortification and revitalization. The idea of erasure lends itself to comparison with certain operations of alchemy that have to do with the processes of mortification, calcination, and dissolution and entering into the blacker-than-black aspect of the nigredo, in which the self is ultimately reduced to no-self. Such a focus emphasizes the death aspect of the opus and the powerful reduction of narcissism. In alchemy, the nigredo is often placed at the beginning of the work, and ultimately the blacker-than-black is thought to be surpassed as blackness lightens and yields to other colors. The changes in coloration reflect subtle changes in the soul.

One reading of this process is that it is linear, progressive, and spiritual. It results in a literal salvational goal in which the lead of the pre-deconstructed or analytic subject is thought to be changed into the gold of a resurrected self, forever beyond further dissolution or mortification. For Hillman, this is a literalized reading of alchemy by which the stain of blackness is forever dispelled. His critique of such a reading parallels the insights of a deconstructive reading in which speaking about a post-deconstructive and/or postanalytic subject is problematic, as if such a self or subject is a fixed outcome or product of such proceedings. There is never simply an "after" of analysis or deconstruction, and expressing it conceptually recreates the illusion of a self-enclosed totality. No one is ever fully analyzed; no deconstruction is ever complete; the unconscious or blackness is never totally eliminated. The alchemical work of James Hillman emphasizes the continuous process of deconstruction while at the same time indicating a transformative process that recognizes a potential for revitalization.

Hillman radicalizes our reading of alchemy and resists any allegorical or salvationist reading of it. His has been an important voice critiquing any reading of steps and stages, emphasizing instead a way of seeing that regards each "phase" for itself. He stays true to alchemy in organizing his work around colors as aesthetic materials reflecting qualities of the soul. In a series of papers he writes about the "Seduction of Black," "Alchemical Blue and the *Unio Mentalis*," "Silver and the White Earth" (parts one and two), and "The Yellowing of the Work." In "Concerning the Stone: Alchemical Images of the Goal," he writes about the *rubedo*, the process of reddening. In all of the works mentioned, he tries to see through the linear progression of a unidirectional model simply progressing through time.

One of the dangers of placing blackness into a process of development is the tendency to move too quickly away from its radicality, its blacker-than-black aspect, its depth, its severity, and the suffering associated with it. The unidirectional, spiritualized version of the alchemical opus wants to move out and away from blackness. Its focus is on the move from black to white, from nigredo to albedo, the classical alchemical formula. Nevertheless, to focus on movement and transition from one state or color to another, useful as this might be, runs the risk of not seeing with that dark eye that sees blackness for itself and not simply as a passage to whiteness, change, and generation.

The temptation to read alchemy in this way has textual support in Edinger: "[T]hat which does not make black cannot make white, because blackness is the beginning of whiteness."[95] "Putrefaction is of so great efficacy that it blots out the old nature and bears another fruit. . . . Putrefaction takes away the acridity from all corrosive spirits of salt, renders them soft and sweet."[96]

The Black Sun (189)

Classic passages such as these may lead one to focus on whiteness, the albedo of new form, and the soft sweetness of renewal. Such passages describe important qualities of alchemical transformation, but they can also lend themselves to readings that can reduce the dark depth of the putrefaction process to a moment of negation in an intellectual dialectic. It is useful to recall Edinger's warnings that the alchemical work is dangerous and requires torture, killing, and death, as well as Hillman's caution that the mortificatio occurs not just once but again and again. Blackness is not just a stage to be bypassed once and for all, but a necessary component of psychological life. The black spot is structurally part of the metaphoric eye itself, a potential inherent in the soul's visual possibility.

Hillman emphasizes that blackness has a purpose: It teaches endurance, warns, dissolves attachments, and "sophisticates the eye" so that we may not only see blackness but actually see by means of it.[97] To see through blackness is to understand its continuous deconstructive activity as necessary for psychological change.[98] To read alchemy this way suggests that its images are "psychic conditions [that are] always available."[99] They do not disappear. Psychologically, it is easy to be seduced. The colors catch our eye as they change from black to white to yellow to red, indicating a movement out of despair to the highest states of psychological renewal (color plate 16). In Hillman's papers, too, one can trace such a movement from the blackest mortifications to where, in blue beginnings, Venus collaborates with Saturn and transforms into the pure whiteness of the albedo.[100] The perfection of white rots but only to yellow, opening the way for rubedo, the reddening, libidinal activity of the soul as it resurrects and revivifies matter, crowning it in beauty and pleasure. In fact, Hillman describes the alchemical process in this way.[101] If one stands back and abstracts his descriptions and places them into a developmental vision, one could say this is in fact what he describes as the alchemical process, however watered down.

Such a reading, however, would interpret Hillman precisely in the way that he would not want to be read. It would impose and carry over a spiritualizing and developmental tendency from the very readings he critiques. To read him in this way would be to follow the linear pull of his work into a banal cliché. It is always too easy to collapse originality and complexity into facile formulations. A careful, serious reading of his work means that, in spite of seeing and "moving beyond" the nigredo, his texts resist any easy exit from blackness. As he moves from color to color, the traces of blackness remain like a subtle body that imbues the soul with its own ongoing essence. In short, he preserves the luminous paradox of blackness.

Consider the following from "Alchemical Blue and the *Unio Mentalis*." Hillman writes, "The transit from black to white via blue . . . always brings black with it. . . . Blue bears traces of the *mortificatio* into the whitening."[102] In "Silver and the White Earth," he states, "'Putrefaction extends and continues even unto whiteness'. . . . We must, therefore, amend our notion of the white earth."[103] Likewise, in the transit from white to yellow, the process is marked by putrefaction, rotting, decay, and death: "Yellow signifies a particular kind of change usually for the worse."[104]

Even in the "final stage" of the alchemical transformation—the reddening—we witness the final dissolution of sunlit consciousness. The reddening of the goal likewise has darkness in its core. So, even while Hillman indicates the soul's movement through the color matrices of alchemy, in each move the subtle essence of blackness works in such a way that the essence of blackness is never left behind.

While Hillman critiques the idea of a literal spiritual and developmental reading of alchemy, still he notes that success in the work depends on the ordering of time, succession, and "stages." The danger is only in literalizing this ordering or totally fixing the colors of psychological experiences into rigid categories of exclusion that would flatten, deplete, and miss their richness and subtlety. When this happens, time, order, succession, and stages are seen as fixed phases—concrete steps toward a literal goal. Such a view leaves us trapped in a linear, historical progression toward some metaphysical illusion stretched out in time rather than grappling in the midst of differentiated, impelling images.

In "Concerning the Stone: Alchemical Images of the Goal," Hillman gives an example of the complexity of an image in which he refuses to separate into "positive and negative, dark and light, death and new birth." The "grit and the pearl, the lead and the diamond, the hammer and the gold are inseparable."[105] For Hillman, "the pain is not prior to the goal, like crucifixion before resurrection"; rather, pain and gold are "co-terminous, co-dependent and co-relative." "The pearl is also always grit, an irritation, as well as a luster, the gilding also a poisoning."[106] It is hard to keep these opposite dimensions of experience in consciousness, but, for Hillman, such a description fits with life, "for we are strangely disconsolate even in a moment of radiance." Our golden experience "again and again will press for testing in the fire, ever new blackness appearing, dark crows with the yellow sun."[107]

On such a basis, I propose that the "light of darkness itself," Sol niger, is such a complex image and that the idea of regeneration is better seen in a deeper consciousness of this paradox than in a moving through and beyond it. The paradox holds the "opposites" of light/dark, visible/invisible, and self and no-self together, and in so doing there is a "light," an effulgence, or a "shine" that is hard to define or capture in any metaphysical language. Taking Hillman's lead, my experience has been to imagine the luster of blackness itself in its multiplicity and, like Hillman and Lopez-Pedreza, to resist as much as possible going to other colors to reflect the complexity of experience. In this way I have attempted to extract the "black" back from the array of colors in order to give full acknowledgement to its subtle presence. While blackness appears somewhat different when seen through blue, white, yellow, and red, its "essence" remains. Here, blackness need not be understood only as a literal color but also as a "qualitative differentiation of intensities and hues, which is essential to the act of imagination."[108] In this way, black remains as a subtle body embracing psyche with its ongoing essence, repeating, deconstructing, tincturing, and making itself felt in the very pigment of the soul. It is an essence of multiple differentiations and layers of meaning. We have seen that writers and painters have long known about the many qualities of blackness. The following is a remark by the famous Japanese painter and printmaker Hokusai: "There is a black which is old and a black which is fresh. Lustrous (brilliant) black and matte black, black in sunlight and black in shadow. For the old black one must use an admixture of blue, for the matte black an admixture of white; for the lustrous black gum (colle) must be added. Black in sunlight must have gray reflection."[109]

In *The Song of Solomon,* Toni Morrison states that "There're five or six kinds of black. Some silky, some wooly. Some just empty. Some like fingers. And it don't stay still. It moves and changes from one kind of black to another. Saying something is pitch black is like saying something is green. What kind of green? . . . Well, night black is the same way. May as well be a rainbow."[110]

Hillman, too, echoes the preceding statements: "There are blacks that recede and absorb, those that dampen and soften, those that etch and sharpen, and others that shine almost with the effulgence—a *Sol niger.*"[111]

In addition to its multiple differentiations, the black essence is also ubiquitous—as John Brzostoski well demonstrates in a piece he wrote called "Tantra Art."[112] In it he demonstrates the all-pervasive infusion of color in our speech. Beginning with black, he highlights its presence in between our words, often invisible to eye and ear when we focus only on the literalizing word or meaning. Here we have a section from Jung's *Psychology and Alchemy* treated to the same technique:

> The (black) *lapis* (black) says (black) in (black) Hermes: (black) 'Therefore (black) nothing (black) better (black) or (black) more (black) worthy (black) of (black) veneration (black) can (black) come (black) to (black) pass (black) in (black) the (black) world (black) than (black) the (black) union (black) of (black) myself (black) and (black) my (black) son.' (black) The (black) Mono-genes (black) is (black) also (black) called (black) the (black) 'dark (black) light.' (black) The (black) *Rosarium* (black) quotes (black) a (black) saying (black) of (black) Hermes: (black) 'I (black) the (black) lapis (black) beget (black) the (black) light, (black) but (black) the (black) darkness (black) too (black) is (black) of (black) my (black) nature.' (black) Similarly (black) alchemy (black) has (black) the (black) idea (black) of (black) the (black) *sol* (black) *niger,* (black) the (black) black (black) sun.

As one reads his description, the narrative force of meaning is frustrated, interrupted, and begins to deconstruct. The flow of ideas is interspersed by a black mantra, a *mortificatio* of narrative articulating

Figure 5.5. Eclipse of the sun. © *1994 Martin Mutti. Used by permission.*

the invisible spaces, which then resists any simple logocentric expression and our ordinary ego desire for clarity. This invisible blackness is not only present in artistic constructions but is also an unconscious dimension of our daily life. Like the musical form of an Indian raga, the drone in the background is all important to the articulation of the individual notes.

If we ignore the black essence by leaving all the blacks out, the narrative becomes clear and distinct. Here is the description without the word "black" interspersed before each word of the narrative: "The *lapis* says in Hermes: 'Therefore nothing better or more worthy of veneration can come to pass in the world than the union of myself and my son.' The Monogenes is also called the 'dark light.' The *Rosarium* quotes a saying of Hermes: 'I the lapis beget the light, but the darkness too is of my nature.' Similarly, alchemy has the idea of *sol niger*, the black sun."[113]

In the first mantra reading, which includes the blackness, one gets the experience of what is being written about in the narrative expression—and more. There is a felt connection between the subtle essence and multiplicity of blackness as it interrupts and tinctures our ordinary discourse through a mortificatio of narrative that then begins to give us a sense of what we might imagine as the dark light itself, formless and animating, producing a deepening pleasure (jouissance) as the demands of linear thought and narrative relativize and diminish.

In this moment, black begins to shine, no longer simply confined in the nigredo, and joy is oddly linked to blackening and deconstruction, or, as Lacan might have said, the lack is linked to jouissance. This black joy is also recognized in the sublime beauty of Hades, where, Jung and Hillman tell us, everything becomes deeper, moving from visible connection to invisible one, and the invisible glows with the presence of the void.

The link between jouissance and blackness is also made by Stanislov Grof and captured in a series of paintings described in *LSD Psychotherapy*. About these images, one of which is presented in figure 5.6 in grayscale, Grof states that through suffering one reaches the Black Sun, "the manifestation of the innermost core of the human being, the divine Self," which he associates with "transcendental bliss," not unlike the descriptions of the Tantric tradition.[114]

The patient whom Grof describes had experienced the destructive power of volcanoes but had come to appreciate the creative aspect of the glowing magma. Giegerich reminds us that this creative fire—a fire that also contains the volcanic metaphor of the stream of lava, the incandescent matter—is at the core of Jung's work.[115] It is an image important to Jung in his vision of the psyche. Even though Grof is aware of both the destructive and creative dimensions of this primordial process, he separates Sol niger, the "destructive" part, from the transcendent black sun. I believe this runs the risk of splitting the archetype apart. As I see it, both experiences are intimately intertwined and present in the blackness of Sol niger as an archetypal image.

For Jung, Hillman, and Giegerich the price of admission to this vision of the soul is the loss of the materialist viewpoint. Only then can the soul show itself as both Hades and Pluto, the dark underworld with its fruitful and shining possibilities. Hillman notes that from one perspective the blackness of night is "the source of all evil," but that from the viewpoint of the Orphics, "Night was a depth of love (Eros) and light (Phanes)."[116]

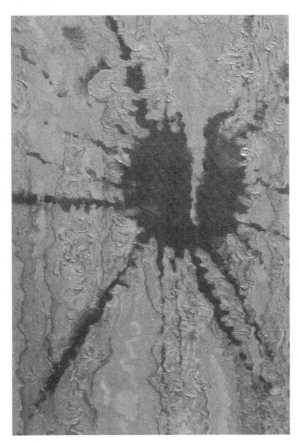

Figure 5.6. Through suffering to the black sun. From S. Grof,
LSD Psychotherapy, *p. 283. Used by permission of Stanislav Grof.*

This mystical love is well described in a study by philosopher George Scheper.[117] Hillman resists proponents of religious darkness and their mystical language, but for Scheper and others, these mystics become our most reliable phenomenologists of a dazzling darkness, of Eros and self-forgetting. In the ancient Hebrew *Song of Songs,* for example, the Shulammite's night quest for her lover reads like a mystic *desendu ad inferno* and, in terms of the poetics of love, the mystic descent into darkness. Whether in the story of Orpheus and Eurydice, Demeter and

Persephone, Ishtar and Dumuzi, all symbolize the overwhelming redemptive power of passion and darkness.

In this spirit, the Hebrew *Song of Songs* resonates with St. John of the Cross, who said:

> *O dark night, my guide*
> *O Sweeter than anything sun rise can discover*
> *Oh night, drawing side to side*
> *The loved and the lover*
> *The loved one wholly ensouling in the lover.*

Mysticism and Black Light

The deepening paradox of Sol niger as a point of conjunction between Hades and Pluto and as an expression of the mystical marriage is deepened in the passion of the mystic's exploration of erotic passion and black light. The passion of ecstatic love is prominent in Sufi mysticism. Henri Corbin links such erotic passion with what the Sufis called black light, considered the highest spiritual stage and the most perilous initiatic step. "The 'black light' is that of the attribute of Majesty which sets the mystic's being on fire; it is not contemplated; it attacks, invades, annihilates, then annihilates annihilation. It shatters . . . the apparatus of the human organism."[118]

This light is considered by the Sufis as "a very delicate spiritual state into which the mystic enters just before the fanâ (annihilation) turns into baqâ (survival)" and marks "a state shared by both."[119] At this moment, the inner eye of the mystic turns dark, and yet it is the point where darkness itself is supreme light.[120] Blackness (Siyâhî), according to Izutsu, in reality is the very light of "the Absolute-as-such" and "corresponds . . . ontologically . . . to the stage of Oneness (aḥadîyah)" or "Supreme Blackness (sawad-e aʿzạm)." " 'The mystic,' Lâhîjî observes, 'does not realize absolute existence unless and until [one] fully realizes absolute Nothingness. . . . Nothingness is in itself the very Existence-by-the-Absolute.' In short, nothingness (or darkness) is in reality existence (light), and light is in reality darkness."[121]

Figure 5.7. Image of the coniunctio. From C. G. Jung, "The Psychology of the Transference," in Practice of Psychotherapy, *p. 249.*

Finally, according to Lâhîjî, there is yet one further ultimate "stage" that can be described—called "annihilation after survival," which Izutsu compares to what Hua Yen Buddhism considers the "ultimate of all ultimate ontological stages, the celebrated *ji-ji-muge-hohkai . . .* [which] represents the extreme limit which our paradox of light and darkness can reach."[122]

In *Dancing Streams Flow in the Darkness,* Shunryu Suzuki comments on a Chinese poem by Sekito Kisen in one of his Zen talks.[123] The poem is called "Sandokai." It is about twelve hundred years old and speaks of the relationship between light and darkness, noting that "In the light there is darkness, but don't take it as darkness. In the dark there is light, but don't see it as light."[124] For Suzuki, the absolute is beyond the limits of our thinking mind and cannot be known. In *Invisible Light,* Paul Murray captures this spirit in a poem titled "Canticle of the Void," part of which follows:

Smaller than the small . . .

I am the seed
of all that is known
and unknown.

I am the root
and stem of meaning,
the ground

of wonder. Through me,
each leading
tendril of desire
is drawn,
and breathes in
consciousness of Being.

And yet when you open
your ears to my voice
and listen with all your hearing
and listen again,
no subtle joining of notes and words,
no vertical song is heard

but silence is singing.

And when you open your eyes
to my appearance
but cannot see me,
or when you close your eyes
and close your ears in concentration
and look with your hands
and turn back again the pages
of sleep's dark scripture,
no great or terrible sign awakes,
no vision burns

The Black Sun (199)

but absence is shining.

Mine is the secret
that lies hidden
like the lustrous pearl
gleaming
within its oyster

the deepest secret
the secret
hidden within the secret.[125]

The following poem by T. S. Eliot expresses similar insights:

I said to my soul, be still, and wait without hope
For hope would be hope for the wrong thing; wait without love
For love would be love for the wrong thing; there is yet faith
But the faith and the love and the hope are all in the waiting.
Wait without thought, for you are not ready for thought:
So the darkness shall be the light, and the stillness the dancing....

In order to arrive at what you do not know
    You must go by a way which is the way of ignorance.
In order to possess what you do not possess
    You must go by the way of dispossession.
In order to arrive at what you are not
    You must go through the way in which you are not.
And what you do not know is the only thing you know
And what you own is what you do not own
And where you are is where you are not.[126]

In Corbin's terms, the invisible black light requires an unknowing that is also a knowing. This state of unknowing is synonymous with the mystical poverty that we attribute to the Sufi, who is said to be "poor in spirit." It is a poverty in which we are reduced to Nothingness and God is no one who can be grasped. In a poem called simply "Psalm," Paul Célan writes:

> No one kneads us again out of earth and clay,
> no one incants our dust. No one.
> Blessèd art thou, No One.
> In thy sight would
> we bloom.
> In thy
> spite.
>
> A Nothing
> we were, are now, and ever
> shall be, blooming:
> the Nothing-, the
> No-One's-Rose.
>
> With
> our pistil soul-bright,
> our stamen heaven-waste,
> our corona red
> from the purpleword we sang
> over, O over
> the thorn.[127]

The Sufi ideas of not knowing and of mystical poverty and black light find their counterparts in the kabbalistic and Chassidic notion of "bittul," the nullification of the ego. In the Chassidic discourse *Basi LeGani*, the nullification of the ego is described as a folly of holiness and self-transcendence, in which the spiritual work of transforming darkness into light is done to the degree where the "darkness itself would be luminous."[128]

Sanford Drob elaborates the kabbalistic recognition of a "darkness that is at the heart of light itself" and finds analogies to the black sun in three moments of negation: in Ayin (as Ein-sof), Tzimtzum, and Shevirah.[129] For Drob, the Ayin suggests "that nothingness is the source of all distinctiveness and difference, and thus of all light, meaning and significance."[130] The Ein-sof is referred to as the "light that does not exist in light," and the Sefirot is spoken of as lights that are concealed or, as in the Zohar, as the light of blackness (Bozina di Kardinuta).[131]

Hasidic teacher Bitzalel Malamud explains that the study of Jewish mysticism involves various classic metaphors that describe supernal dynamics. The Sun is one such metaphor, referring to a nonapprehensible level of infinite light "which in its source is completely nullified and non-existent but which nevertheless emanates as a ray to create and enliven all creation, spiritual as well as the physical." The metaphor, however, does not tell the whole story because we are thinking about an infinite "sun" that, if revealed as the direct source of the ray, would leave it and creation no room to exist with any independence. Malamud explains that in order to allow a place for separate existence, the infinite sun needs to be completely contracted. In the language of the kabbalist, this is called the Tzimtzum, which is basically the hiding of godliness.[132]

In other words, Tzimtzum refers to the contraction of God's infinite light in order to create a space or black void so that there is room for creation. Shevirah refers, on the other hand, to a brilliant spark that exists like a scintilla in the sea of darkness that can serve as a basis for redemption. In the kabbalistic universe, light and dark exist in an invisible interpenetration that, like Sol niger, might well be referred to as Divine Darkness.

A friend and colleague, Robert Romanyshyn, knew of my work on the black sun and had himself been working on a book of poems called *Dark Light.* He told me that he had no idea why the title had come to him, and he sent me the following dream of a black sun:

> V. and I awaken in a hotel room. It is dark outside, and I am surprised because it feels as if it should be morning. It feels that we have slept and the night has passed. I call the hotel desk to ask the time and someone tells me it is 9 A.M. Then the person says, "Haven't you heard? Scientists are saying there's something wrong with the sun."

In a half waking state, a kind of reverie, the dream seems to continue:

I have the sense that the world now will be lit by a *dark light*.

I also have the sense that these scientists have determined that there is much less hydrogen (fuel) and/or much less mass to the sun than they had previously expected. The world is going to become increasingly dark and cold.

But then the dark, nearly black light becomes blue/violet/purple. A blue sun, a beautiful aura of blue color bathes the world. I think of the color of the tail of the Peacock in alchemy.

In a letter to me he comments that he was left wondering whether the world were entering into a dark sun (apart, of course, from wondering about the personal meaning of the dream for his own life). Although it is not my intent to comment on this dream with regard to Romanyshyn's personal life, I would like to amplify it a bit by noting that in *The Soul in Grief: Love, Death, and Transformation,* he discusses the tragic death of his wife.[133] Unflinchingly, he lived through a most profound darkness and emerged with a sense of gratitude and the renewal of life. Likewise, in this dream, the darkness of Sol niger transforms into an array of colors associated with an alchemical symbol of transformation, the peacock's tail, or *cauda pavonis:* The peacock's tail in traditional alchemy is said to occur "immediately after the deathly black stage" of the *nigredo.* "After the *nigredo,* the blackened body of the Stone is washed and purified by the mercurial water during the process of *ablution.* When the blackness of the *nigredo* is washed away, it is succeeded by the appearance of all the colours of the rainbow, which looks like a peacock displaying its luminescent tail."[134]

This appearance is "a welcome sign that the dawning of the albedo is at hand, that the matter is now purified and ready for re-animation by the illuminated soul."[135] Looking at this image in the light of our exploration of Sol niger, it is not the case that when the nearly black light becomes a blue violet and/or purple sun bathing the world in color, that blackness disappears any more than the loss of a loved one ever vanishes, but that "blue is 'darkness made visible.'"[136] This is an idea reminiscent of Jung's now famous saying that "one does not become enlightened by imagining figures of light, but by making the darkness conscious." For Hillman, "the transit from black to white via blue implies that blue always brings black with it."[137]

The image in figure 5.8 emerged at the end of a long-term analysis of a woman artist. Suffering through the multiple mortifications that analysis requires to be successful allows a fuller flowering of the imagination, which shows itself here in a creative combination of peacock and owl feathers. The image emerged after a couple of dreams, the first about the end of a love affair and the second her "first flying dream ever."

Resonant with the cauda pavonis of alchemy, the image's multicolored eyes are prominent. For my patient, the eyes were cat's eyes and represented a more independent way of seeing that emerged after deep disillusionment. The owl feathers reminded her of night vision, of being able to see in the dark of the transcendence of the starred heavens, and of the goddess Athena, to whom the owl was sacred. The owl's eyes were Athena's eyes and as such became related to nocturnal studies, to the academy, and to wisdom. The owl also has many other mythological references, including a relationship to the dead sun and to healing.[138]

For Hillman, before healing can take place and the blackness of the nigredo can be transformed into the *terra alba,* or white earth, one must be able to see through multiple eyes and from many perspectives. From one point of view, the emergence of the white earth leaves the blackness behind, but as we have seen in numerous ways, the terra alba and the darkness against which it defines itself form an intimate and indissoluble relationship so that the white earth "is not sheer white in the literal sense but a field of flowers, a peacock's tail, a coat of many colors."[139]

Hillman explains that the multiple eyes of cauda pavonis reflect the full "flowering of imagination [that] shows itself as the qualitative spread of colors so that imagining is a coloring process, and if not in literal colors, then as the qualitative differentiation of intensities and hues which is essential to the art of imagination."[140]

Ultimately, for Hillman, these colors are not the same as in the subjectivist philosophies of Newton and Locke or of Berkeley and Hume, where colors are considered as only secondary qualities brought about by the mind and senses of the observer. Here he reverses the history of

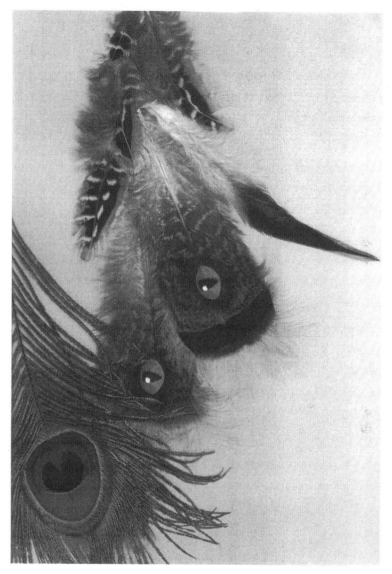

Figure 5.8. Variation of the peacock tail. Artwork by analysand. Used by permission.

philosophy. Color is now seen as a "primary quality" of the thing itself, not in a naturalistic sense but as "*phainoumenon* on display" at the heart of matter itself, prior to all abstraction.[141]

In my patient's image of cauda pavonis, the eyes become prominent. They look back at the dreamer, the artist, and us with an intensity that suggests we are living in an animated, conscious, living universe that not only we see but that also sees us. I remember Edinger once commenting that after years of analysis and looking at dreams, it occurred to him that the dreams also see us and that this is the awakening of what Jung meant by psychic reality. Hindu artists were well aware of this phenomenon as can be seen in the image of multiple perspectives and eyes we see in figure 5.9. It is with the constellation of psychic reality that psychological events come to life.

When my Jungian colleague Harry Wilmer heard I was working on a book on the black sun, he told me that he had been making yarn paintings and sewing on canvas since 1941 and that he had recently made one titled *The Black Hole* (color plate 17a). He sent me a picture of his image and stated that the band across the middle is the Milky Way and the large sphere in the right lower corner is the Earth. The row of lights are the aurora borealis, and the gray explosions are gases believed to be released at the event horizon.

Wilmer also commented that this image shows the ultimate black sun that we can expect when the end of time comes. He goes on: "At that time, theory tells us that the gigantic black hole will suck in the entire Milky Way, the Earth and our entire galaxy, including the Sun. . . . The red dot is the 'singularity,' the most dense gravitational body possible."[142]

I imagine Wilmer's vision as an ultimate Sol niger image, not reducible to either psychological or physical reality. His description is ominous and black, but his image is filled with color and life. I remembered an article in the *New York Times* by James Glanz. In the article Glanz describes how black holes have been seen as "windowless cosmic dungeons, ultracompressed objects with gravity so powerful that anything that plummets through their trapdoors—surfaces called event horizons enshrouding each one—is forever lost to the rest of the

Figure 5.9. The multiple eyes of psychic reality. From author's personal collection.

universe. Scientists believe that not even light beams can escape once they are inside."[143]

He goes on, however, to report a surprising, new find by astronomers who, using an X-ray observatory in orbit around the Earth, have discovered an intense glow, a glow with the intensity of ten billion suns, burning just outside the event horizon of a huge but very distant black hole (color plate 17b). In other words, for the first time, these astronomers have seen energy and light pouring out of a black hole and into the surrounding universe.

These observations have given rise to many speculations and probably will for the foreseeable future.[144] The interpenetration of darkness and light in Wilmer's vision and the paradox of the enigma of the black hole is reminiscent of a dream of Jung's, which he reported in a letter to Father Victor White on December 18, 1946.[145] The letter was written sometime after Jung had a second heart attack. Jung writes:

> It is a mightily lonely thing, when you are stripped of everything in the presence of God. One's wholeness is tested mercilessly. . . .
> I had to climb out of that mess and I am now whole again. Yesterday I had a marvelous dream: One bluish diamond, like a star high in heaven, reflected in a round quiet pool—heaven above, heaven below. The *imago Dei* in the darkness of the earth, this is myself. This dream meant a great consolation. I am no more a black and endless sea of misery and suffering but a certain amount thereof contained in a divine vessel.

In a similar fashion, at the end of his life

> the French poet Victor Hugo at the age of eighty three had a stroke. Four days later, during his death struggles, he, like Goethe, spoke of light, saying, "Here is the battle of day against night." Hugo's last words continued what in life he had always done: searching the darkest recesses of human nature for its brightest treasures. As he died he whispered, "I see black light."[146]

I read Jung's dream and Hugo's comment in the spirit of Lao Tzu, who wrote that "mystery and manifestation arise from the same source. This source is called darkness. . . . Darkness within darkness, the gateway to all understanding."[147]

I would like to end with a quote from Arthur ZaJonc, who wrote a book called *Catching the Light: The Entwined History of Light and Mind:* "As we leave light's expansive dominions, the heavens dim and darkness quietly falls. Within that darkness there is a silent murmur, a still voice that whispers of yet another and unsuspected part to light, for even utter darkness shimmers with its force."[148]

So our journey to the black sun ends with a whisper that began and ends in darkness, a darkness no longer light's contrary but a point of possibility in which light and dark both have their invisible origin, a simulacrum of substance in a world without foundations.

EPILOGUE

We began our exploration of the black sun as an experiment in alchemical psychology. It begins and ends with an enigma, with a movement from the nigredo of light to the mystery of an illuminated darkness. Imagined in juxtaposition to light, darkness casts a shadow and sets the stage for a new Faustian bargain, not with the forces of darkness but with the forces of light. In so doing, the primacy of light is declared, and the values of science, technology, rational order, patriarchy, and progress lead the way into modernity with its astonishing contributions to the spread of civilization and to consciousness itself. We have noted, however, that if light and the sun have led us into the present, it has also led to a massive repression and devaluation of the dark side of psychic and cultural life and displayed a blind spot with regard to vision itself. Philosophical and cultural critics of our time have pointed to the shadows of phallocentrism, logocentrism, and heliopolitics, driven by the violence of light, a condition we have considered psychologically and symbolized by a one-sided identification with King/ego and the tyrannical power of an undifferentiated, unconscious shadow. We have noted that the despotic King as prima materia must be relativized, and we have examined the alchemical phenomenology of the mortificatio in which this primitive King is tortured, beaten, humiliated, poisoned, drowned, dissolved, calcined, and killed.

These alchemical operations lead to a nigredo, or descent into darkness, that ultimately empties the soul and leaves only skeletal remains and the infernal light of Sol niger. Sol niger has been a difficult image to throw light upon since, like a black hole, it sucks all light into itself. Thus, in alchemy and, following it, in the depth psychology of Jung, the black sun has been associated with darkness almost exclusively.

Our strategy has been to stick with this image and to resist any salvationist attempt to reach beyond it. Rather, our work has been to hesitate before the darkness, to pause and enter its realm, following it in alchemy, literature, art, and clinical expressions. Entering this world of darkness, we have encountered Sol niger in its blacker-than-black aspects and seen its most literal and destructive dimensions associated with narcissistic mortification, humiliation, delusion, despair, depression, physiological and psychological decay, cancer, psychosis, suicide, murder, trauma, and death.

In short, we have followed it into the heart of darkness, into the worlds of Hades and Ereshkigal, to Kali's cremation ground and Dante's world of ice, where puer visions of light and eternity give way to Saturnian time and the perils of night. Here, rational order breaks down, and traumatogenic defenses come into play to prevent the unthinkable, but the unthinkable itself presents us with a mystery, the mystery of a death that is not simply literal, but also symbolic. Alchemy portrays such mysteries in a strange and paradoxical confluence of images: corpses and coffins with sprouting grains and black suns that shine. It is a mystery that calls for more than defense and constellates a necessity that must be entered. As such, we have conceived of it as an ontological pivot point, marking a desubstantiation of the ego that exhibits both death and new life, light and darkness, presence and absence, the paradoxical play intrinsic to Sol niger as a black sun.

For the alchemists, the unrepresentable can be perceived only by the inward person and was considered a mystery at the heart of nature itself. Its odd light, the lumen naturae, was considered to be a divine spark buried in darkness and could be found in both the prime matter of the alchemist's art and in the *soma pneumatikon*, or subtle body. We have traced the images of the subtle body in many esoteric traditions as well as in the imagery of contemporary patients.

For all of the traditions we have explored, the subtle body is a microcosm of a larger universe and an image of the divine in human form. This form has shown itself in symbols of the primordial human being, who, understood psychologically, is an expression of the Self. For Jung, the Self is an idea that attempts to reflect the wholeness of the human psyche. It is intended to designate a structure that includes both consciousness and the unconscious, light and dark, and was considered a central, ordering principle at the core of psychic life. The Self as a transcendental and superordinate structure cannot be made totally conscious. At its core, it was always considered to be an unknown mystery that disseminated itself in multiple archetypal images across time and culture. We have seen how these archetypal images more or less adequately represent the wholeness of the archetypal structure that they attempt to express. For Jung, the Self is a psychological lens through which to consider these expressions. These images, perhaps by necessity, always fall short of full expression of the archetype of wholeness. We have considered that the same limitations may apply to the concept of the Self.

Concepts as well as symbols of wholeness and expressions of totality have a tendency to degenerate and move toward abstraction as idealized and rational conceptualizations that seduce us into forgetting that they fundamentally reflect an unknown. With regard to the psyche, Jung writes, "The concept of the unconscious *posits nothing*, it designates only my *unknowing*."[1] We have noted the importance of preserving this mystery that constitutes the strangeness and miracle of perception at the heart of the mysterium coniunctionis. We have concluded that if we speak of unity or wholeness, it is important not to lose sight of stubborn differences and the monstrous complexities that, if true to the phenomenon, lead to humor, astonishment, and at times divine awe. As noted, the idea of the Self is Jung's attempt to capture this complexity, but as his theories became assimilated and familiar, his concept is subject to the same fate as all fundamental ideas. That is, they soon lose their original profundity, mystery, and unknown quality.

In our attempt to speak the unspeakable, we have noticed that the Self, too, casts a shadow, and we have focused on this shadow, recognizing the unnamable, invisible, and unthinkable core of the idea, which some have referred to as a Divine Darkness while others have called it a non-Self. The non-Self is not another name for the Self but is founded in the recognition of the problematics involved in any representation of wholeness and a mark for the profound expression of this mystery. All of the attempts to name this mystery might be said to leave traces in the language in which we have attempted to speak it. No signifier proves to be adequate to capture the fullness of human experience. The idea of the Self, like a shooting star of darkness, leaves a trail of metaphor in a variety of images inscribed in the margins of our experience. One might imagine these images as traces of silence at the heart of what we have imagined as the Self.

In an attempt to speak about the Self, we have sought to find innovative ways to preserve its mystery, paradox, and unknown quality. Borrowing from postmodern philosophy, the Self has been imagined as a ~~Self~~ under erasure, as an idea and image that has the mortificatio and self-deconstruction at its heart. Such a ~~Self~~ is always a non-Self also. It is a darkness that is light and a light that is darkness, and in this way of imagining it we have a glimpse of Sol niger.

Experientially, these two poles of the archetype, light and dark, are in an eternal embrace, crossing one another in a dance that might look like the structure of DNA. It appears to me now that Sol niger might be considered an archetypal image of the non-Self, having two integrated poles and multiple differentiations. At one end, the non-Self can be seen in its most literal form locked into the nigredo and the mortification of the flesh. Here the non-Self leans toward physical annihilation and literal death. At its other pole, however, the archetypal image is no longer confined to the nigredo and reflects itself in a different light, where annihilation is linked to both the presence of the void understood as absence, Eros, and self-forgetting and a majesty that sets the soul on fire.

In all, there is an alchemy and art in darkness, an invisible design rendering and rending vision, calling it to its sourceless possibility. The light of Western metaphysics has obscured darkness; sedimented reason has thrown it to the shadows, naming it only as its inferior counterpart. But darkness is also the Other that likewise shines; it is illuminated not by light but by its own intrinsic luminosity. Its glow is that of the lumen naturae, the light of nature, whose sun is not the star of heaven but Sol niger, the black sun.

NOTES

Introduction

1. Zenkei Shibayama, *Zen Comments on the Momonkan*, p. 28.
2. C. G. Jung, *Visions: Notes of the Seminar Given in 1930–1934*, vol. 2, ed. Claire Douglas, p. 1132.

Chapter 1

1. C. G. Jung, *C. G. Jung Speaking: Interviews and Encounters*, p. 228.
2. Ibid.
3. Ibid., p. 229.
4. C. G. Jung, *Mysterium Coniunctionis, Collected Works*, vol. 14, p. 255, para. 345.
5. C. G. Jung, *Memories, Dreams, Reflections*, p. 268.
6. Ibid.
7. Ibid., p. 269.
8. Ibid.
9. C. G. Jung, *Psychology and Alchemy, Collected Works*, p. 13, para. 14.
10. J. Hillman, "The Seduction of Black," p. 45.
11. J. Derrida, *The Margins of Philosophy*, p. 251.
12. M. Eliade, *Patterns of Comparative Religions*, p. 124.
13. Janet McCritchard, *Eclipse of the Sun: An Investigation into the Sun and the Moon Myths*.
14. Madronna Holden, "Light Who Loves Her Sister, Darkness," *Parabola* (Spring–Summer, 2001): 38.
15. R. Moore and D. Gillette, *King, Warrior, Magician, Lover: Rediscovering the Archetypes of the Mature Masculine*, p. 52.
16. D. Levin, *Modernity and the Hegemony of Vision*, p. 6.
17. Cf. J. Derrida, *Writing and Difference*, p. 84.
18. E. Edinger, *Anatomy of the Psyche*, p. 150.

19. Ibid., p. 148.

20. Ibid.

21. Edinger, *The Mysterium Lectures: A Journey through C. G. Jung's Mysterium Coniunctionis*, p. 20.

22. Stolcius, *Vividarium Chymicumm*, 1624.

23. Michael Maier, *Atlanta Fugiens*, 1618.

24. Edinger, *Anatomy of the Psyche*, p. 150.

25. Arthur Edward Waite, *The Hermetic Museum* (York Beach, Me.: Samuel Weiser, 1990), p. 278.

26. Edinger, *Anatomy of the Psyche*, p. 154.

27. Ibid.

28. Cf. Jung, "The Psychology of Transference."

29. L. Abraham, *A Dictionary of Alchemical Imagery*, p. 93.

30. Stanton Marlan, ed., *Salt and the Alchemical Soul: Three Essays by Ernest Jones, C. G. Jung, and James Hillman*, p. xxiv.

31. J. Hillman, "Silver and White Earth (Part Two)," p. 22.

32. Edinger, *Anatomy of the Psyche*, p. 156.

33. Jung, *Psychology and Alchemy*, p. 52, para. 61, ftn. 2.

34. Dante, *The Divine Comedy*, trans. by Lawrence White, p. 1.

35. Edinger, *Melville's Moby Dick: A Jungian Commentary*, p. 21.

36. Ibid.

37. Excerpt from T. S. Eliot, "The Hollow Men," in *Collected Poems 1909–1962* (New York: Harcourt, 1963).

38. Johannes Fabricius, *Alchemy: The Medieval Alchemists and Their Royal Art*, p. 103.

Chapter 2

1. Hillman, "The Seduction of Black," p. 50.

2. W. Rubin, preface to *Ad Reinhardt*, p. 29.

3. Edinger, *Melville's Moby Dick*, p. 21.

4. Jung, *Letters of C. G. Jung*, vol. 1, 1906–1950, ed. Gerhard Adler; trans. R. F. C. Hull. Feb. 28, 1932, p. 89.

5. Edinger, *Goethe's Faust: Notes for a Jungian Commentary*, p. 8.

6. Johann Wolfgang von Goethe, *Goethe, The Collected Works*, vol. 2, *Faust I & II*, translated by Stuart Atkins (Princeton: Princeton University Press, 1984), lines 354–76, 298–405, 410–17, 640–46, 664–67.

7. Hillman, "The Imagination of Air and the Collapse of Alchemy," p. 274.

8. Ibid.

9. Cf. Plato, *Phaedrus*, 246d-e.

10. Samuel Hazo. "The Feast of Icarus." *The Rest Is Prose*, p. 3.

11. Phillip Maverson, *Classical Mythology in Literature, Art, and Music*, p. 320.

12. Ibid.

13. Andrea De Pascalis, *Alchemy, the Golden Art*, p. 54, references Maier's 1617 text, *Symbola aureae mensae* for the same material.

14. Giles Clarke, "A Black Hole in Psyche," p. 67.

15. Ibid., p. 69.

16. Ibid.

17. R. D. Laing, *The Divided Self*, p. 204.

18. Von Franz, M.-L., *Alchemy: An Introduction to the Symbolism and the Psychology*, pp. 156–57.

19. Laing, *Divided Self*, p. 205.

20. T. Folly and I. Zaczek, *The Book of the Sun*, p. 112.

21. Hillman, "The Seduction of Black," p. 49.

22. G. Woolf, *Black Sun: The Brief Transit and Violent Eclipse of Harry Crosby*, p. 174.

23. E. Germain, *Shadows of the Sun: The Diaries of Harry Crosby*, p. 7.

24. Woolf, *Black Sun*, 197.

25. Ibid., p. 197–98.

26. Ibid., p. 198.

27. Ibid.

28. Quoted in J. Kristeva, *Black Sun: Depression and Melancholy*, p. 141.

29. Ibid., p. 13.

30. Ibid., p. 12.

31. Ibid., p. 151.

32. Ibid.

33. Ibid., p. 143.

34. Ibid.

35. Ibid., p. 144.

36. Cf. Hillman, "On Senex Consciousness," p. 24.

37. Cf. Jung, *Aion: Researches into the Phenomenology of the Self*, p. 911; Von Franz, *Alchemy*, p. 156.

38. Hillman, "On Senex Consciousness," p. 20.

39. Ibid., p. 21.
40. Gary Snyder, *Earth House Hold*, p. 118.
41. Steven Lonsdale also richly amplifies the deep origins of dance in his books *Animals and the Origins of Dance* and *Dance and Ritual Play in Greek Religion*.
42. V. S. Gregorian, A. Azarian, M. B. Demaria, and L. D. McDonald, "Colors of Disaster: The Psychology of the 'Black Sun,'" p. 1.
43. Ibid., p. 4.
44. Ibid.
45. Book of Joel 2:10 (Holy Bible: Revised Standard Version).
46. Revelations 6:12.
47. Gregorian, Azarian, Demaria, and McDonald, "Colors of Disaster," p. 13.
48. Ibid.
49. Jung, *Mysterium Coniunctionis*, p. 144, para. 172.
50. Dieter Martinetz and Karl Kernz Lohs, *Poison: Sorcery and Science, Friend and Foe*, p. 136.
51. *Outlines of Chinese Symbolism and Art Motives*, C. A. S. Williams (Rutland, Vt., and Tokyo: Charles E. Tuttle, 1974), p. 187.
52. Ibid.
53. Abraham, *A Dictionary of Alchemical Imagery*, pp. 26–27.
54. Silvia Brinton Perera, *Descent to the Goddess: A Way of Initiation for Woman*, p. 24.
55. Ibid., pp. 24–25.
56. Ajit Mookerjee, *Kali: The Feminine Force*, p. 61.
57. E. Harding, *Kali: The Black Goddess of Dakshineswar*, p. 38.
58. Swami Vivekananda, *In Search of God and Other Poems*, p. 25.
59. May Sarton, "The Invocation to Kali, part 2," courtesy of W.W. Norton & Co.
60. Hillman, *The Dream and the Underworld*, p. 168.
61. Helen Luke, *From Darkwood to White Rose Journey and Transformation in Dante's Divine Comedy*, p. 41.
62. E. M. Cioran, *On the Heights of Despair*. Note on back cover.
63. Ibid., p. 23–28.
64. Giegerich discusses the painful limitation in the chapter titled "No Admission" in *The Soul's Logical Life*.
65. Selection from Stephen Mitchell, trans., *The Book of Job*, p. 13–14.

Chapter 3

1. Edinger, *Anatomy of the Psyche,* p. 148.
2. In any case, for many alchemists, the boundaries between the images and overt reality were not so hard and fast as they are for modern consciousness.
3. R. Bosnak, *A Little Course in Dreams: A Basic Handbook of Jungian Dreamwork,* pp. 60–68.
4. Miriam Van Scott, *Encyclopedia of Hell,* p. 6.
5. P. Tatham, "A Black Hole in Psyche: One Personal Reaction," p. 122.
6. Ibid., p. 123.
7. Scott, *Encyclopedia of Hell,* p. 14.
8. William Blake, *The Book of Urizen,* from *The Complete Poetry and Prose of William Blake,* ed. by David V. Erdman (Berkeley: University of California Press, 1982), pp. 74, 75.
9. D. Kalsched, *The Inner World of Trauma: Archetypal Defenses of the Personal Spirit,* p. 1.
10. Ibid, p. 4, quotes L. Stein, "Introducing Not-Self," *Journal of Analytic Psychology* 12, no. 2 (1967): 97–113.
11. Ibid., p. 3.
12. Ibid., p. 4.
13. Ibid.
14. Ibid., p. 5.
15. Ibid.
16. For Kalsched, the self-care system is an archetypal defense structure composed of mythological images of "the progressed and regressed aspects of the psyche" in conflict, but "maintaining an energetic organization" (3).
17. Ibid., p. 4.
18. Ibid., p. 206
19. Ibid.
20. These considerations give rise to many compelling questions. For example, is the equation of the *personal* spirit with the Self in Jung's sense—something transcendent and partially beyond the psychic realm—an adequate one? Are the organizations of defenses protective of the Self or of the ego? Does the Self feel anxiety over trauma, or is anxiety, as Freud suggests, in the seat of the ego, which is then protected by archetypal processes of differing kinds? Does it make a difference who the "child" or "animal" is that's

being attacked? Can the child at times reflect an innocence that must be killed, as alchemy would have it, or is the animal the kind that likewise must die? Is every child of the psyche a "divine child" and every animal a reflection of the Self? Can the Self be killed? Does it die when a person dies? In raising these questions, I am implicitly suggesting my uncertainty over what Kalsched has described (important contribution though it is) as an adequate basis for understanding the archetypal meaning of Sol niger seen only through the eyes of defense.

21. Cf. Richard Booth, *Death and Desire: Psychoanalytic Theory in Lacan's Return to Freud*.

22. Rosen, *Transforming Depression*, p. xxvi.

23. Ibid., p. 34.

24. Cf. Rosen, *Transforming Depression*, p. 65.

25. Kalsched, *Inner World of Trauma*, p. 215.

26. Mark Welman, "Thanatos and Existence: Towards a Jungian Phenomenology of the Death Instinct," p. 123.

27. Ibid., p. 127.

28. Ibid., quoting Jung, *Memories, Dreams, and Reflections*.

29. Ibid., p. 128.

30. Cf. Hillman, *The Dream and the Underworld*, p. 64.

31. Ibid.

32. Ibid., p. 65.

33. Ibid., p. 49.

34. Ibid.

35. Ibid.

36. Ibid., p. 46.

37. Ibid., p. 47.

38. Ibid.

39. Ibid., p. 67.

40. Jung, "Psychology of Transference," p. 257.

41. Jung, "Psychology of Transference," in *Practice of Psychotherapy*, p. 265.

42. Jeffrey Raff, *Jung and the Alchemical Imagination*, p. 82.

43. Ibid., p. 80.

44. Stanislas Klossowski de Rola, *The Golden Game: Alchemical Engravings of the Seventeenth Century*, p. 8.

45. Ibid.

46. Edward Kelly, "The Terrestrial Astronomy of Kelly series," sixteen engravings, http://www.levity.com/alchemy/emblems.html (accessed May 7, 2004). The site author credits the image to Edward Kelly, *Tractatus duo egregii, de Lapide Philosophorum, una cum Theatro astronomica terrestri, cum Figuris, in gratiam filiorum Hermetis nunc primum in lucem editi, curante J. L. M. C (Johanne Lange Medicin Candito)*, Hamburg, 1676.

47. Adam McLean, ed., *The Hermetic Garden of Daniel Stolcius: Composed of Flowerlets of Philosophy Engraved in Copper and Explained in Short Verses Where Weary Students of Chemistry May Find a Treasure House and Refresh Themselves after Their Laboratory Work*, emblem 99.

48. Ibid., p. 108.

49. Ibid.

50. Mona Sanqvist, "Alchemy and Interart," p. 276.

51. Ibid.

52. J. Gage, *Color and Meaning: Art, Science, and Symbolism*, p. 234.

53. Ibid.

54. Cf. ibid., p. 235.

55. Ibid., p. 236.

56. Ibid., p. 240.

57. M. E. Warlick, *Max Ernst and Alchemy: A Magician in Search of Myth*, p. 1.

58. Anna C. Chave, *Mark Rothko: Subjects in Abstraction*, p. 181.

59. Ibid., p. 184.

60. Ibid.

61. Ibid., p. 196.

62. Ibid.

63. Ibid.

64. Ibid., p. 193.

65. Ibid.

66. Barbara Rose, *Art-as-Art: The Selected Writings of Ad Reinhardt*.

67. Ibid., p. 81.

68. Ibid.

69. Ibid., p. 82.

70. R. Smith, "Paint in Black: Ad Reinhardt at Moca," pp. 1, 9.

71. Naomi Vine. "Mandala and Cross: Ad Reinhardt's Black Paintings," pp. 124–33.

72. Ibid., p. 128.

73. D. Kuspit, "Negativity Sublime Identity: Pierre Soulages's Abstract Paintings."
74. Ibid.
75. Ibid., p. 17.
76. Robert Rauschenberg, "Black Painting," p. 136.
77. Meir Ronnen, "Kiefer on Kiefer: The Impossibility of Making an Image."
78. J. Flam, 1992, "The Alchemist."
79. Rafael Lopez-Pedraza, *Anselm Kiefer: The Psychology of "After the Catastrophe,"* p. 79.
80. Ibid., p. 82.
81. Ibid., p. 87.
82. Janet Towbin, *The Seduction of Black.* Artist's statement.

Chapter 4

1. Jung, *Alchemical Studies,* pp. 160–61.
2. Edinger, *Anatomy of the Psyche,* p. 20–21.
3. Abraham, *A Dictionary of Alchemical Imagery,* p. 5.
4. Indra Sinha, *Tantra: The Cult of Ecstasy,* p. 52.
5. Mookerjee, *Kali: The Feminine Force,* p. 64.
6. Edinger, *Anatomy of the Psyche,* p. 21, citing Jung, *Psychology and Alchemy,* paragraphs 484–85.
7. The process of the albedo is complex and has been the topic of many commentaries. See Edinger's *Anatomy of the Psyche* (40–41) for further elaboration. Also see Hillman's essays "Silver and White Earth," parts one and two, and Abraham's *Dictionary of Alchemical Imagery.*
8. Hillman, "Silver and White Earth," part two, p. 33.
9. Ibid., p. 34.
10. Jung, *Alchemical Studies,* p. 125.
11. Ibid., p. 126, citing Mylius, *Philosophia reformata,* p. 244.
12. Ibid., p. 131.
13. Derrida, *Disseminations,* p. 89.
14. Martin Jay, p. 510.
15. Derrida, *Writing and Difference,* p. 86. Derrida also cites Plato, *The Republic,* 508a–509.
16. Cf. Jung, *Alchemical Studies,* p. 125, paragraphs 161–63.
17. Corbin uses the term *mundus imaginalis* in his discussion of Sufi mysticism. Hillman picks it up in his elaboration of archetypal psychology. It refers to

an intermediary kind of imagination not reducible to either nature or spirit but residing instead in between as an intermediary phenomenon of the imaginal.

18. In *Archetypal Psychology: A Brief Account*, Hillman credits Corbin, who was primarily known for his interpretations of Islamic thought, for also being the "second immediate father" of *Archetypal Psychology* (3). In his own work, Hillman goes on to elaborate the notion of the mundus imaginalis.

19. Jung, "On the Nature of the Psyche," p. 195, quoting *Liber de Caducis*.

20. Kalsched, p. 64.

21. G. R. S. Mead, *The Doctrine of the Subtle Body in the Western Tradition*, p. 11.

22. In addition to Jung's work on the subtle body, the writing of Nathan Schwartz-Salant particularly makes use of the concept with regard to clinical practice. Cf. Schwartz-Salant, *The Mystery of the Human Relationship: Alchemy and the Transformation of the Self.*

23. James E. Siegel has put forth an interesting variation on the idea of the microcosm in "The Idea of the Microcosm: A New Interpretation." He states, in contrast or complement to Jung, "Whether or not the collective unconscious is a microcosm, the psyche in its entirety is a microcosm with the body as the earth element," and he feels that "this finding may have important consequences for our understanding of the human condition as well as for our appreciation of Jungian thought" (52). In that article he speaks of an inner sun and moon, inner weather and climate, inner oceanography, and so on and concludes that we reside in an inner world in which "the inner sun can be regulated to . . . access the unconscious and to influence if not control the inner weather. This article's microcosm concept is perhaps the opposite side of the same coin as analytical psychology, and it can perhaps help to further establish the reality of the psyche" (72).

24. Sanford Drob, *Symbols of the Kabbalah: Philosophical and Psychological Perspectives*, p. 186. Drob cites Giovanni Filoramo, *A History of Gnosticism*, p. 56.

25. Ibid., p. 187.

26. Ibid.

27. *Ezekiel* commentary, pp. 7–8.

28. Ibid., p. 188.

29. Since 1933 the Eranos meetings have been held annually in late August at the home of Olga Froebe-Kapteyn, at the northern end of Lago Maggiore near

Ascona, Switzerland. In this setting scholars from around the globe present their work. Lectures are delivered in German, English, Italian, and other languages, and these lectures are published in the form of the *Eranos Jahrbücher* [yearbooks]. Rudolf Otto suggested the Greek word *eranos*, which means a meal to which each person contributes a share. Jung was a regular and influential participant in these meetings. For more information, see the preface by Joseph Campbell in *Spirit and Nature: Papers from the Eranos Yearbooks* (New York: Pantheon Books/Bollingen Press, 1954).

30. A great deal of uncertainty exists about the origins of Jewish mysticism and Kabbalah. Gershom Scholem writes about this issue in his book *Origins of the Kabbalah*. He notes, "The question of the origin and early stages of the Kabbalah, that form of Jewish mysticism and theosophy that appears to have emerged suddenly in the thirteenth century, is indisputably one of the most difficult in the history of the Jewish religion after the destruction of the Second Temple" (3). Different traditions of Jewish mysticism have dated the origins to much earlier sources, but such attributions are difficult to authenticate.

31. Drob describes the sefirot as "the traits of God and the structural elements of the world" and notes that "they should be capable of providing us with insight into both God and the totality of the created world" (*Kabbalistic Metaphors*, p. 49).

32. Two sources for further elaboration of this theme are *The Tree of Life*; Chayyim Vital's *Introduction to the Kabbalah of Issac*; Luria's *Palace of Adam Kadmon*; and the *Gates of Light*, by Joseph Gikatilla.

33. From von Rosenroth, *Kabbala de Nudate*, Frankfurt, 1684; referenced by Kurt Seligman in *The History of Magic*.

34. Seligman, *History of Magic*, p. 352.

35. Drob, *Symbols of the Kabbalah*, p. 200.

36. Alex Grey, *Sacred Mirrors: The Visionary Art of Alex Grey*, p. 36.

37. Ibid.

38. David V. Tansley, *Subtle Body: Essence and Shadow*, p. 46.

39. "The halo is inscribed with signs of contemplation from six different paths: the symbols of Yin and Yang from Taoism; a description of the magnitude of Brahman from Hinduism; the watchword of the Jewish faith, 'Hear Oh Israel, the Lord our God, the Lord is One'; the Tibetan Buddhist mantra,

'Om Mani Padme Hum,' a prayer for the unfolding of the mind of enlightenment; Christ's words of the 'Lord's Prayer' in Latin; and a description of Allah along with the Islamic prayer, 'There is no God but God, and Muhammad is his messenger'" (Gray, *Sacred Mirrors*, opposite plate of "Praying"). Grey says he attempted in his image to depict the spiritual core of light that transcends, unites, and manifests in the various religious paths.

40. Phillip Rawson, *The Art of Tantra*, p. 154.

41. Rawson, *Art of Tantra*, p. 168.

42. Erwin Rouselle, "Spiritual Guidance in Contemporary Taoism."

43. Ibid., p. 75.

44. Little and Eichman, *Taoism*, p. 350.

45. Rousselle, "Spiritual Guidance," p. 71.

46. Cf. ibid., p. 83, 82.

47. *The White Cloud Daoist Temple*, p. 2.

48. This description of my visit to China is recounted in my article, "Jung in China: The First International Conference of Jungian Psychology and Chinese Culture. A Personal Account." *The Round Table Review* 6, no. 4 (March–April 1999): 24.

49. Little and Eichman, *Taoism*, p. 348. I also appreciate the help extended to me by Heyong Shen, professor of psychology, and Fu Jian Pinga, a respected specialist in classical Chinese culture at South China Normal University in Guang Zhov China, as well as Donald Sutton, professor of history at Carnegie Mellon University.

50. The most important of these was Huang Zhijie, a Taoism master of the Zhongyee Temple. Ren Farong, from Louguam Temple in Shaanxi, China, has written a book on the *I Ching* and internal alchemy in which he summarizes a lifetime of practice.

51. Stanton Marlan, "The Metaphor of Light and Renewal in Taoist Alchemy and Jungian Analysis," p. 266.

52. C. G. Jung, *Alchemical Studies*, p. 266, para. 337.

53. Rebekah Kenton, "A Kabbalistic View of the Chakras," at http://www .kabbalahsociety.org/ (accessed May 9, 2004).

54. P. Tatham, "A Black Hole in the Psyche: One Personal Reaction," p. 120.

55. G. Elder, *The Body: An Encyclopedia of Archetypal Symbolism: The Archive for Research in Archetypal Symbolism*, p. 411.

56. Von Franz, *Archetypal Dimensions of the Psyche*, p. 89.

57. Phillip Rawson and Laszlo Legeza, *Tao: The Chinese Philosophy of Time and Change*, p. 25.

58. Edinger, *Anatomy of the Psyche*, p. 211.

59. Ibid., p. 210.

60. Adam McClean discusses the important alchemical theme of bird symbolism in "The Birds in Alchemy." Moreover, Lyndy Abraham writes:

> Birds of all kinds appear in alchemical texts. The birth of the philosopher's stone from the union of the male and female substances at the chemical wedding is frequently compared to the birth of a bird or chick from the philosopher's egg or vessel. Some of the vessels in which this opus is carried out are named after birds: the pelican . . . , the cormorant and the stork. . . . The four main stages of the opus are likewise symbolized by birds: The black nigredo by the crow or raven, the multi-coloured or rainbow stage by the argus, peacock or peacock's tail, the white albedo by the swan or dove, and the red rubedo by the phoenix." (23)

61. Jung, *Psychology and Alchemy*, p. 243, para. 357. The images are located on pp. 245 and 257, respectively.

62. Cf. ibid., p. 256.

63. Jung, *Alchemical Studies*, figures 26 and 28.

64. Eden Gray, *A Complete Guide to the Tarot*, p. 34.

65. Ad de Vries, *Dictionary of Symbols and Imagery*.

66. Ibid., p. 319.

67. Ellen Frankel and Betsy Protkin-Teutsch, *The Encyclopedia of Jewish Symbols*, p. 98.

68. Ibid., p. 100.

69. Ibid.

70. Ananda Coomaraswamy, "The Inverted Tree."

71. Jung, *Alchemical Studies*, pp. 313–14.

72. Ibid., p. 311.

73. Ibid.

74. Ibid., p. 312. A similar resonance can be found in the pictograph of the Tao as pointed out in David Rosen's *Tao of Jung: The Way of Integrity*, pp. xvi–

xvii: "On the right side [of the pictograph] is a head with hair which is associated with heaven and interpreted as the beginning or source."

75. Ibid., p. 312n. 11, and 313.

76. From Prabhavananda and Isherwood, *Bhagavad-Gita*, p. 146. Quoted in Jung, *Alchemical Studies*, p. 313.

77. Hillman, "Senex and Puer" in *Puer Papers*, p. 30.

78. Cf. Mitchell Walker, "The Double: Same-Sex Inner Helper," pp. 48–52; Lyn Cowan, "Dismantling the Animus"; Claire Douglas, *The Woman in the Mirror: Analytical Psychology and the Feminine*; Christine Downing, *Myths and Mysteries of Same-Sex Love*; and Claudette Kulkarni, *Lesbians and Lesbianism: A Post-Jungian Perspective*.

79. Hillman, *A Blue Fire: Selected Writings of James Hillman*, p. 82.

Chapter 5

1. Jung, *Psychology and Alchemy*, p. 82, para. 112.

2. De Pascalis, *Alchemy: The Golden Art*, p. 32.

3. Ibid.

4. Jung, "Concerning the Self," p. 11.

5. Cf. Jung, *Psychology and Alchemy*, p. 82.

6. Jung, "Concerning the Self," p. 12.

7. Ibid.

8. Ibid.

9. Ibid.

10. Ibid., p. 16.

11. Ibid., p. 19.

12. Ibid., p. 20.

13. Jung and Edinger both attempt to deal with this apparent paradox. Edinger quotes Jung's *Mysterium Coniunctionis*:

> I must point out to the reader that these remarks on the significance of the ego might easily prompt him to charge me with grossly contradicting myself. He will perhaps remember that he has come across a very similar argument in my other writings. Only there it was not a question of ego but of the *self*. . . . I have defined the self as the totality of the conscious and the unconscious psyche, and the ego as the central reference-point of consciousness. It is an essential part of the self,

and can be used *pars pro toto* [part for the whole] when the significance of consciousness is borne in mind. But when we want to lay emphasis on the psychic totality it is better to use the term "self." There is no question of a contradictory definition, but merely of a difference of standpoint. (*Mysterium Lectures,* 93, para. 133)

Edinger himself goes on to note the following: "So the sun as the symbol of consciousness represents both the ego and the Self. The reason for that double representation is that the Self cannot come into conscious, effective existence except through the agency of an ego. Needless to say it can come into plenty of effective existence without an ego but it can't come into *consciously* effective existence without the agency of an ego. That's why it is unavoidable that the symbolism of Sol, as the principle of consciousness, represents both the ego and the Self" (94).

14. Niel Micklem, *Jung's Concept of the Self: Its Relevance Today,* papers from the public conference organized in May, 1990, by the Jungian Postgraduate Committee of the British Association of Psychotherapists.

15. Niel Micklem, "I Am Not Myself: A Paradox," in *Jung's Concept of the Self: Its Relevance Today,* papers from the public conference organized in May, 1990, by the Jungian Postgraduate Committee of the British Association of Psychotherapists, p. 7.

16. Ibid., p. 8.

17. Ibid.

18. Ibid.

19. Ibid., pp. 8–9.

20. Ibid., p. 10.

21. The coniunctio has been described as "an alchemical symbol of a union of unlike substances; a marrying of the opposites in an intercourse which has as its fruition the birth of a new element. . . . From Jung's point of view, the coniunctio was identified as the central idea of alchemical process. He himself saw it as an archetype of psychic functioning, symbolizing a pattern of relationships between two or more unconscious factors. Since such relationships are at first incomprehensible to the perceiving mind, the coniunctio is capable of innumerable symbolic projections (i.e., man and woman, king and queen, dog and bitch, cock and hen, Sol and Luna)." From A. Samuels, B. Shorter, and F. Plaut's *Critical Dictionary of Jungian Analysis,* p. 35.

22. Micklem, "I Am Not Myself," p. 11.

23. Cf. Edinger, *Mysterium Lectures*, p. 132.

24. Ibid., p. 134.

25. Ibid., pp. 134–35.

26. Jung, *Alchemical Studies*, caption below frontispiece.

27. Ibid.

28. Edinger, *Mysterium Lectures*, p. 135.

29. Ibid., p. 135.

30. Ibid., p. 136.

31. Hillman, "Silver and the White Earth (Part Two)," p. 56.

32. Hillman, "Peaks and Vales," p. 57.

33. Hillman, "Silver and the White Earth (Part Two)," pp. 56–67.

34. Ibid., p. 57.

35. Ibid.

36. From "The Secret of Freedom," verse 1, in *The Secret of the Golden Flower: The Classic Chinese Book of Life*, trans. by Thomas Cleary, p. 39.

37. Ross, Nancy Wilson, *The World of Zen: An East-West Anthology*, p. 259.

38. From poem, "Immortal Sisters," by Sun Bu-er, in Cleary, *Secret of the Golden Flower*, p. 103.

39. Ibid., pp. 41–42.

40. Ibid., p. 101.

41. Oscar Mandel, *Chi Po and the Sorcerer: A Chinese Tale for Children and Philosophers*.

42. Ibid., pp. 25–27.

43. Edinger, *Anatomy of the Psyche*, p. 165.

44. Ibid., p. 167.

45. Jung, *Mysterium Coniunctionis*, p. 546, para. 778.

46. Edinger, *Anatomy of the Psyche*, 167.

47. Ibid., p. 168.

48. Hillman, *Archetypal Psychology: A Brief Account*, p. 18.

49. Cf. Hillman, "The Seduction of Black," p. 45. The word "alchemy" is said to derive from the root *khem* or *chemia* [black] and to refer to Egypt, the land of black soil.

50. *The American Heritage Dictionary of the English Language*, 3d ed. (Boston, New York, and London: Houghton-Mifflin Press, 1992).

51. M. Merleau-Ponty, *Phenomenology of Perception*, p. 228.

52. Ibid., p. 229.

53. Fabricius, *Alchemy*, p. 60.

54. Ilan Chelners, *Oxford Dictionary of Twentieth-Century Art*, p. 399.

55. Jung, *Mysterium Coniunctionis*, pp. 247–48, para. 332.

56. Julia Kristeva, *Black Sun: Depression and Melancholia*, p. 147.

57. From personal correspondence, although the pastor is quoting Kallistos Ware in *The Orthodox Way*.

58. E. Stein, *Knowledge and Faith*, p. 87.

59. Pseudo-Dionysius the Areopagite, *Pseudo-Dionysius: The Complete Works*, p. 265.

60. Pseudo-Dionysius, *The Mystical Theology and the Celestial Hierarchies*, p. 9.

61. Pseudo-Dionysius, *Pseudo-Dionysius*, p. 132.

62. Ibid., p. 136, citing Bartholemew.

63. Pseudo-Dionysius, "The Mystical Theology," in *Pseudo-Dionysius: The Complete Works*, p. 141.

64. Even when the Divinity is not able to be called forth in manifestation and remains silent, the Divine essence is "present." Jung notes, "Summoned and not summoned, God will be there" (Jung, *Memories, Dreams, Reflections*, illustration 13, p. xviii).

65. Cf. Hillman, "Silver and the White Earth," part one, p. 21.

66. See *Collected Poems of Theodore Roethke*, p. 31.

67. M. Stein, *Jung's Map of the Soul: An Introduction*, p. 154, quoting Jung, *Memories, Dreams, and Reflections*.

68. C. G. Jung, *Aion, Collected Works*, vol. 9ii.

69. Roger Brooke, *Jung and Phenomenology*, p. 131.

70. D. Miller, "Nothing Almost Sees Miracles! Self and No-Self in Psychology and Religion," p. 15.

71. Ibid., p. 14, quoting Jung, *Mysterium Coniunctionis*, para. 190.

72. Cf. ibid., p. 13.

73. Ibid., p. 15.

74. Sean Kelly, "Atman, Anatta, and Transpersonal Psychology," pp. 188–99.

75. Ibid., p. 197.

76. Ibid., p. 198.

77. Jung also uses the word "complementarity," which for him was a bit too mechanical and functional and for which compensation is "a psychological refinement" ("On the Nature of the Psyche," p. 287).

78. Cf. Hillman, *The Myth of Analysis*, pp. 207–208.

79. Hillman, "Peaks and Vales," p. 67.

80. Lacan's "petite a" is a profoundly polyvalent concept and the subject of literally thousands of pages of exegesis in Lacan's work. That said, Bruce Fink discusses it in terms of "the residue of symbolization—the real that remains, insists, and ex-sists after or despite symbolization—as the traumatic cause, and as that which interrupts the smooth functioning of law and the automatic unfolding of the signifying chain" (Bruce Fink, *The Lacanian Subject: Between Language and Jouissance*, p. 83).

81. Jung, *Mysterium Coniunctionis*, p. 98, para. 117.

82. Ibid., p. 97, para. 117.

83. Derrida, "How to Avoid Speaking: Denials," in *Languages of the Unsayable: The Play of Negativity in Literature and Literary Theory*, p. 4.

84. Derrida, *Of Grammatology*, p. xvii.

85. Ibid., p. 19.

86. Cf. Stuart Sim, *Derrida and the End of History*.

87. Hillman, "Concerning the Stone: Alchemical Images of the Goal," p. 256.

88. Ibid.

89. Simon Critchley and Peter Dews, eds., *Deconstructive Subjectivities*, pp. 25–26.

90. Ibid.

91. Murray Stein, *Jung's Map of the Soul*, p. 152.

92. Ibid.

93. Cf. Critchley and Dews, *Deconstructive Subjectivities*, p. 26.

94. Lévinas, for instance, criticizes Heidegger's transsubjective concept of *Dasein* by noting that "Dasein is never hungry" (Critchley and Dews, p. 30), and Hillman chooses to rely on the word "soul" as opposed to Self because it retains a connection with the body, with physical and emotional concerns above love and loss, life and death. "It is experienced as a living force having a physical location" and is more easily expressed in psychological, metaphoric and poetic descriptions (Hillman, *The Myth of Analysis*, p. 207).
    Both Lévinas and Hillman share a number of overlapping concerns. Both are critical of the primacy of a theoretical model of consciousness in which the subject maintains an objectifiying relation to the world mediated through representation. Both support a movement toward a revisioned subject as an embodied being of flesh and blood, a subject who is fully sen-

tient and in touch with sensation and who is "vulnerable" and "open to wounding" (E. Lévinas, *Otherwise than Being or Beyond Essence*, p. 15), filled with "*jouissance* and *joie de vivre*" (Critchely and Dews, p. 29).

In addition, both Lévinas and Hillman share a unique, ethical sensibility. For Lévinas, ethics is fundamental, and the entire thrust of his *Otherwise than Being* is to "found ethical subjectivity in sensibility and to describe sensibility as a proximity to the other" (ibid., p. 30). What this means for Lévinas is very different from our usual understanding of ethics. For him, "Ethics is not an obligation toward the other mediated through" formal principles or "good conscience." Moral consciousness is not an experience of values but an access to exterior being—to what he calls the Other. From a psychological point of view, this begins to sound like the capacity to see beyond our narcissistic self-enclosure and actually to have contact with something outside of our own egos. The subject is subject to something that exceeds us (ibid., p. 26). The "deep structure of subjective experience"—the responsibility or responsivity to the other—is what Lévinas calls Psyche (ibid., p. 31). Likewise, the thrust of Hillman's archetypal psychology is a movement beyond the narcissistic enclosure in which the aim is a "psychotherapeutic cure of 'me,'" in which all the me-ness has been cooked out of our emotions (Hillman, "Concerning the Stone," p. 259).

This comparison of Lévinas with Hillman is not meant in any way to equate their thought. A real comparison of their work would require an independent study of what each thinker means by terms they use in common. For instance, the subject for Lévinas is an embodied "me" and nobody else, whereas, as we have seen, for Hillman the "me" is what is to be "cured" and "cooked." This may or may not be more than a terminological difference since, for both, the "psyche" is not an instance of some general concept or genus of the human being: an ego, self-consciousness, or thinking thing, and "both move beyond a concept of an abstract and universal 'I.'"

For Lévinas, the subject is not hard and autonomous but soft, weak, passive, sensual, and fleshy. In Jungian terms, such a subject is one who has integrated the feminine, the *anima*, the soul. In *The Myth of Analysis*, Hillman puts it this way: "[P]sychotherapy achieves its ultimate goal in the wholeness of the conjunction [in the] incarnation of durable weakness and unheroic strength" (p. 293). For him this means an end to the "repudiation of femininity" and a termination of misogyny, when we "take Eve back into

Adam's body, when we are no longer decided about what is . . . inferior, what superior, what exterior, what interior; when we have taken on and taken in all those qualities not *per se* female but which have been projected onto women and seen as inferior." To take back this "inferiority" leads toward the therapeutic goal of the coniunctio, which would now be experienced as a weakening—rather than an increase—of consciousness. This means "the sacrifice of the mind's bright eye" and a "loss of what we have long considered to be our most precious human holding: Apollonian consciousness" (ibid., p. 295). Since women as well as men are subject to the influences of modernism, their consciousness can likewise be dominated by Apollonian identifications, and a similar integration of anima values can lead to a coniunctio that sacrifices the bright eye, which stands above its objects in a specular way. Hillman and others have stated that the anima is linked not only to the psyche of men (Hillman, *Anima: An Anatomy of a Personified Notion*, pp. 53–55).

"A therapy that would move toward this coniunctio would be obliged to stay always within the mess of ambivalence, the comings and goings of the libido, letting interior movement replace clarity, interior closeness replace objectivity, the child of psychic spontaneity replace literal right action" (Hillman, *Myth of Analysis*, p. 295).

In Hillman's emphasis on closeness, movement beyond objectivity, and spontaneity, his thought resonates with that of Lévinas. The subject Hillman describes is resonant with Lévinas's postdeconstructive subjectivity of a "subject *after* deconstruction" (Critchely and Dews, p. 39).

95. Edinger, *Anatomy of the Psyche*, p. 148, quoting *The Lives of the Alchemystical Philosophers*, p. 145.
96. Ibid., p. 149, quoting Paracelsus, *Hermetic and Alchemical Writings*, 1:153.
97. Hillman, "Seduction of Black," p. 49.
98. Cf. ibid., pp. 49–52.
99. Hillman, "Concerning the Stone," p. 243.
100. Hillman, "Alchemical Blue and the *Unio Mentalis*," in C. Eshleman, ed., *Sulfur I: A Literary Tri-Quarterly of the Whole Art*, p. 36.
101. Cf. Hillman, "Concerning the Stone," pp. 261, 265.
102. Hillman, "Alchemical Blue," p. 35.
103. Hillman, "Silver and the White Earth (Part Two)," pp. 33–34.
104. Hillman, "The Yellowing of the Work," p. 78.

105. Hillman, "Concerning the Stone: Alchemical Images of the Goal," p. 243.

106. Ibid.

107. Ibid.

108. Hillman, "Alchemical Blue and the *Unio Mentalis*," p. 41.

109. Gage, *Color and Meaning*, p. 239.

110. Toni Morrison, *The Song of Solomon*, p. 40.

111. Hillman, *Seduction of Black*, p. 51.

112. J. Brozostoski, "Tantra Art."

113. Jung, *Psychology and Alchemy*, pp. 105–106. Jung evaluates three printed editions of the *Tractatus aureus* and concludes that the proper translation of Hermes/Venus's comment is 'I beget the light, and darkness is not my nature . . . therefore no thing is better or more worthy of veneration than the conjunction of myself and my brother.'

114. Stanislav Grof, *LSD Psychotherapy*, p. 283.

115. Cf. W. Giegerich, *The Soul's Logical Life*, p. 61.

116. Hillman, *Dreams and the Underworld*, p. 34.

117. Scheper, G., "Illumination and Darkness in the Song of Songs."

118. Henry Corbin, *The Man of Light in Iranian Sufism*, p. 108.

119. Shikiko Izutsu, "The Paradox of Light and Darkness in the Garden of Mystery of Shabastori," pp. 300–301.

120. A further elaboration of black light and luminous night has been written by Tom Cheetham in an article titled "Black Light: Hades, Lucifer, and the Secret of the Secret, a Contribution to the Differentiation of Darkness."

121. Ibid., pp. 303–304.

122. Ibid., p. 304.

123. Shunryu Suzuki, *Branching Streams Flow in the Darkness: Zen Talks on the Sandokai*.

124. Ibid., p. 111.

125. Paul Murray, "Canticle of the Void," pp. 25–27.

126. T. S. Eliot, *Four Quartets*.

127. Paul Celan, "Psalm," in *Selected Poems and Prose of Paul Celan*. My thanks go to Peter Thompson.

128. Josef V. Schneersohn and Uri Menachem Schneersohn, *Basi LeGani: Chasidic Discourses*, p. 24.

129. Personal correspondence, April 11–15, 2001.

130. Personal correspondence, April 11–15, 2001.

131. Personal correspondence, April 11–15, 2001.

132. Personal communication. Bitzalel Malamud is a Hasid who specialized in the study of an untranslatable Chasidic work titled *The Mitzava Is a Candle and the Tora Is a Light,* subtitled *The Gate of Unity* by Mittler Rebbe (Dov Ber of Lubavitch). This text has an extensive commentary by Reb Hillel.

133. Robert Romanyshyn, *The Soul in Grief: Love, Death, and Transformation.*

134. Abraham, *A Dictionary of Alchemical Imagery,* pp. 141–42.

135. Ibid.

136. Hillman, "Alchemical Blue and the *Unio Mentalis,*" p. 37.

137. Ibid., p. 35.

138. Ad de Vries, *Dictionary of Symbols and Imagery,* pp. 353–54.

139. Hillman, "Alchemical Blue and the *Unio Mentalis,*" p. 41.

140. Ibid.

141. Ibid.

142. Personal letter from Harry Wilmer, Dec. 24, 2002. He references Kip Thorn in his book *Black Holes and Time Warps: Einstein's Outrageous Legacy.*

143. James Glanz, "Bright Glow May Change Dark Reputation of Black Hole."

144. This image is an artist's rendition of recent observations. "Artist's View of Black Hole and Companion Star GRO J1655-40," at http://hubblesite.org/newscenter/archive/2002/30/image/a (accessed May 10, 2004).

145. Jung, *C. J. Jung Letters,* vol. 1, *1906–1950,* pp. 449–50.

146. Arthur ZaJouc, *Catching the Light: The Entwined History of Light and Mind,* pp. 325–26.

147. Ibid., p. 325.

148. Ibid.

Epilogue

1. Jung to Max Frischknect, Feb. 8, 1946, in *Letters of C. G. Jung,* p. 411.

BIBLIOGRAPHY

Abraham, Lyndy. *A Dictionary of Alchemical Imagery*. Cambridge: Cambridge University Press, 1998.

Barnes, Susan. *The Rothko Chapel: An Act of Faith*. Houston: Rothko Chapel, 1989.

Blake, William. *The Book of Urizen*. London, 1794.

Book of Joel. *The Holy Bible: Revised Standard Version*. New York: Thomas Nelson and Sons, 1953.

Booth, Richard. *Death and Desire: Psychoanalytic Theory in Lacan's Return to Freud*. New York: Routledge, 1991.

Bosnak, R. *A Little Course in Dreams: A Basic Handbook of Jungian Dreamwork*. Boston: Shambhala, 1986/1988.

Brewer, B. *Eclipse*. Seattle: Earthview, 1978/1991.

Brooke, Roger. *Jung and Phenomenology*. New York: Routledge, 1991.

————, ed. *Pathways into the Jungian World: Phenomenology and Analytic Psychology*. London and New York: Routledge, 2000.

Brzostoski, J. "Tantra Art." *Arts Magazine*. New York,: Art Publishers, [n.d.].

Cabala Mineralis Manuscript. http://www.levity.com/alchemy/cab_min1.htm (accessed September 2, 2004).

Cavendish, Richard, ed. *Man, Myth, and Magic: An Illustrated Encyclopedia of the Supernatural*, vol. 20. New York: Marshall Cavendish, 1970.

Celan, Paul. "Psalm." In *Selected Poems and Prose of Paul Celan*, trans. John Felstiner. New York: W. W. Norton, 2001.

Chave, Anna C. *Mark Rothko: Subjects in Abstraction*. New Haven: Yale University Press, 1989.

Cheetham, Tom. "Black Light: Hades, Lucifer, and the Secret of the Secret: A Contribution to the Differentiation of Darkness." *Spring 68: A Journal of Archetype and Culture*. Woodstock, Conn.: Spring Publications, 2001.

Chelners, Ilan. *Oxford Dictionary of Twentieth-Century Art*. New York: Oxford University, 1998.

Cioran, E. M. *On the Heights of Despair,* trans. Ilinca Zarifopol-Johnston. Chicago: University of Chicago Press, 1992. Originally published in the *Boston Phoenix.*

Clarke, Giles. "A Black Hole in Psyche." *Harvest* 29 (1983):67–80.

Cleary, Thomas, trans. *The Secret of the Golden Flower: The Classic Chinese Book of Life.* San Francisco: HarperSanFrancisco, 1991.

Coomaraswamy, Ananda. "The Inverted Tree." *Quarterly Journal of the Mythic Society* 29, no 2 (n.d.): 111–49.

Corbin, Henry. *The Man of Light in Iranian Sufism.* Boulder: Shambhala, 1978.

Cowan, Lyn. "Dismantling the Animus." Lecture originally delivered in October, 1991; later revised and expanded into an unpublished paper.

Critchley, Simon, and Peter Dews, eds. *Deconstructive Subjectivities.* Albany: State University of New York Press, 1996.

Dante. *The Divine Comedy,* trans. Lawrence Grant White. New York: Pantheon, 1948.

De Pascalis, Andrea. *Alchemy, The Golden Art: The Secrets of the Oldest Enigma.* Rome: Gremese International, 1995.

Derrida, J. *Disseminations,* trans. Barbara Johnson. Chicago: University of Chicago Press, 1981.

———. "How to Avoid Speaking: Denials." In *Languages of the Unsayable: The Play of Negativity in Literature and Literary Theory,* ed. Sanford Budick and Wolgang Iser. New York: Columbia University Press, 1989.

———. *The Margins of Philosophy,* trans. Alan Bass. Chicago: University of Chicago Press, 1982.

———. *Of Grammatology,* trans. Gayatri Spivak. Baltimore: Johns Hopkins University Press, 1967/1997.

———. *Writing and Difference,* trans. Alan Bass. Chicago: University of Chicago Press, 1967/1976.

de Vries, Ad. *Dictionary of Symbols and Imagery.* Amsterdam: Worth Holland, 1974.

Douglas, Claire. *The Woman in the Mirror: Analytical Psychology and the Feminine.* Boston: Sigo, 1990.

Downing, Christine. *Myths and Mysteries of Same-Sex Love.* New York: Continuum; Boston: Sigo, 1989.

Drob, Sanford. *Symbols of the Kabbalah: Philosophical and Psychological Perspectives*. Northvale, N.J.: Jason Aronson, 2000.

———. *Kabbalistic Metaphors: Jewish Mystical Themes in Ancient and Modern Thought*. Northvale, N.J.: Jason Aronson, 2000.

Edinger, Edward F. *Anatomy of the Psyche: Alchemical Symbolism in Psychotherapy*. LaSalle, Ill.: Open Court, 1985.

———. *Goethe's Faust: Notes for a Jungian Commentary*. Toronto: Inner City Books, 1990.

———. *Melville's Moby-Dick: A Jungian Commentary: An American Nekyia*. New York: New Directions, 1975.

———. *The Mysterium Lectures: A Journey through C. G. Jung's Mysterium Coniunctionis*. Toronto: Inner City Books, 1995.

Elder, George. *The Body: An Encyclopedia of Archetypal Symbolism: The Archive for Research in Archetypal Symbolism*. Boston: Shambhala, 1996.

Eliade, M. *Patterns of Comparative Religions*, trans. Rosemary Sheed. New York and Cleveland: Meridian, World Publishing, 1958/1971.

Eliot, T. S. *Four Quartets*. New York: Harcourt, Brace, 1943.

Eshleman, C., ed. *Sulfur I: A Literary Tri-Quarterly of the Whole Art*. Pasadena: California Institute of Technology Press, 1981.

Fabricius, Johannes. *Alchemy: The Medieval Alchemists and Their Royal Art*. London: Diamond Books, 1994.

Filoramo, Giovanni. *A History of Gnosticism*, trans. A. Alcock. Cambridge: Basil Blackwell, 1990.

Fink, Bruce. *The Lacanian Subject: Between Language and Jouissance*. Princeton: Princeton University Press, 1995.

Fisch, S. *Ezekiel*. London: Soncino Press, 1950/1968.

Flam, J. "The Alchemist." *New York Review*, February 13, 1992.

Folly, T., and I. Zaczek. *The Book of the Sun*. Philadelphia: Courage Books, 1997.

Frankel, Ellen, and Betsy Plotkin-Teutsch. *The Encyclopedia of Jewish Symbols*. London: Jason Aronson, 1992.

Gage, John. *Color and Meaning: Art, Science, and Symbolism*. Berkeley: University of California Press, 1999.

Germain, E. *Shadows of the Sun: The Diaries of Harry Crosby*. Santa Barbara: Black Sparrow Press, 1977.

Giegerich, W. *The Soul's Logical Life*. Frankfurt: Peter Lang, 1998.

Gihalilla, Joseph. *Gates of Light,* trans. and introduction by Avi Weinstein. San Francisco: Harper Collins, 1994.

Glanz, James. "Bright Glow May Change Dark Reputation of Black Hole." *New York Times,* October 22, 2001.

Goethe, Johann Wolfgang. *Goethe, The Collected Works,* vol. 2, *Faust I & II.* Translated by Stuart Atkins. Princeton: Princeton University Press, 1994.

Gray, Eden. *A Complete Guide to the Tarot.* New York: Crown, 1970.

Gregorian, V. S., A. Azarian, M. B. Demaria, and L. D. McDonald. "Colors of Disaster: The Psychology of the 'Black Sun.' " *The Arts in Psychotherapy* 23, no. 1 (1996): 1–14.

Grey, Alex. *Sacred Mirrors: The Visionary Art of Alex Grey.* With essays by Ken Wilbur, Carlo McCormick, and Alex Grey. Rochester, Vt.: Inner Traditions International, 1990.

Grof, Stanislav. *LSD Psychotherapy.* Pomona, Calif.: Hunter House, 1980.

Halevi, Z'ev ben Shimon. *Kabbalah: Tradition of Hidden Knowledge.* London: Thames and Hudson, 1979.

Harding, E. *Kali: The Black Goddess of Dakshineswar.* York Beach, Me.: Nicholas-Hays, 1993.

Hawley, J., and D. Wulff. *Devi: Goddess of India.* Berkeley: University of California Press, 1966.

Hazo, Samuel. "The Feast of Icarus." *The Rest Is Prose.* Pittsburgh: Duquesne University Press, 1980.

Hillman, J. *Anima: An Anatomy of a Personified Notion.* Dallas: Spring Publications, 1985.

———. *Archetypal Psychology: A Brief Account.* Dallas: Spring Publications, 1983.

———. *A Blue Fire: Selected Writings of James Hillman.* New York: Harper and Row, 1989.

———. "Concerning the Stone: Alchemical Images of the Goal." *Sphinx 5: A Journal for Archetypal Psychology and the Arts,* ed. Noel Cobb with Eva Loewe. (1993): 234–65.

———. *The Dream and the Underworld.* New York: Harper and Row, 1979.

———. "The Imagination of Air and the Collapse of Alchemy." In *Eranos Yearbook.* Frankfurt: Insel, 1981.

———. *The Myth of Analysis: Three Essays in Archetypal Psychology.* Evanston, Ill.: Northwestern University Press, 1972.

————. "On Senex Consciousness." In *Fathers and Mothers,* ed. P. Berry, 18–36. Dallas: Spring Publications, 1990.

————. "The Seduction of Black." In *Fire in the Stone: The Alchemy of Desire,* ed. and introduction by Stanton Marlan, 42–53. Wilmette, Ill.: Chiron, 1997.

————. "Silver and White Earth, Part Two." *Spring* (1980): 21–63.

————. "The Yellowing of the Work." In *Paris '89: Proceedings of the Eleventh Congress for Analytical Psychology,* ed. M. A. Mattoon, 77–102. Einsiedeln, Switzerland: Daimon, 1991.

Holden, Madronna. "Light Who Loves Her Sister, Darkness." *Parabola* (Spring–Summer, 2001).

Izutsu, Toshihiko. "The Paradox of Light and Darkness in the Garden of Mystery of Shabastori." In *Anagogic Qualities of Literature,* ed. Joseph Strelka, 288–307. University Park: Pennsylvania State University Press, 1971.

Jay, Martin. *Downcast Eyes: The Denigration of Vision in Twentieth-Century French Thought.* Chicago: University of Chicago Press, 1994.

Jung, Carl Gustav. *Aion: Researches into the Phenomenology of the Self.* Princeton: Princeton University Press, 1959.

————. *Alchemical Studies: Collected Works,* vol. 13, trans. R. F. C. Hull. Princeton: Princeton University Press, 1967.

————. "Concerning the Self," trans. Hildegard Nagel. *Spring* (1951). Reprint, Nendeln, Liechtenstein: Kraus, 1977.

————. *Letters of C. G. Jung,* vol. 1, 1906–1950, ed. Gerhard Adler; trans. R. F. C. Hull. Princeton: Princeton University Press, 1973.

————. *Memories, Dreams, Reflections,* recorded and ed. Aniela Jaffé; trans. Richard Winston and Clara Winston. New York: Pantheon, 1961/1983.

————. *Mysterium Coniunctionis: Collected Works,* vol. 14. Princeton: Princeton University Press, 1955/1963.

————. "On the Nature of the Psyche." In *The Structure and Dynamics of the Psyche.* Princeton: Princeton University Press, 1960/1969.

————. *Psychology and Alchemy: Collected Works,* vol. 12, trans. R. F. C. Hull. Princeton: Princeton University Press, 1953/1968.

————. *Psychology and Religion: West and East.* Princeton: Princeton University Press, 1958/1963.

————. "The Psychology of Transference." In *The Practice of Psychotherapy: Collected Works,* vol. 16. Princeton: Princeton University Press, 1954/1966.

―――. *Visions: Notes of the Seminar Given in 1930–1934*, vol. 2, ed. Claire Douglas. Princeton, N.J.: Princeton University Press, 1997.

Kalsched, D. *The Inner World of Trauma: Archetypal Defenses of the Personal Spirit*. New York: Routledge, 1996.

Kelly, Sean. "Atman, Anatta, and Transpersonal Psychology." *Hindu-Buddhist Interactions*. Delhi: Ajanta, 1993.

R. Klibansky, F. Saxl, and E. Panofsky. *Saturn and Melancholy: Studies in the History of Natural Philosophy, Religion and Art*. New York: Basic Books, 1964.

Klossowski de Rola, Stanislas. *Alchemy: The Secret Art*. New York: Bounty Books, 1973.

―――. *The Golden Game: Alchemical Engravings of the Seventeenth Century*. New York: George Braziller, 1988.

Kristeva, Julia. *Black Sun: Depression and Melancholy*, trans. Leon S. Roudiez. New York: Columbia University Press, 1989. Originally published in *Les Filles du Feu*, 1854.

Kulkarni, Claudette. *Lesbians and Lesbianism: A Post-Jungian Perspective*. New York: Routledge, 1997.

Kuspit, D. "Negativity Sublime Identity: Pierre Soulages's Abstract Paintings," http://www.artnet.com (accessed April 23, 2004).

Laing, R. D. *The Divided Self*. Baltimore: Pelican Books, 1965.

Levin, D. *Modernity and the Hegemony of Vision*. Berkeley, Los Angeles: University of California Press, 1993.

Lévinas, E. *Otherwise than Being or Beyond Essence*, trans. Alphonso Lingis. The Hague: Martinus Nijhoff, 1981.

Little, Stephen, with Shawn Eichman. *Taoism and the Arts of China*. Chicago: Art Institute of Chicago, with the University of California Press, 2000.

Lonsdale, S. *Animals and the Origins of Dance*. New York: Thames and Hudson, 1981.

―――. *Dance and Ritual Play in Greek Religion*. Baltimore: Johns Hopkins University Press, 1993.

Lopez-Pedraza, Rafael. *Anselm Kiefer: The Psychology of "After the Catastrophe."* New York: Thames and Hudson, 1996.

Luke, Helen. *From Darkwood to White Rose: Journey and Transformation in Dante's Divine Comedy*. New York: Parabola, 1989/1995.

Mandel, Oscar. *Chi Po and the Sorcerer: A Chinese Tale for Children and Philosophers*. Portland, Vt.: Charles E. Tuttle, 1964.

Marlan, Stanton. "The Metaphor of Light and Its Deconstruction in Jung's Alchemical Vision." In *Pathways into the Jungian World: Phenomenology and Analytical Psychology*, ed. R. Brooke, 181–96. London and New York: Routledge, 2000.

———. "The Metaphor of Light and Renewal in Taoist Alchemy and Jungian Analysis." *Quadrant: Journal of the C. G. Jung Foundation for Analytical Psychology* 31, no. 2 (Summer, 2001).

———, ed. *Fire in the Stone: The Alchemy of Desire*. Wilmette, Ill.: Chiron, 1997.

———, ed. *Salt and the Alchemical Soul: Three Essays by Ernest Jones, C. G. Jung, and James Hillman*. Woodstock, Conn.: Spring Publications, 1995.

Martinetz, Dieter, and Karl Kernz Lohs. *Poison: Sorcery and Science, Friend and Foe*. Leipzig: Edition Leipzig, 1987.

Maverson, Phillip. *Classical Mythology in Literature, Art, and Music*. Lexington, Mass.: Xerox College Publishing, 1971.

McCritchard, Janet. *Eclipse of the Sun: An Investigation into the Sun and the Moon Myths*. Glastonbury, Somerset: Gothic Image Publications, 1990.

McDermott, Rachel Fell. "The Western Kali." In *Devi: Goddesses of India*, ed. J. Hawley and D. Wulff, 281–313. Berkeley: University of California Press, 1996.

McGuire, W., and R. F. C. Hull, eds. *C. G. Jung Speaking: Interviews and Encounters*. Princeton: Princeton University Press, 1952/1977.

McLean, Adam. "The Birds in Alchemy." *Hermetic Journal* 5 (1979).

———, ed. *The Hermetic Garden of Daniel Stolcius: Composed of Flowerlets of Philosophy Engraved in Copper and Explained in Short Verses Where Weary Students of Chemistry May Find a Treasure House and Refresh Themselves after Their Laboratory Work*, by Daniel Stolcius, trans. Patricia Tahil. Edinburgh: Magnum Opus Hermetic Sourceworks, 1980.

———, ed. *The Rosary of the Philosophers*. Edinburgh: Magnum Opus Hermetic Sourceworks, 1980.

Mead, G. R. S. *The Doctrine of the Subtle Body in the Western Tradition*. London: J. M. Watkins, 1919.

Merleau-Ponty, Maurice. *Phenomenology of Perception*, trans. Colin Smith. New York: Routledge and Kegan Paul, 1962.

———. *The Visible and the Invisible*. Chicago: Northwestern University Press, 1969.

Micklem, Niel. "I Am Not Myself: A Paradox." In *Jung's Concept of the Self: Its Relevance Today*. Papers from the Public Conference Organized in May, 1990, by the Jungian Postgraduate Committee of the British Association of Psychotherapists. [CITY]: British Association of Psychotherapists, 1990.

Miller, D. "Nothing Almost Sees Miracles! Self and No-Self in Psychology and Religion." *Journal of Psychology and Religion* 4–5 (1995): 1–25.

Mitchell, Stephen, trans. *The Book of Job.* New York: Harper Perennial, 1979/1987.

Mookerjee, Ajit. *Kali: The Feminine Force.* New York: Destiny Books, 1988.

———. *Tantra Art: Its Philosophy and Physics.* New York: Kumar Gallery, 1966.

Moore, R., and D. Gillette. *King, Warrior, Magician, Lover: Rediscovering the Archetypes of the Mature Masculine.* San Francisco: HarperSanFrancisco, 1990.

———. *The King Within: Accessing the King in the Male Psyche.* New York: William Morrow, 1992.

Morrison, Toni. *The Song of Solomon.* New York: Signet/Penguin, 1977; originally published by Knopf, Toronto.

Munch, E. *The Cry.* Oslo: National Museum, 1897; reprinted in *Graphic Works of Eduard Munch.*

Murray, Paul. "Canticle of the Void." In *Invisible Light: Poems about God,* ed. Diana Culbertson. New York: Columbia University Press, 2000.

Opus Magnum. Prague, Czech Republic: Trigon Press, 1997.

Perera, Sylvia Brinton. *Descent to the Goddess: A Way of Initiation for Woman.* Toronto: Inner City Books, 1981.

Poncé, Charles. *Kabbalah: An Introduction and Illumination for the World Today.* Wheaton, Ill.: Theosophical Publishing, 1973.

Powell, Neil. *Alchemy: The Ancient Science.* Garden City and New York: Doubleday, 1976.

Prabhavananda, Swami, and Christopher Isherwood, trans., *Bhagavad-Gita: The Song of God.* Hollywood: Vedanta Press, 1989.

Pseudo-Dionysius, the Areopagite. *The Mystical Theology, and the Celestial Hierarchies* of Dionysius the Areopagite. Fintry, England: Shrine of Wisdom, 1949.

———. *Pseudo-Dionysius: The Complete Works,* trans. Colm Luibheid. Classics of Western Spirituality series. New York: Paulist Press, 1987.

Raff, Jeffrey. *Jung and the Alchemical Imagination.* York Beach, Me.: Nicolas-Hayes, 2000.

Rauschenberg, Robert. "Black Painting." *Art in America* 77 (June, 1989).

Rawson, Phillip. *The Art of Tantra.* Greenwich, Conn.: New York Graphic Society, 1973.

———. *Tantra: The Cult of Ecstasy.* New York: Bounty, 1973.

————, and Laszlo Legeza. *Tao: The Philosophy of Time and Change.* London: Thames and Hudson, 1973.

Roethke, Theodore. *The Collected Poems of Theodore Roethke.* Garden City, N.Y.: Anchor Press, 1975.

Romanyshyn, Robert. *The Soul in Grief: Love, Death, and Transformation.* Berkeley: Frog, 1999.

Ronnen, Meir. "Kiefer on Kiefer: The Impossibility of Making an Image." *The Jerusalem Post,* international edition, June 2, 1990.

Rose, Barbara. *Art-as-Art: The Selected Writings of Ad Reinhardt.* New York: Vicky Press, 1975.

Rosen, D. *The Tao of Jung: The Way of Integrity.* New York: Penguin Arkana, 1997.

————. *Transforming Depression: Healing the Soul through Creativity.* York Beach, Me.: Nicolas-Hays, 2002.

Ross, Nancy Wilson, ed. *The World of Zen: An East-West Anthology.* New York: Random House, 1960.

Rouselle, Erwin. "Spiritual Guidance in Contemporary Taoism." In *Spiritual Disciplines: Papers from the Eranos Yearbook,* ed. Joseph Campbell. New York: Pantheon, 1960.

Rubin, W. Preface to *Ad Reinhardt.* New York: Rizzoli Press, 1991.

Samuels, A., B. Shorter, and F. Plaut. *A Critical Dictionary of Jungian Analysis.* London and New York: Routledge and Kegan Paul, 1991.

Sanqvist, Mona. "Alchemy and Interart." In *Interart Poetics: Essays on the Interrelations of the Arts and Media,* ed. Ulla-Britta Lagerroth, Hans Lund, and Erik Hedling, 269–81. Amsterdam: Rodopi, 1997.

Scheper, G. "Illumination and Darkness in the Song of Songs." In *Analecta Husserliana: The Yearbook of Phenomenological Research,* vol. 38, ed. Anna-Teresa Tymieniecka, 315–36. Dordrecht: Kluwer Academic Publishers, 1992.

Schneersohn, Josef V., and Uri Menachem Schneersohn, both of Lubavitch. *Basi LeGani: Chasidic Discourses.* Brooklyn: Kaploun Kehot Publication Society, 1990.

Scholem, Gershom Gerhard. *Origins of the Kabbalan.* Jewish Publication Society. Princeton: Princeton University Press, 1962.

Schwartz-Salant, N. *The Mystery of e Human Relationship: Alchemy and the Transformation of the Self.* New York and London: Routledge, 1986.

————. "On the Subtle-Body Concept in Clinical Practice." In *The Body in Analysis,* ed. Nathan Schwartz-Salant and Murray Stein, 19–58. Chiron Clinical series. Wilmette, Ill.: Chiron, 1986.

Seligman, Kurt. *The History of Magic*. New York: Pantheon, 1948.

Shibayama, Zenkei. *Zen Comments on the Momonkan*. New York: Harper and Row, 1974.

Siegel, James E. "The Idea of the Microcosm: A New Interpretation." *Spring 67*. Woodstock, Conn.: Spring Publications, 2000.

Sim, Stuart. *Derrida and the End of History*. New York: Totem, 1999.

Singh, Madanjeet, comp. *The Sun: Symbol of Power and Life*. New York: Harry N. Abrams, 1993.

Sinha, Indra. *The Great Book of Tantra*. Rochester, Vt.: Destiny, 1983.

———. *Tantra: The Cult of Ecstasy*. London: Hamlyn, 2000.

Smith, R. "Paint in Black: Ad Reinhardt at Moca." *Artweek* 22 (November 14, 1991).

Snyder, Gary. *Earth House Hold*. New York: New Direction Books, 1957.

Stein, E. *Knowledge and Faith*, trans. Walter Redmond. *The Collected Works of Edith Stein*, vol. 8. Washington, D.C.: ICS Publications, Institute of Carmelite Studies, 2000.

Stein, Murray. *Jung's Map of the Soul: An Introduction*. Chicago and LaSalle, Ill.: Open Court, 1998.

Stolcius, Daniel. *The Hermetic Garden of Daniel Stolcius: Composed of Flowerlets of Philosophy Engraved in Copper and Explained in Short Verses Where Weary Students of Chemistry May Find a Treasure House and Refresh Themselves after Their Laboratory Work*, ed. Adam McLean, trans. Patricia Tahil. 1627. Reprint, Edinburgh: Magnum Opus Hermetic Sourceworks, 1980.

Suzuki, Shunryu. *Branching Streams Flow in the Darkness: Zen Talks on the Sandokai*, ed. M. Weitsman and M. Wenger. Berkeley: University of California Press, 1999.

Tansley, David V. *Subtle Body: Essence and Shadow*. New York: Thames and Hudson, 1984.

Tatham, P. "A Black Hole in the Psyche: One Personal Reaction." *Harvest* 30 (1984): 120–23.

Thorn, Kip. *Black Holes and Time Warps: Einstein's Outrageous Legacy*. New York: Norton, 1994.

Towbin, Janet. "The Seduction of Black." Artist's statement, unpublished document.

Trismosin, Solomon. *Splendor Solis: Alchemical Treatises of Solomon Trismosin, Adept and Teacher of Paracelsus*. London: Kegan Paul, Trench, Trubner, 1921.

van Löbensels, Robin, and V. Walter Odajnyk, eds. *Quadrant: Journal of the C. G. Jung Foundation for Analytical Psychology* 31, no. 2 (Summer, 2001).

van Scott, Miriam. *Encyclopedia of Hell*. New York: Thomas Dunne, 1998.

Vine, Naomi. "Mandala and Cross: Ad Reinhardt's Black Paintings." *Art in America* 79 (November, 1991).

Vivekananda, Swami. *In Search of God and Other Poems*. Calcutta: Advaita Ashrama, 1968.

von Franz, Marie-Louise. *Alchemy: An Introduction to the Symbolism and the Psychology*. Toronto: Inner City Books, 1980.

———. *Archetypal Dimensions of the Psyche*. Boston: Shambhala, 1997.

von Rosenroth, Knorr. *Kabbala De Nudate*. Frankfurt, 1684; cited by Kurt Seligman in *The History of Magic*. New York: Pantheon, 1948.

Wagner, R. *The Ring of the Nibelung*. Illus. Ul de Rico. Foreword by Sir George Solti. London: Thames and Hudson. 1980.

Waite, A. E., ed. *The Hermetic Museum*. York Beach, Me.: Samuel Weiser, 1990.

Waite, A. E., ed. and trans. *Paracelsus, Heremetic, and Alchemical Writings of Paracelsus*. New Hyde Park, N.Y.: University Books, 1967.

Walker, Mitchell. "The Double: Same-Sex Inner Helper." In *Mirrors of the Self: Archetypal Images That Shape Your Life*, ed. Christine Downing, 48–52. Los Angeles: Tarchter, 1991.

Ware, Kallistos. *The Orthodox Way*. Crestwood, N.Y.: St. Vladimir's Seminary Press, 1995.

Warlick, M. E. *Max Ernst and Alchemy: A Magician in Search of Myth*. Austin: University of Texas Press, 2001.

Welman, Mark. "Thanatos and Existence: Towards a Jungian Phenomenology of the Death Instinct." In *Pathways into the Jungian World: Phenomenology and Analytic Psychology*, ed. Roger Brooke. London and New York: Routledge, 2000.

The White Cloud Daoist Temple. Beijing: Chinese Daoist Association, 1994.

Woolf, G. *Black Sun: The Brief Transit and Violent Eclipse of Harry Crosby*. New York: Vintage, 1976.

ZaJouc, Arthur. *Catching the Light: The Entwined History of Light and Mind*. New York and Oxford: Oxford University Press, 1993.

INDEX

Italics indicate pages with images.

analysis (*continued*)
within, 187–88. *See also* clinical
cases

Anatomy of the Psyche (Edinger), 17–19, 97

animal instinct and awakening imagery, 122, *123*

Annata vs. Atman (non-Self vs. Self), 179–81

antagonism and complementarities in Self/non-Self, 180–81

Apollonian vision, 14–15, 37, 67, 232–33*n* 94

arche-trace and archetype, 184–85

archetypes: absent presence of, 184; nigredo as, 27–30; Sol niger as, 6, 195

art and artists: death symbolism, 66; Sol niger symbolism, 79–96

Art-as-Art: The Selected Writings of Ad Reinhardt (Rose), 89

astral man (Primordial Man of Light), 99, *100*, 101–5, 109

Athena, 204

Atman vs. Annata (Self vs. non-Self), 179–81

aurum philosophicum, 9

awakening, psychic, 122–25, plate 10

Ayin, 202

Azarian, A., 48

balance vs. fusion in union of opposites, 167. *See also* differential conjunction

Basi LeGani, 201

Bhagavad-Gita, 136

biblical references: earthquakes and dark sun, 49–50; Ezekiel's vision of astral man, 103; Job's despair, 62–64

birds in alchemical symbolism, 128, *129*, 130, 225–26*n* 60, plate 11

birth imagery, 86, 99–102, 112, *113*, 132–35

blackening process, 17, 162–63. *See also nigredo*

blacker-than-black, nigredo experience as, 56, 188

black holes: and fears of loss of consciousness, 171–72; luminescence of, 206, 208, plates 17a–17b; and Sol niger imagery, 36, 37

The Black Hole (Wilmer), 206, plate 17a

black light, 84–85

blackness, independent transformational purpose of, 189–95. *See also* darkness

black-on-black painting, 86–90

black sun. *See* Sol niger

Black Sun: Depression and Melancholy (Kristeva), 43–44

Blake, William, 38, *39*, 68

The Body of Abel Found by Adam and Eve (Blake), *39*

Bond, Stephenson, 14

Book of Lambspring, 19

Bosnak, R., 66–67

Bowen, Matreya, 57, plate 4

Brant, Sebastian, 154

Broken Flowers and Grass (Kiefer), 93, *94*

Brooke, Roger, 178

Brueghel, Pieter, 33

Brzostoski, John, 193

regeneration/rebirth, 57, 66, 73–75, 76, 81–82, 98, 125–28, 172–73; and Self-discovery, 163, 177–78; unity in, 63. *See also mortificatio*

Death and the Landsknecht (Dürer), 46

death instinct, Freudian, 71, 73, 74–75, 78, 88

"Death of the King" (Stolcius), 19

decay and decomposition. *See putrefactio*

deconstruction in nigredo experience, 178–82, 185, 193–94, 195, 214

defense against darkness: critique of Kalsched's strategy, 68–72, 75, 212; ego vs. Self as source of, 219n19; Lacan's challenge to, 73; non-being as escape from despair, 62–64

DeMaria, M. B., 48

depression: as defense against trauma, 70, 71; and egocide, 73–75; and nigredo experience, 24; and struggle with Sol niger, 37–40, 167–75; and symbolic journey to underworld, 77

Derrida, Jacques, 13, 17, 88, 101, 183–87

Descent to the Goddess (Perera), 24

despair and descent into darkness, 23, 60–64

developmental model and loss of darkness's true role, 188–92

differential conjunction: importance of, 192, 213; and invisibility of inner light, 101–2; and shadow integration, 99; vs. unity/sameness, 138–42, 149–59, 212, 213, 233n94, plate 12, plate 14

Directions for Endowment and Vitality, 112

The Divided Self (Laing), 36–37

Divine Comedy (Dante), 23

divine darkness in theology, 173–79, 202, 208. *See also* God/gods

Doré, Gustave, *28, 60*

double nature of light, 102. *See also* luminous darkness

doubling vs. unity/sameness, 138, *139,* 140–42, plate 12

Douglas, Claire, 142

dragon symbolism, 19

Dreams and the Underworld (Hillman), 77–79

dreams as observers of humanity, 206

Drob, Sanford L., 102, 201–2

Duchamp, Marcel, 165

Dürer, Albrecht, *46*

Earth and soul connection to embodied experience, 33

earthquakes and Sol niger, 49–50

Edinger, Edward: burning in alchemical process, 97; on Christian symbolism, 151–55; cluster thinking and alchemical process, 17–19; on coniunctio, 124; and descent to darkness, 23, 24; on dreams as observers of humanity, 206; mysterious nature of opposites, 185; on Sun as both ego and Self, 227–28n13; on universality of nigredo experience, 24–25; and value of blackness, 189–90

ego: and attachment to salvation, 62; avoidance of unresolved opposites, ego (*continued*)

151, 152, 153; and dangers of soul flight, 32; death of, 19, 25, 72–79, 83, 163–64, 211, 212; and defense against trauma, 70–71; and displacement of subject, 187; dissolution of, 20–21, 201, 212; fears of unconscious, 161–62; and King vs. Tyrant, 14, 17; meditative challenges to, 108; as seat of anxiety, 219n19; vs. Self, 38, 40, 163, 227–28n13; and worship of light, 16–17, 211; wounding of innocence in, 23

ego psychology, challenge to, 72–73, 78

Ein-sof, 202

"El Desdichado" (Nerval), 43–44

Eliade, Mircea, 13–14

Eliot, T. S., 25, 200

elixir field and subtle body theory, 112

embodied experience, Self/soul connection to, 32–33, 181, 187, 231n94

emotions in nigredo journey, 66–67, 111, 170–71

energy body. *See* subtle (illuminated) body

erasure: and paradox of non-Self, 184–85; of subject, 187–88, 188

Ereshkigal, 24, 56, 69

Ernst, Max, 85–86

escape from suffering, strategy of, 33, 62–64, 67–68, 71, 151. *See also* defense against darkness

ethical theory and moral consciousness, 17, 231–32n94

eye symbolism, 206, 207

Ezekiel, 103

Fabricius, Johannes, 165

fading star imagery for descent to darkness, 24, 25

Fall of Icarus (Stevens and Momper), 33

Faust (Goethe), 24

Faust (Rembrandt's painting), 31

Feast of Icarus (Hazo), 32

feminine psyche: birthing role in alchemy, 86; Christian struggle to integrate, 152, 153; and creativity from mortification, 128, 130; masculine rejection of, 169, 170, 232–33n94; mythical association with death, 24, 56–59, 69, 98, plates 4 and 6; vs. sun king patriarchy, 14; transformation of repressed sexuality, 121–25, plate 10; and unification of sames, 142

filius philosophorum (philosophical child), 86, 99–102, 132–35

Fink, Bruce, 230–31n80

The Five Poisons (Williams), 55

Flam, Jack, 91

Flamel, Nicholas, 56

flying symbolism, 30 32–33, 128, 129, 130–31

Fontana, Lucio, 91

The Forest (Doré), 28

For Luck (Landerer), 55

Foucault, Michel, 130–31, 187

fragmentation of psyche, traumatic defensive organization of, 69–72

Freud, Sigmund, 71, 76, 78

fullness of nothingness paradox, 179

Gage, John, 84

Germain, Edward, 41–42

Giegerich, Wolfgang, 62
Gillette, Douglas, 14, 15–16
Glanz, James, 206, 208
Gnosticism, Primordial Man in, 103
God/gods: as absent presence, 184; and
    Apollonian vision, 14–15, 37, 67,
    232–33*n* 94; and feminine aspect of
    death, 24, 56–59, 69, 98, plates 4 and
    6; and flight to Sun, 32–33; founda-
    tion in divine darkness, 173–79, 202,
    208; Greco-Roman, 37, 44–45, 152,
    204, plate 14; holistic concept of,
    152; and inner light sources of subtle
    body, 105; Self as inner god, 70, 208.
    See also mythological expressions;
    religions
Goethe, Johann Wolfgang, 24, 27–32
Good, the, Platonic sun as, 101
Gray, Eden, 132
green lion symbol, 22, plate 1
Gregorian, V. S., 48
Grey, Alex, 105–7, plates 7–8 and 15
grieving process, getting stuck in, 43–44
Grof, Stanislov, 195, *196*
grounding, psychological, 32–33, 181,
    187, 231*n* 94

Hades, symbolic journey to, 77–78
halos and subtle body inner light, 107
Harvest (Clarke), 36
Hasidic discourse and journey in dark-
    ness, 201–2
Hazo, Sam, 32
head symbolism, 162–63
healing and poisons, 55
heart symbolism, 133, 171

Heemskerck, Marten van, 44
Heidegger, Martin, 76
Hermes, *152*, plate 14
The Hermetic Garden (Stolcius), 81–
    82, *83*
The Hermetic Museum, 73, 75
Hexastichon (Brant), 154
Hillman, James: and death as meta-
    phor, 77–79; hero's journey vs. de-
    scent to underworld, 59–60; on
    human preference for light, 13; on
    illuminated lunacy, 177; on integra-
    tion of shadow, 99; on multiple per-
    spectives in healing process, 204,
    206; and opposite properties within
    objects, 186; on problems with sal-
    vationist goal, 188–89, 232–33*n* 94;
    on Saturn, 45; on Self's lack of con-
    nection to embodiment, 181, 231*n*
    94; on soul's nigredo journey to de-
    spair, 23; on union of sames, 141–42,
    154–55; and value of blackness, 190–
    92, 193; on wings and flying, 30
Hinduism, 105–9, 136, 179–81, 206. *See
    also* Tantra
Hokusai, 192
Holbein, Hans, 19–20
Holden, Madronna, 15
"The Hollow Men" (Eliot), 25
hope, dangers of, 70
"How to Avoid Speaking: Denials"
    (Derrida), 183
Hugo, Victor, 208
humanistic view of psychology: chal-
    lenge to, 72–73, 78; difficulties with
    abstract art, 90

Index (259)

objectified vs. lived body, 164–65

On the Heights of Despair (Cioran), 60–62

ontological pivotal point, 87, 88, 212

opposites, dance of: as artistic subject, 90–91; balancing of, 88, 150, 167, 212; and black sun as paradox, 84, 86–88, 148–49; complementarities in, 180–81, 182; ego discomfort with, 151, 152, 153; as inexpressible paradox, 182–87; marriage and creation, 99, 101–2; as necessary life rhythm, 15, 37, 60–62; in nigredo experience, 94–95; Self as, 99–102; and Sun imagery, 82; transcendence of, 140–42, 177–78; Western separation in, 97, 99. *See also* union of opposites

The Orthodox Way (Ware), 175

Ovid, 32–33

painful experiences. *See* suffering

Pandora (Reusner), 151–52

Paracelsus, 102

paradox: of absent presence, 88, 183–87; black sun as, 4, 5, 6, 11–12, 84, 86–88, 148–49, 192; of differentiated union, 155–56; fullness of nothingness, 179; integration of, 163–64; and linguistic limitations, 32, 182–87; and transformation of soul, 150–51, 212

passion and joy of blackness, 195–209, 214

patriarchy and worship of light, 14–16, 211

peacock tail symbolism, 203–6

perception, transformation of, 164–65

Perera, Sylvia, 24, 56

Perry, John, 14

personal spirit, 71, 72, 219n19

"petite a" concept, 182, 230–31n80

pharmakon (elixir), 20

philosopher's stone, 10, 73, 86, 187–88

Philosophia Reformata (Mylius), 81

philosophical child, 86, 99–102, 132–35

philosophical tree symbolism, 128

physical illness and nigredo experiences, 36, 47, 171

pinkness in subtle body clinical case, 122, 125

Plato, 30, 32, 101, 136

pleasures of union, 157–59

pleroma concept, 178

poetry: death as release to poetic life, 76, 83; linguistic paradox of, 32; as nigredo expression, 50–51, 59; and paradox of unity, 156; and passion of darkness, 198–201; Sol niger's role in creative process, 44

poison symbolism, 19–20, 54–56

poststructuralist view of subjects, 187

prayer/meditation, 107–8, 174

Praying (Grey), 107, plate 8

presence and absence, paradox of, 88, 183–87

Primordial Man of Light, 99, *100*, 101–5, 109

"Psalm" (Célan), 201

Pseudo-Dionysius the Areopagite, 175–79

psyche: activation center in solar plexus, 115–18; as larger than ego,

solar plexus role in nigredo experience, 112–18, *119*, 130–31, 160, 162

solificatio, 148–49, plate 13

Sol niger: as archetypal image, 6, 195; artistic interpretations of, 79–96; in birth of filius philosophorum, 133; as black hole, 36, 37; and burning out of soul, 26, 37–40, plate 2; challenge to Western tradition, 188; coldness symbolism, 59–60; complementarities with Sol, 182; creativity role of, 42, 43–44; and defense against trauma, 71–72; depressive struggle with, 37–40, 41, 167–75; destructive side of, 33–36, 37–56, plate 3; escape strategy, 67–68; as feminine aspect of death, 57; flying dream encounter, 30; integration role of, 10–11, 159–67; introduction, 3–7; as irreducible to reality, 206; as non-Self, 149; as paradox, 4, 5, 6, 11–12, 84, 86–88, 148–49, 192; in Platonic metaphor, 101; in psychic progress, *137, 138, 139;* Romanyshyn's dream of, 202–3; as shadow, 10–11, 37–56; and solar plexus energy center, 113–14, 160, 162; as source of new Self, 142; spiritual experience of, 175–78, 201–2; and subtle body in analysis, 114–32; summary of journey, 211–14. *See also* luminous darkness

soma pneumatikon (subtle body), 102. *See also* subtle body

The Song of Solomon (Morrison), 193

Song of Songs, 196

soul: burning out of, 26, 37–40, 42, 97–98, plate 2; color symbolism for, 189; as embodied experience, 32–33, 181, 187, 231*n* 94; harmonization through sex, 124; light as goal of, 13; loss of innocence, 23–24; and paradox, 150–51, 212; and Self, 181, 231*n* 94; transformation of, 62, 83, 91; underworld images for afterlife of, 78; unification as goal of, 10

Soulage, Pierre, 90–91

The Soul in Grief: Love, Death, and Transformation (Romanyshyn), 203

sous rapture, 184–87

"Spiritual Guidance in Contemporary Taoism" (Rousselle), 109

spirituality: Asian perspective on Self/non-Self, 179–81; and black-on-black paintings, 89–90; Chinese, 109–14, *115,* 123–24, 155–56, 176; contribution to value of darkness, 196–97; and inversion of consciousness, 136; and nigredo experience, 173–78, 201–2; overemphasis on salvationist goal, 189, 190–92. *See also* mysticism; mythological expressions

Splendor Solis (Trismosin), 20, *21,* 26, 130, plate 2

The Starred Heaven (Kiefer), 91, *92*

star symbolism, *24, 25,* 101

Stein, Edith, 175–76

Stein, Murray, 178

Stevens, Petrus, 33

Stolcius, Daniel, 19, 33, *34,* 81–82, *83*

subject, transformation of, 187–88, 231–33*n* 94

Trismegistus, Hermes, *141*
Trismosin, Solomon, 20, *21*, 26, 130, plate 2
Tyrant, 14, 17
TzimTzum, 202

Unamuno, Miguel de, 4–5
uncertainty and life/death ambiguity, 125–28
unconscious: alchemical metaphor for, 9–12; as balancer of consciousness, 180; blackness as metaphor for, 194; and destructiveness of static psyche, 37; as Great Mother, 134–35; as home of monstrosities, 151–55, 159–75; instinctual state, 19, 54, 122, *123*, *137*; and King as only light, 17; roots symbolism for, 131; Sol niger as metaphor for, 11; and suffering, 5. *See also nigredo;* Self
uncreated light, 174
undecidability in Rothko's art, 87–88
underworld, symbolic journey to, 59–60, 77–79, 172–73
unidirectional model of development, dangers of, 188–92
union of opposites: as alchemical goal, 10; vs. black sun paradox, 6; complexity of, 165, *166*, 167, 180–81, 191–92, 213; dark light as product of, 86; as monstrosity, 151–55; as mysterium coniunctionis, 5, 76, 177, 185; sexual symbolism of, 107, 124, *198*, 228*n* 21; vs. unity/sameness, 141–42, 150, 151, 213. *See also coniunctio;* differential conjunction

unity: and alchemy metaphor, 10, 11, 86; artistic irresolution in, 87; in death, *63;* vs. doubling of opposite properties, 99, 101–2; ego vs. Self, 72–73; and sameness, 138–42, 149–59, 212, 213, 233*n* 94, plates 12 and 14
unknowing, darkness/cloud of, 175, 177, 179, 185, 200–201, 213
unus mundus as illusion, 155. *See also* unity

Van Rijn, Rembrandt, *31*
Vine, Naomi, 89–90
violence of light in Western tradition, 16–17, 211
Virgil, 67
virgin's milk, 22–23
Viridarium Chymicum (Stolcius), 33, *34*
Vividkananda, Swami, 57–58
volcanic metaphor, 195
Von Franz, Marie-Louise, 37, 122
vulnerability and defense against trauma, 70

Ware, Kallistos, 175
Warlick, M. E., 85
Welman, Mark, 75–77
Western tradition: *coniunctio* vs. Eastern spiritual sexuality, 124; polarity of opposites in, 97, 99; Sol niger's challenge to, 188; splitting of God image in, 152; and worship of light, 16–17, 211, 214, 232–33*n* 94. *See also* modernity
whitening in alchemy, 54, 97–99, 130, 189–90, 203–4

wholeness, 10, 76, 149, 150. *See also* integration; union of opposites

Williams, C. A. S., 55

Wilmer, Harry, 206

wing symbolism, 30, 32

Winnicott, Donald W., 69

wise old man archetype, 130–31, 132–33

Wolff, Geoffrey, 42

wounding: alchemical healing of, 188; and black sun dreams, 203; and defenses against trauma, 68–72; and mortification process, 22–23; mourning and fear of loss, 43–44, 47; and philosophical tree symbol, 128

Writing and Difference (Derrida), 17

ZaJonc, Arthur, 209

Zen Buddhism and paradox of Sol niger, 4